Scholarship
and
Character

75 Years of Alpha Chi

ROBERT W. SLEDGE

ALPHA CHI COLLEGE HONOR SCHOLARSHIP SOCIETY

PUBLISHED BY
THE NATIONAL COUNCIL OF ALPHA CHI
COLLEGE HONOR SCHOLARSHIP SOCIETY
BOX 2249 HARDING UNIVERSITY
SEARCY, ARKANSAS 72149

ALPHA CHI IS A MEMBER OF THE
ASSOCIATION OF COLLEGE HONOR SOCIETIES

PRINTED BY
HARDING PRESS
SEARCY, ARKANSAS 72149

CONTENTS

INTRODUCTION

Authorization

It has now been seventy-five years since the February day in 1922 when representatives from several colleges gathered at Southwestern University, Georgetown, Texas, to found a general scholarship honor society for the "Class A" colleges of the state. In 1995, as the members of the executive committee of Alpha Chi met in Philadelphia to begin planning the 1997 National Convention, they recollected that 1997 would be the 75th anniversary of the founding of the society. The committee believed that it would be the appropriate time to introduce a comprehensive history of the organization.

Several previous short essays on this subject had been attempted, but no major effort had ever been undertaken. In his 1954 address to the society, Regional President Troy Crenshaw of Texas Christian University said:

> A definitive history of our Society is yet to be written. The records of our proceedings show that in our annual meeting in 1951, Miss Bessie Shook spoke of the need of a history of Alpha Chi, and Dr. Claud Howard added that such a history should be undertaken during the lifetime of Dr. Bishop [the founder of the Southwestern University Scholarship Society in 1915] so that he might prepare the first part of it. A motion was then passed to appoint a committee to prepare the history, but I have so far been unable to trace the subsequent development of the matter.[1]

Tied up with the technicalities of dividing into two regions, the convention took little notice of this call except to appoint Dr. Crenshaw historian for the society. No significant developments emerged from this initiative and the project was largely forgotten in official circles until 1995.

Once the executive committee agreed to recommend proceeding with this history, President Robert W. Sledge offered to undertake authorship. By mail ballot, the National Council granted formal authorization to continue. A Publication Committee was appointed to oversee the work.

The committee met at the national headquarters in Searcy, Arkansas, in March, 1996, to establish parameters that would allow for completion in time for the 1997 Convention. This committee was composed of Dr. Dennis Organ, Alpha Chi executive director, as chair; Dr. Barbara Clark, former National Council secretary; Dr. Joseph E. Pryor, former National Council secretary-treasurer and the society's first executive director; Dr. Paul Michelson, Region IV secretary-treasurer; and Dr. Christine Condaris, National Council member.[2]

Each of these persons made valuable comments about the manuscript. Dr. Clark read almost the entire manuscript and found numerous potential problems in the first draft. Dr. Organ was especially helpful in copy editing, selecting title and pictures, and in seeing the work through the press. He is the de facto publisher of the book. A word of gratitude is in order to Mrs. Lara Noah (Arkansas Eta, 1992), administrative assistant of Alpha Chi, for her services in many areas, but particularly in setting up the manuscript for printing. My appreciation also goes to my wife, Marjorie (Texas Alpha, 1956), and my student secretary, Virginia Doggett (Texas Upsilon, 1997), for proofreading and setting up the reference notes, respectively. The shortcomings in this work, however, are the responsibility of the author and not of the committee or the national office.

Author's Frame of Reference

This essay must begin with a personal note, almost an apology, in the classic sense of the term. Major obstacles confront anyone who attempts to write about events in which he or she may play a personal role. The goal of being objective is clearly unobtainable, because one recalls events in certain ways, and it is difficult to dissuade the memory merely on the basis of documented facts. People see events from different angles, and each perception may be true, while being at least slightly at variance with the others.

Second, there is a fine line to walk between excessive modesty and the need to tell the story as it was. Partly, one encounters this dilemma in deciding whether to use first person pronouns. Partly, it has to do with separating the narrator from the participant in terms of the perspective from which the story is told. In the matter of citing references, one may assert something to be so on the basis of one's memory, but there is no way of offering documentation for memory.

A third problem in the preparation of this work was time. The decision to prepare a history was made less than a year from the time completion was due, which is a very short time frame. Further, problems of personal and family illness at precisely the period budgeted for the writing severely restricted the contemplation necessary for a truly adequate work.

These difficulties are reflected in what has ended up being only a partial job of research. The Alpha Chi archives at Southwestern University are only started; much material needs to be gathered for them. The sources that are available there relate principally to the story of Alpha Chi at the national and regional levels. For these stories, there are adequate written resources. But the real story of the organization lies in the local chapters, where the majority of the individuals who make up the society have their principal relation to Alpha Chi. Here, information is much harder to come by. Thus, the work is guided by its sources, and becomes much less a grassroots account than the author would desire.

The fact that the author has strong Texas ties may be adduced to suggest a regional bias in this presentation. Alpha Chi, for much of its existence, was a regional organization. Persons from other sections of the country may become impatient with hearing the word "Texas," particularly in the early chapters. The author knows no solution for this problem and begs the reader's patience for this and any other flaws.

The author was inducted into Texas Alpha chapter of Alpha Chi in the fall of 1951 while a student at Southwestern University. He attended the regional/national meeting on the Southwestern campus in 1953 but remembers very little about it. Subsequently, he became professor of history (with an emphasis on modern American social/intellectual history) at McMurry College, Texas Upsilon chapter. He became head sponsor of Texas Upsilon in 1969. He has served as vice president and president of Region I. In 1973, the author was elected as an at-large member of the National Council, becoming vice president of the Council to fill an unexpired term in 1981 and succeeding to the presidency in 1983. At the end of that term in 1987, he rotated off the Council. In 1989, he was reelected to the Council and named to fill out another unexpired term, this time as secretary. In 1991, the National Council elected him president, with another four-year term added in 1995. In these roles, he has been privy to much of the inner working of the National Council for a third of the life of the society.

Additionally, the author has had the privilege of knowing a substantial number of the early student members of the organization as they rose to positions of prominence in educational, ecclesiastical, and business circles during the author's youth.

These close ties are presented as both assets and liabilities in the preparation of this story. It is hoped that the former will predominate.

References and Notes

While this work seeks to adhere to the canons of scholarly documentation, reference notes are kept to a minimum. Much of the information contained herein comes from the official publications of the society, the *Proceedings*, the *Recorder*, and the *Newsletter*. No reference notes are utilized when these documents are obviously the source of information, unless the need to list exact pages makes it appropriate.

The bulk of the sources consulted are documents published by the society. These official publications include the following:

(1) A "Minute Book" containing the unpublished and published annual accounts of the society's functioning through 1932;

(2) Annual paperbound booklets called *Proceedings* which reported the official minutes of the organization and reprinted major speeches and papers. These appeared each year from 1933 to 1956, except for three years during World War II;

(3) The *Recorder*, a more extensive record of official proceedings and selected articles. From 1957 through 1969, the society sought to publish the *Recorder* semi-annually, and did so with only occasional lapses to an annual publication; from 1970 to 1994, the *Recorder* appeared annually. Beginning in 1995, the society produced three annual editions, one focused on official proceedings, one composed of student essays and productions, and one appealing to alumni interests;

(4) A separate publication was the "Supplement," beginning in 1970 as an annual flyer centering on chapter activities and announcements. No issue was published in 1974 and, from 1975 on, the society changed the periodical's name to the *Newsletter* and produced it semi-annually through 1994. The following year, it too appeared three times a year, with one issue dedicated each year to alumni matters; and

(5) A number of other public materials, such as the randomly republished "Alpha Chi Constitution" and *Manual of Rituals*.

Another type of source for this essay is the archival material found in several libraries. These contain correspondence files, miscellaneous holdings of official publications which duplicate the material noted above, and mementos such as banquet programs, place cards, and official badges. For Alpha Chi the most important of these are:

(1) The Center for American History at the University of Texas at Austin, which contains some of the collected papers of Harry Y. Benedict, Homer P. Rainey, and John C. Granbery, Jr.;

(2) The Alpha Chi archive in the Special Collections room of the A. Frank Smith, Jr. Library at Southwestern University, which contains collections of official publications, national secretary-treasurer correspondence (mainly 1969-73), and presidential-vice presidential papers (mainly 1981-87). Upon the completion of this book, all materials gathered in the course of the research will be deposited in the archive;

(3) The archive of Southwest Texas State University, containing the correspondence, scrapbooks, and miscellaneous publications of Alfred E. Nolle;

(4) The university archive at Texas Christian University, which contains a most enlightening Alpha Chi file for the period 1956-64.

(5) There are doubtless other correspondence materials in other institutions and in private hands. These remain largely unexplored.

The memories of pivotal persons, living and dead, who contributed to this story in interviews and reminiscences constitute a third category of resource. Such recollections are occasionally apparent in the account, but most are anonymous. Members of the Publication Committee are among these, as they corrected mistaken statements on the basis of their memories as participants.

NOTES

[1] *Proceedings*, 1954, p. 13.
[2] See 1996 *Recorder*, Proceedings issue, p. 2.

CHAPTER 1 (1915-22)
CONCEPT AND CONCEPTION

The Southwestern University Scholarship Society

The signs on the highway outside Georgetown, Texas proclaimed the community as the home of Southwestern University, "Texas' Oldest University." (Student pranksters regularly painted over the "l" in "oldest" to make it read "Oddest." The school just as regularly restored the signs to their original condition.) The claim was based on the chartering of an institution called "Rutersville College" by the Republic of Texas in 1840. Rutersville and three other similar institutions of the Methodist Episcopal Church, South all but vanished during the strains of the Civil War and a yellow fever epidemic that followed it. In 1873 the Methodists of the state founded the consolidated successor to the other schools at Georgetown, thirty miles north of Austin. It was styled "Texas University," and grew under that title until the state requested the use of the name for its new school in Austin. The trustees acceded to this request, and renamed the denominational college "Southwestern University."

By 1910 the school had grown and prospered and had produced distinguished graduates like J. Frank Dobie. But there was a growing conviction in the minds of many of its constituents that it could never aspire to greatness until it left the backwater county seat town of Georgetown and relocated in a more accessible and prestigious city such as Fort Worth or Dallas. Southwestern's board debated such a proposal at length but eventually turned it down by a narrow margin. A principal proponent of the plan to move the school was Southwestern's president, the brilliant physicist Robert Stewart Hyer. Along with a minority of the board, and with substantial encouragement from the city of Dallas, Hyer resolved to begin a new Methodist institution in Dallas anyway. This event coincided with the Methodist Episcopal Church, South's impending divestiture of its connection with Vanderbilt University as its flagship school. The Methodists believed that Vanderbilt's semi-autonomous governing body was leading the Nashville school too far from its denominational

1

roots. To replace it, they created two more controllable universities, one east of the Mississippi (Emory in Atlanta) and a new one to be created west of the river. Hyer was named founding president of the new school in Dallas, Southern Methodist University in 1911.[1]

Upon the defection of the president, and the loss of much of the school's support along with him, Southwestern was in dangerous waters. To guide it safely through the shoals of the coming years, the trustees picked Charles McTyeire Bishop. As Southwestern's president, Bishop's challenge was to foster the survival of the school and to create a new mission for it.

Charles Bishop was probably destined to be a leader of a Methodist college from birth. His middle name honored the southern Methodist bishop who was the founder of Vanderbilt University. His only son was named Eugene Hendrix Bishop after the man for whom Hendrix College in Arkansas is also named. Both McTyeire and Hendrix were leaders in the educational emphasis of the Methodist Episcopal Church, South.

A native of North Carolina, Bishop earned his B.A. and M.A. degrees from Emory and Henry College in Virginia. He was ordained a Methodist minister and eventually appointed to churches in North Carolina and Missouri. Already prominent in denominational affairs, he was pastor of the M.E. Church, South in the university town of Columbia, Missouri, when he was called to the presidency of Southwestern.[2]

After several years at the college, Bishop sought to fill a gap he perceived in the life of the campus, the absence of a general society honoring scholarship. Such an organization did exist elsewhere. It was Phi Beta Kappa, but it was very exclusive and far beyond the ambitions of an obscure denominational college in the southwest. (Southwestern received a chapter of Phi Beta Kappa in 1995.) Bishop resolved to create a local society at Southwestern patterned after Phi Beta Kappa. A preliminary meeting with four students explored the possibilities of such a society. Given the intense rivalry on campus between "Greeks" (members of fraternities and sororities) and "Barbarians" (independents), the students cautioned him to make its objectives clear so that he would not be suspected of trying to build a new "Greek" club among the independents.

At this initial meeting Bishop gave the four (L.U. Spellman, Florence Ryan, and two other male students) the proposed rules for the new society and a secret handshake. The quartet approved the idea, and Bishop proceeded to the next step.[3]

Together with Professors R.J. Eddy and J.L. McGhee, the two faculty members who held membership in Phi Beta Kappa, President Bishop invited fifteen students to join a group whose goal was "the encouragement and promotion of scholarship and high character among its members and the students of Southwestern University." The name for the new group was "Southwestern University Scholarship Society."[4] Bad weather interfered with the plan to hold a symbolic beginning under an oak tree on the campus where the original meeting to plan a college in Georgetown had been held in 1870. The alternative was to hold the meeting in the president's parlors in Snyder Hall.[5]

Each member pledged "to encourage the diligent pursuit of scholarship, the observance of worthy standards of personal conduct, and the cultivation of a worthy college spirit among the younger members of the student body."[6] Student officers elected were Otto W. Moerner, Eldora Meachum, Bliss Woods, and George Pierce.[7] A tentative constitution established the ground rules for subsequent elections of faculty and students to membership. According to the rules of the new society, "only Seniors—or in exceptional cases, Juniors—are eligible."[8] Another provision allowed both faculty and students to serve as officers. In 1916 they elected Dr. Bishop to be president and Dr. McGhee to be secretary, along with three students in other offices. Also in 1916 they elected, as their bylaws allowed, two more faculty to membership—Dean A.S. Pegues and the newly-arrived Dr. John C. Granbery. In addition, the venerable C.C. Cody, recently retired as dean of the school, received "honorary membership."[9]

The purposes of the new society were thus three in number. First, the new organization was deliberately patterned after Phi Beta Kappa in seeking to recognize academic achievement. Second, it focused not only on scholarship but also on character. Third, it expected its members to leaven the academic atmosphere of the campus.

The Market for a General Honor Society

The three aims of the Southwestern Scholarship Society corresponded to the felt needs on many college campuses of the day. They also expanded the society beyond the focus of Phi Beta Kappa, creating the possibility for a different type of organization.

Like Phi Beta Kappa, the society gave recognition to accomplishments in scholarship. Symbols of scholarly achievement were relatively few in that era. Men who had earned the right proudly and routinely displayed their Phi Beta Kappa keys on watch chains draped across their vests for all to see. Phi Beta Kappa membership was even more prestigious at the beginning of the twentieth century than at its end.

Among other things, it represented a much more narrow cross section of the population. In 1920 only one American in six was even graduating from high school. The levels for college graduation were even lower; 3.3 percent of the 23-year-olds that year had graduated from college, in an era when the normal age for graduation was 20 or 21. This meant that only the intellectual elite and/or the children of the well-to-do were matriculating in college at all, much less graduating. By comparison, a half century later, around a fourth of Americans were graduating from college in timely fashion.[10] Finally, there were not very many schools authorized to establish a chapter of Phi Beta Kappa. This exclusiveness created only a very limited opportunity for Phi Beta Kappa membership and helped give rise to the feeling that such a privilege needed to be extended to equally worthy students at less prestigious schools. Membership in a college honor society, even if not quite Phi Beta Kappa, would grant a lofty cachet to its holders. The word "honor" here corresponded to a fixation on reputation in the South. Honor was principally the province of the gentleman, the elite, the person of distinction. These descriptions certainly encompassed the college graduate.

The term "honor" reflected the presence on many Southern campuses, including Southwestern, of an "honor system" aimed at maintaining the highest standards of integrity. This was closely congruent with the second aspect of the honor society's charter, namely, character. Character was a legitimate concern for a southern denominational college. Less obviously, but no less truly, it was also a concern for state-supported schools, which were not so secular as might be supposed. The American society that emerged from World War I was in a state of ethical flux. One symbol of this moral confusion was the emergence on college campuses of the "flappers," the coeds who smoked and drank almost as freely as their male counterparts had before the war. Fashion trends among young women included a hemline that rose year by year between 1918 and 1926 from ankle length to knee length and higher. The founding date of the new honor society coincided with the coming

of age of the "lost generation" of the cynical, hedonistic youth carica-
tured in the writings of F. Scott Fitzgerald. While college life was understood as a time for sowing wild oats, colleges took very seriously their
responsibilities to be "*in loco parentis*" to their students and circum-
scribed student behavior rather severely. An honor society which fos-
tered respect for character development would be a welcome ally in such
a cause.

In many ways, students of the 1920s were more disciplined and dignified than the popular image might suggest. Rigid rules of conduct were
a standard part of the college scene. Male students routinely wore coats
and ties to class. Female students, and often males as well, were subject
to restrictive curfews. On the other hand, pranks were commonplace and
offenders were not severely disciplined. College administrators accepted
hazing as a normal means of initiating persons into the various institutions of collegiate life. This tolerance applied to honor societies as much
as to other groups.

The third emphasis for ranking scholars at Southwestern was their
role as leaven on the campus. The first two strands survived rather ex-
plicitly in the structures of modern Alpha Chi. The task of serving as role
models for younger students also survived, though implicitly rather than
overtly. Many chapters today plan programs that allow them to promote
scholarship among the freshman and sophomore classes. Other chapters
hold forth membership in Alpha Chi as an incentive to promote the highest forms of academic accomplishment. The initiation ceremony for new
members includes the injunction to "wear the Recognition Pins for one
week when you are on campus, not for self-glorification, but to aid in
making the aims and ideals of Alpha Chi better known in this center of
education."[11]

A Statewide Honor Society

The society at Southwestern continued to flourish through the remainder of the decade. It honored successive classes of students and
additional faculty with membership. Word of its value reached other
schools in the state, including the University of Texas. The opportunity
for like-minded institutions to share in a statewide association for the
promotion of scholarship was not long in coming.

Early in 1922 the "class A" colleges and universities in the state of

Texas received an invitation to a meeting at Southwestern for the purpose of expanding the Southwestern concept beyond the local level. The
apparent moving force behind this initiative was the collaboration between Dean Harry Y. Benedict of the University of Texas and Dr. John
C. Granbery of Southwestern. President Bishop was not involved, having resigned in 1921 to accept the task of becoming founding president
of a state college in Lubbock, which would, in 1923, become Texas Technological College and eventually Texas Tech University. Granbery and
Benedict envisioned an alliance of scholarship societies that would encompass, at least initially, all the major institutions of the state that engaged in liberal arts education.

The University of Texas, in those days, was the unrivaled center of
higher education in the state. Though several other schools, such as Baylor
and Southwestern, adopted term "university" in their names, most citizens of the state referred to the school in Austin as, simply, "The University." As head of academics at "The University," Dean Benedict could
lay claim to being the top educator in the state. His prestige and influence were enormous.

Benedict was impressed by the honor society he saw at neighboring
Georgetown. He hoped to expand the idea, creating an organization that
would allow recognition of distinguished undergraduate achievement at
schools in the state that could not qualify for Phi Beta Kappa chapters.
Phi Beta Kappa was conservative in its expansion policies, and it seemed
likely that many very good students in good colleges would never be
able to qualify because their schools could not attain recognition from
Phi Beta Kappa. The University of Texas had the only chapter in the
state at the time.

Dean Benedict's expectation was that Texas, the premier university
of the state, would act as senior partner for the proposed statewide organization. He further expected the "Scholarship Societies of Texas," as
the new body was to be named, would serve as a model for other states
who would in due course organize their own, independent alliances. "I
had rather wanted," he wrote, "the Texas Scholarship Societies to remain in Texas, giving room for the development of similar organizations in the different states . . . ."[12] This concept was in fact the operational principle under which the society began. The University of Texas
never had a chapter of its own because, as Benedict explained, the institution already had Phi Beta Kappa and a host of disciplinary honor soci-

eties.[13] Nevertheless, Texas hosted several general meetings of the organization, including the 1923 meeting where full organization was completed and, on an emergency basis, the 1935 meeting where members of the local Phi Beta Kappa chapter served as hosts for the younger society.

We cannot tell whether Granbery's vision for the new organization stopped at the state boundary, but he was not favorably inclined toward including the state's normal schools (teacher training colleges). He anticipated creating a more exclusive body. In an early letter to Benedict, Granbery said, "although the normal schools now give the A.B. degree, I suppose we would not consider them A class colleges for our purposes."[14] In the outcome this point of view did not prevail, and the scope of the proposed organization was open to most baccalaureate institutions in the state. As it turned out, four of the first ten members were normal schools. In spite of slightly differing visions for the new society, the two saw eye to eye on nearly everything else and no friction between them is apparent in the record. With the concurrence of Benedict, Granbery issued invitations to several Texas colleges to attend a meeting at Southwestern to discuss the matter. The scheduled time for the meeting was February 22, 1922.

NOTES

[1] Ralph Wood Jones, *Southwestern University, 1840-1961* (Austin: San Felipe Press, 1973), passim.

[2] *Who Was Who In America*, Vol. 2 [1943-50] (Chicago: A.N. Marquis Co., 1950), p. 63).

[3] Interview, L.U. Spellman, January 11, 1983.

[4] *Megaphone* [Southwestern University student newspaper], April 23, 1915.

[5] Ibid.

[6] *Megaphone*, June 13, 1916.

[7] *Megaphone*, April 23, 1915.

[8] Ibid.

[9] *Megaphone*, June 13, 1916.

[10] *Historical Statistics of the United States* (Washington: U.S. Government Printing Office, 1975), Series H-600, H-755.

[11] *The Alpha Chi Handbook* (Searcy, AR: National Council of Alpha Chi, [1996]), p. 54.

[12] H.Y. Benedict to Dr. U.W. Lamkin, President, Northwest Missouri State Teachers College, April 20, 1934, Box 2B64, H.Y. Benedict Papers, The Center

for American History, University of Texas at Austin.

[13] Ibid.

[14] J.C. Granbery, Jr., to H.Y. Benedict, May 18, 1922; Benedict Papers, UT, Box 2P 379.

Focus On . . .

A LITTLE PHI BETA KAPPA?

In the beginning the scholarship society movement at Southwestern and beyond had in mind emulating Phi Beta Kappa. A 1916 newspaper article explained that the Southwestern Scholarship Society would be similar to Phi Beta Kappa.[1] The two faculty invited by President Bishop to share in the founding of the society were the two Phi Beta Kappa key holders at the school.

When Harry Benedict became interested in the idea, it was because of his ties to Phi Beta Kappa that he signed on to the effort to build a state-wide society honoring distinguished baccalaureate scholars. "Having for a long time been Secretary of the Phi Beta Kappa Chapter at this institution [the University of Texas] and believing in Phi Beta Kappa, and believing further that high rank students should be suitably acknowledged and if possible rewarded, I became secretary of the Scholarship Societies of Texas . . . ."[2]

A generation later Prof. Bessie Shook, long-time recording secretary of the society, produced an essay entitled "Why Alpha Chi?" for the *Recorder*. Shook spent half the article detailing the history of Phi Beta Kappa, noting that the society was a major element in the inspiration of Alpha Chi. She then asked herself, "Will Alpha Chi ever become Phi Beta Kappa?" Explaining her negative answer, she went on, "Alpha Chi tries to reach the schools that do as good work as any in the country, but will have to wait for several generations, maybe forever, to be received into the older organization. Alpha Chi is approachable; it is democratic."[3]

Benedict would have agreed with this. Earlier he had written, "Alpha Chi is designated for that great body of substantial colleges and universities that can not hope for early consideration by such an exclusive organization as Phi Beta Kappa. It aspires to the same function in its field as does Phi Beta Kappa in its realm."[4]

Alpha Chi later began to see itself in a different light. In 1955 the National Council decided that it would try to recruit chapters at institutions where Phi Beta Kappa existed. The Council believed that Alpha Chi's emphasis on chapter activities and student participation made the younger society qualitatively different from Phi Beta Kappa. The two may have served similar constituencies, but they provided different services and opportunities.

At the approach of the seventy-fifth anniversary of the founding of Alpha Chi, the society understood itself to be self-sufficient, no longer a small school Phi Beta Kappa, meaningful in and of itself. Some campuses have chapters of both societies, and the two are able to coexist at those institutions. Alpha Chi sees itself as having other functions and values than recognition alone. It fosters leadership opportunities and provides forums for student scholarship. It may seem contradictory to take Prof. Shook's comment about Alpha Chi being democratic and place it alongside the society's purpose to recognize only an elite minority. Nevertheless, Alpha Chi understands the paradox and is content with it.

NOTES

[1] *Megaphone*, June 13, 1916.

[2] Benedict to Dr. U.W. Lamkin, President, Northwest Missouri State Teachers College, April 20, 1934, Benedict Papers, University of Texas, Box 2B64.

[3] *Recorder*, Autumn 1958, pp. 3-5.

[4] Typescript ca. late 1934 in Benedict Papers, University of Texas, Box 2B64.

CHAPTER 2 (1922-27)
THE SCHOLARSHIP SOCIETIES
OF TEXAS

Robert S. Hyer, who, according to college legend, made a wireless broadcast before Marconi, was professor of physics and president at Southwestern in the closing years of the nineteenth century. This universal genius was also an architect of some skill, and it was he who designed the "Ad Building" which still dominates the campus. Construction began in 1898 and, within two years, the building was ready for use. Two decades later, the massive Victorian edifice was the site of the first meeting of the organization that was to become Alpha Chi.

The First Meeting - 2/22/22

The new society had an unpromising beginning, if judged by the attendance. Although invitations were broadcast to more than two dozen schools statewide, only five sent representatives to the meeting, and of those conferees, two ended up not joining at all. Present for the small gathering, which convened at 9:30 a.m., were faculty and students from the University of Texas, Southern Methodist University, Southwestern University, Baylor College (now University of Mary Hardin-Baylor), and Texas Woman's College (now Texas Wesleyan College). The body selected Dr. Granbery to preside and student delegate Christine Hutchison of Texas Woman's College as secretary. Each school was officially represented by a faculty and a student delegate, with several visitors from the host institution and Baylor College.

Each of the delegations expressed its interest and enthusiasm for the proposed society and the body proceeded to the next step, the creation of a constitution. At this point, the meeting recessed to give time for a committee to draw up a constitutional plan. Appointed to the committee were Dean Benedict and Dr. Granbery, the originators of the idea, and student Joe Connally of SMU.

10

At the afternoon session the committee reported a tentative plan, which Benedict and Granbery must surely have had in mind all along. The plenary voted to establish a statewide society and authorized the immediate organization of local chapters based on the partially completed constitution. The constitution committee received instructions to continue their work, with an eye to a second meeting a little later in the year. Dean Benedict invited the conferees to Austin on April 21, a timetable that would allow the constitution committee to complete its work, and a date that coincided with a "Conference on the Teacher Problem in Texas" in Austin. With this, the founding meeting adjourned.[1]

Though some had to leave, most of the delegates remained in Georgetown for an evening banquet held at Southwestern's women's dormitory. Joined by members of the host school's honor society, the guests sat down to a gaily decorated table, "attractively decorated with pot hyacinths and blooming begonias intertwined with ferns and foliage. Numerous red candles in crystal holders cast a cheerful glow over the tables. Places were found by the aid of dainty place cards bearing the name of the individual and appropriate Washington birthday decorations, hatchets, and cherry branches. . . . Flags, red, white and blue candles and 'Uncle Sams' were used as plate favors." Musical groups entertained between courses, and Granbery, who was presiding, invited several short speeches. Altogether, thirty-five delegates and guests enjoyed the evening.[2]

Austin: The Second Founding

Secretary Christine Hutchison sent out invitations to the Austin meeting in April over her name and Granbery's as chairman. The dateline of the letter, April 17, was just four days prior to the proposed gathering, and this late notice may account for a relatively small attendance there too. The Committee on Constitution would present a preliminary report, she said, but there were constitutional issues that needed input from all the participants, and those would be part of the agenda. She invited the delegates to gather at Room 223 of the University of Texas Education Building at 5 p.m.[3]

The meeting was a shambles. It is probable that Miss Hutchison herself was not present, since the minutes of this meeting are in Harry Benedict's handwriting. "Owing to various conflicts with the other meetings held in Austin on the same day," he wrote, "the meeting held at 5 P.M. was very thinly attended." Only eight persons showed up, representing six colleges. However, Benedict noted that he and Granbery had held conversations with a number of other persons who, while unable to make the scholarship society meeting, were very interested in the outcome. The eight delegates received copies of the proposed constitution and suggested changes. Granbery continued as temporary chairman of the proposed organization and Benedict became the de facto secretary.[4]

In spite of poor attendance at the two meetings, prospects for establishing the society were not completely bad. Benedict and Granbery had a network of friends and colleagues across the state. They pressed on through these informal contacts and through formal communications from Benedict to the several institutional presidents. Dean Benedict mailed a long letter to the presidents in May 1922 in which he expanded on the trend in American life to think and speak disparagingly of honor students on the ground that "mastery of a great division of human knowledge is inferior in importance to acquaintance with classmates." Charging that colleges were complacent in the face of "this harmful propaganda," Benedict asserted that there were only a very few exceptions to the thesis that success in college presaged success in life. "Were this not the fact," he wrote, "our colleges would be in desperate need of thorough going reform."

Benedict continued by saying that while colleges were expending extra help on the weak student, they were neglecting the good student: "Our courses, our degrees, are adjusted to the average student, not to him." But, he went on, there is a trend afoot to change that in such schools as Johns Hopkins, Yale, Lehigh, Smith, and Barnard. Acknowledging that there are a variety of ways by which colleges could encourage fine students, Benedict invited the schools of Texas to join in one of the better ways, namely, the establishment of an organization honoring scholarly achievement: "What is being attempted is . . . to establish in our Texas Colleges an undergraduate scholarship society of such merit and standing that membership in it will be valued and sought by our capable students, an objective incentive to hard study."[5]

On December 12, 1922, Benedict dispatched a copy of the letter to "all the Class A 4-Year Texas Colleges." He noted that some schools were not going to participate, Rice because it was not interested, Texas A&M because it did not grant the B.A. degree, and Sul Ross, Tarleton and Grubbs Vocational College because they were junior colleges.[6]

Yet again in February 1923, the call went out to all who had not responded inviting them to share in the proposed organization. The cover letter announced that "most of the Texas Colleges of the First Class" had agreed to participate and would send delegates to a meeting at the University of Texas on February 22, 1923. The invitation requested that a student and a faculty delegate be sent, but that at least one be present if at all possible.[7]

1923: The Firm Foundation

Dean Benedict probably already knew that the 1923 meeting was going to be successful before it ever began. His correspondence would have told him that more than a dozen schools expected to send delegations and that several others, while sending their regrets about attendance, stood ready to participate immediately at the local level. So, when the body convened at 10 a.m., Room 207 of the Education Building was crowded with participants. The roll call elicited responses from delegates representing Austin College, Baylor College, Baylor University, Daniel Baker College, Our Lady of the Lake College, Southwestern University, Texas Christian University, Texas Presbyterian College, Trinity University, the University of Texas, Sam Houston Normal, Southwest Texas Normal, and West Texas Normal. Benedict announced that letters of support were in hand from Simmons College, Sul Ross Normal, East Texas Normal, North Texas Normal, Texas Woman's College, and Southern Methodist University.

Benedict, the host and prime mover, served as temporary chairman of the meeting. He traced the history of the movement thus far, including the steps taken in developing a constitution. This constitution, begun at Georgetown and further expanded at Austin the previous year, had received still more extensive revision by correspondence. When most chapters appeared to be satisfied, Benedict had printed it and sent it out to the delegates in advance of the 1923 meeting.

At this point Benedict called for election of permanent officers, who would serve, under the terms of the proposed constitution, for one year terms. Granbery, who was not one of Southwestern's voting delegates, was elected president, with Dr. S.I. Hornbeak of Trinity as vice president and Dean Benedict as secretary-treasurer.

The business of the meeting consisted mainly in the perfecting of the proposed constitution. Several modifications ensued, mostly rearranging various elements already in the document. Upon perfection and adoption of the constitution, the session confirmed previously elected officers in their positions. On motion, charter membership was held open until June 1, 1923. The chair appointed several committees to clear up outstanding details. When Baylor University extended an invitation to the society to meet in Waco in 1924, the session agreed unanimously to accept. At 4 p.m., the meeting adjourned and the organization of the Scholarship Societies of Texas was complete.[8]

Not only was the society now firmly established constitutionally, but it contained most of the faculty members who would lead it for the next decade and beyond. In addition to Dr. Granbery, delegates E.H. Sparkman of Baylor University, Earl Huffor of Sam Houston Normal, Alfred H. Nolle of Southwest Texas Normal, W.P. Davidson of Southwestern, and Harry Benedict of the University of Texas would each serve as president in the next few years. Dean Benedict served as secretary-treasurer (which was arguably a more influential position than president) until his selection to be president of the University of Texas in 1928, at which point Dean Alfred Nolle accepted the responsibility, a post which he served with distinction for the next forty years.[9]

No clear canon of the "charter" chapters appears in the minutes. In 1925 the society studied the sequence of participation of its member schools and gave them a numerical designation. On the basis of that standard, there were fifteen schools that qualified as charter members. These were, in order of number: Southwestern University, Baylor College (now University of Mary Hardin-Baylor), Baylor University, Texas Presbyterian College (school now merged with another), Trinity University, West Texas State Normal (now West Texas A&M University), North Texas State Normal (now North Texas State University), College of Industrial Arts (now Texas Women's University), Southwest Texas State Normal (now Southwest Texas State University), Austin College, East Texas State Normal (now Texas A&M at Commerce), Texas Woman's College (now Texas Wesleyan University), Our Lady of the Lake College, Texas Christian University (withdrawn in early 1960s), and Sam Houston State Normal (now Sam Houston State University).[10]

The Constitutional Structure

The "Constitution of the Scholarship Societies of Texas" basically consisted of two parts, one outlining the statewide organization and the other specifying the nature of local chapter organization.

The overall governing body was the Council, composed of one faculty member from each chapter, serving a three-year term, and one student member from each chapter, serving a one-year term. The Council met annually to accept new members, hear reports from the local chapters, make legislative enactments for the furtherance of the society, and suspend delinquent chapters. The Council would be represented in the interval between its meetings by the Executive Committee, which could act and speak for the society. The three officers elected annually by the Council composed the Executive Committee. In addition, the new constitution contained the usual provisions for amendments, quorum, and financial resources.

Local chapter organization included five officers (two secretaries among them) and three committees: Membership, Program, and Social. A Faculty Advisory Committee of three persons consisted of the faculty member of the Council and two others to be elected by the membership of the chapter. In addition, the rules specified that there be monthly meetings and at least one "public meeting" each year where a guest speaker would address an appropriate topic.

The local chapter article of the constitution also spelled out the specifications for membership. It provided for three classes of membership, namely Junior membership, Senior membership, and Graduate membership. The first was based on grade average at the end of two years, the second on grade average at the end of three years, and the third based on grade average at the end of four years. Students had to retain their standing in the class to be elected to the next level of membership. The top ranking 10 percent of the classes were eligible for membership, except that juniors with a 90 average and seniors with an 87 average could be included, even if they fell below the top decile of the class. Considerable debate, and several revisions of the Constitution over the next few years, centered on the complexity of this article.

The provision indicated that there was no concern for the "grade inflation" of subsequent years. It also indicated that colleges and universities, in Texas at least, graded on a percentage scale alone, not awarding letter grades or establishing "grade point averages." In addition to the scholarship standard, students had to be approved by the faculty of their schools, thus permitting disqualification on the basis of character and reputation, a criterion found in the Southwestern society's objectives, but not mentioned in the statewide body's constitution. That document said that the objective—the *only* objective—of the organization was "the promotion of scholarship among undergraduate students in the academic division of Texas Colleges."[11]

Covering the State

Invitations to the 1924 meeting of the Scholarship Societies of Texas went out over the signatures of Dean Benedict and two officers of the host chapter at Baylor University, president Arthur Strain and secretary Dixon Wecter. (Wecter subsequently became a prominent historian, with major works on Mark Twain and the Great Depression.)

The meeting began at 10 a.m. on February 22 at Baylor's Model School Building. With President Granbery in the chair, fifteen delegations answered the roll call, representing all but one of the established chapters plus one non-established chapter (H.Y. Benedict of the University of Texas).

In addition, the host school turned out in force, with fifteen faculty and thirty-eight student scholarship society members in attendance at the opening session.

After opening greetings from the president of Baylor University and two musical numbers, the meeting got down to business. Dr. W.P. Davidson reported for the "badge committee," noting that they had approved a design by the A.H. Fetting Company of Baltimore and "members are now wearing the badges." The committee, also charged with selecting a motto for the organization, noted that there had been considerable debate over the matter in both the badge committee and the organizations's executive committee, and asked for more time to deliberate. This request was granted, and the committee returned to the afternoon session with a proposal. They recommended a passage from the King James version of the Bible, John 8:32, "Ye shall know the truth and the truth shall make you free."

The committee also went on to recommend that the reverse of the badge (sometimes called the key or the charm) contain the initials of the school, the initials of the member, and the date "February 22, 1922." It would be understood that only the members would wear the badge. Further, the committee called for the preparation of a shingle signed by the general officers to be presented to each member.

The Council agreed that the executive committee would be the interpreter of the Constitution between meetings of the Council. This was occasioned by the continuing confusion over the meaning of the article on membership qualifications.

The chapter at Sam Houston State Teachers College (all the state normal schools were renamed in 1923) invited the Council to meet with them in Huntsville in 1925. After accepting this invitation, the Council elected officers for the coming year. The nominating committee proposed Dr. E.H. Sparkman, sponsor of the host chapter, for president; Dean A.H. Nolle of Southwest Texas State Teachers College for vice president; and for re-election, Dean Benedict as secretary-treasurer. The Council accepted the report and outgoing President Granbery declared them duly elected.[12]

The meeting of 1925 convened on February 21 because February 22 was a Sunday. Because of inconvenient train schedules in and out of Huntsville, the Council held afternoon and evening sessions rather than the traditional morning and afternoon meetings. Eleven member schools had representation, but delegates were also present from two applicant schools, Howard Payne and Simmons colleges, as well as observers from the University of Dallas, Southern Methodist University and Rice Institute, along with Dean Benedict from Texas.

Benedict recorded that "the presence of representatives from 'Simmons' and 'Howard Payne' with informal applications for charters caused some confusion. They were very welcome but the Constitution requires that applications for new charters be made two months in advance of the regular annual meeting."[13] The two delegations in question withdrew from the room while the Council debated the issue. They finally decided to bypass the constitution to the extent of recognizing the two as regular members of the meeting, with their applications to be considered approved when they were properly presented to Dean Benedict. Dean Julius Olsen of Simmons College made such an impression on the Council that they elected him vice president of the society for the coming year, although his chapter had not technically yet been approved. Of course, Harry Benedict's school never had a chapter at all, and the Constitution did not spell out anything more than that the officers be elected "from and by the Council."[14]

Information on local activities, which was the forum in which most students encountered the Scholarship Societies, is hard to come by, so an accounting of some of these in the minutes of the general meeting is welcome. Baylor University and several other schools reported that their local meetings were primarily social. The TCU chapter conducted a "know-your-own-college" program. Texas Presbyterian focused on awarding prizes to aspiring underclassmen as a means of promoting scholarship. Southwestern worked on the problems of recognition of superior students. All agreed that a program worked best with continuity, a commodity that only the faculty could provide, since student tenure was necessarily limited to two years at most.

It was pointed out that the Constitution made no provision for alumni or honorary membership, but the Council took no action of the matter at that time. The Council elected host sponsor Earl Huffor as president for the coming year, to serve with Dean Olsen and Dean Benedict.

Baylor College (for the second year), North Texas State, and Southwestern asked for the privilege of hosting the 1926 meeting of the Council. The first two withdrew in favor of the "mother society," as they called it, and Southwestern received the honor.

Since most of business was completed in the afternoon session, the delegates visited Sam Houston's home and "other points of interest" in the community. The college hosted an evening banquet with Dean Benedict as the featured speaker.[15]

In the interval between meetings, Dean Benedict dispatched a letter to the chapters with proposed clarifications in the membership article of the constitution. This issue was to come up for consideration at the next meeting of the Council. He also noted that charters had been prepared for the member societies and he was in the process of mailing them. Further, he noted that he was "trying earnestly to have a permanent card for each member of each society." He reminded the local secretaries to prepare these individually for submission to the central office, instead of simply listing all of the chapter's inductees on a single sheet of paper.[16]

The Scholarship Societies of Texas returned to its birthplace for the 1926 meeting. Earl Huffor returned to his alma mater as president of the society founded at his college, a society which was about to break the original bounds it had set for itself. Several new schools sent applications for membership and representatives to plead their cases. The new members accepted at the meeting were Stephen F. Austin State Teachers College, St. Edward's University, McMurry College, Incarnate Word College, and Sul Ross State Teachers College. This represented substantial growth, and placed chapters of the society on campuses all across the state.

The applications that caused the most commotion were from two schools that did not even send delegates. These were Centenary College in Shreveport, Louisiana, and Hendrix College in Conway, Arkansas. The obvious problem they created was that they wanted to join the "Scholarship Societies of *Texas*." After some debate, however, the Council agreed to accept the two schools, subject to their meeting the same general standards that the Texas schools attained. The question of the organization's name was easy enough to resolve, but it required a major readjustment in thought, a readjustment that could take place over a year's time. Further, if a name change was taken up at the 1927 meeting, Centenary and Hendrix could give valuable insights in the selection process.

The annual debate over the membership article erupted yet again when the committee appointed to clarify the matter returned a report that was not entirely satisfactory to the Council. The Baylor College chapter proposed some changes that seemed to have merit, and eventually the Council referred the whole matter back to committee *again*.

Southwestern's Panhellenic Council sponsored a reception for the delegates after adjournment and the "mother chapter" hosted the evening banquet at a building in downtown Georgetown. This banquet was unusual in that no less than fifteen persons were recognized to make remarks. At the banquet the Council accepted the report of its nominating committee, electing J.C. McElhannon of Baylor College as president for the coming year, with John Lord of TCU as vice president and Harry Benedict continuing as secretary-treasurer. Lord subsequently served a term as president and sixteen more years as vice president, fifteen of them consecutively. For several of those years, he was the de facto head of the organization, with the post of president left vacant.

Closing the Books on the Scholarship Societies of Texas

The final meeting of the Council of the Scholarship Societies of Texas convened in Fort Worth on February 26, 1927. Delegates from twenty-five member or applicant schools answered the roll call, plus, of course, Dean Benedict of the University of Texas. This represented 100 percent attendance. In a break with tradition, President McElhannon appointed Mrs. Ethel Garrett of Sam Houston State to take the minutes, freeing Dean Benedict to participate more freely in the discussions. Brite Chapel on the Texas Christian University campus was the site of the proceedings.

After opening greetings, Benedict reported on the financial status of the organization for the first five years. In that span, the organization had taken in $594.00 and spent $368.03.

On motion, the president appointed a committee to propose a name for the newly expanded organization. In due course, the committee returned with a recommendation in two parts. First, they proposed the name "Scholarship Societies of the South" for the organization as a whole. The Council voted down an amendment that would have changed that to "Southern Scholarship Societies" and adopted the committee's original suggestion, thirty to six. The second part of the motion called for the local chapters to adopt a Greek letter name, Alpha Pi Omega. This idea drew heated debate and ended up being referred to a committee by a vote of twenty-four to ten.

In other business the Council granted membership to Abilene Christian College and South Texas State Teachers College (now Texas A&M at Kingsville).

The membership article finally came up for consideration. It did little to clear up the complicated structure of eligibility. One provision held that "small colleges may elect in excess of the top tenth of a class, using due moderation, but larger colleges are expected to adhere more strictly to this limit."[17] The most striking new membership provision came from the floor, calling for the election to honorary membership of faculty who show a "marked interest." This provision, when adopted the following year, restored the practice of the mother chapter in the years before the creation of the statewide organization.

The new officers reflected tradition and a radical break with the past.

The first president of the Scholarship Societies of the South was to be Dean Alfred Nolle of Southwest Texas State. By this action, Nolle became the first person to be elevated from vice president to president, although two years intervened between the terms. Vice president Edna Graham from West Texas State was the first woman named to the executive committee. Harry Benedict accepted another year as secretary-treasurer, but it turned out that this time he would be unable to complete his term.

Non-business items included a drive to Lake Worth for the delegates and a banquet in the TCU cafeteria. By this time a banquet and a tour of the sights of the host city had become something of a tradition for the Scholarship Societies of Texas. Perhaps they would continue to be the same for the Scholarship Societies of the South.[18]

NOTES

[1] "Scholarship Society Convention A Success," *Megaphone*, February 28, 1922.

[2] "Scholarship Guests Are Given Banquet," ibid.

[3] John C. Granbery and Christine Hutchison to Dean H.Y. Benedict, April 17, 1922. The letter is incorporated in the "Minute Book of the Scholarship Societies of Texas," partly handwritten and partly typed, hereafter referred to as "Minute Book." The original is in the Alpha Chi archive at Southwestern University.

[4] "Minutes of the Meeting of April 21, 1922" in "Minute Book," p.4. Benedict appears to have reconstructed these minutes from memory, since an entry to the title page of the "Minute Book" states, "Book begun March 1924." An incomplete list of conferees included on page 4 also suggests that Benedict's memory of the event was dimming.

[5] Benedict and Granbery to "the President and faculty of _____ " May, 1922, reproduced in "Minute Book," p. 5.

[6] Ibid.

[7] "Minute Book," p.7. The founders already had noted the auspicious nature of February 22 in scheduling this meeting, and subsequent annual meetings conformed as closely as possible to that date for several years thereafter.

[8] "Minute Book," pp. 9, 11.

[9] "Minute Book," p. 9. Also see Appendix.

[10] "Minute Book," p. 39.

[11] "Minute Book," pp. 13-15.

[12] "Minute Book," pp. 25-31.

[13] "Minute Book," p. 39.

[14] Article III.

[15] "Minute Book," pp. 35-43.

[16] H.Y. Benedict to the Secretaries of the Scholarship Societies of Texas, September 19, 1925 in "Minute Book," p. 45.

[17] "Minute Book," p. 73.

[18] "Minute Book," pp. 63-75.

Focus On . . .

JOHN COWPER GRANBERY, JR.

The founding president of the Scholarship Societies of Texas was Dr. John Cowper Granbery, Jr. In 1922 Granbery was a busy man, with fingers in several pies at the time of the founding of the statewide scholarship organization. He was an outspoken liberal in a conservative region, and thus constantly involved in controversy. Southwestern's historian said of him, "the university faculty never possessed a more free-tongued, articulate, unshrinking, free-thinking, iconoclast member than John C. Granbery, Texas' famed editor, owner, publisher of The Emancipator."[1]

Granbery was born in Richmond, Virginia, in 1874. His father was a wounded Confederate veteran, professor at Vanderbilt, Methodist pastor and bishop, and founder of the Methodist mission in Brazil. The bishop's wife, a native of central Missouri, was a great-granddaughter of Patrick Henry. She bore him eight children, of whom only three survived childhood.

John Granbery, Jr. became one of the highly educated men of his generation, with degrees from Randolph-Macon (A.B.), Vanderbilt University (B.D.) and the University of Chicago (A.M., Ph.D.).[2] In 1913 Southwestern's president Charles Bishop invited him to become head of the department of economics and sociology. Though his doctoral work was in theology, Granbery was well-versed in sociology. A friend of Jane Addams, he was a frequent correspondent with many of the leaders of the social gospel movement, including Walter Rauschenbusch. At Southwestern, he became active in state politics, agitating for schools for Hispanic children, prohibition, heavy inheritance taxes, improved working conditions for women and children, high taxes on large land holdings, and a cooperative economic system with no leisure class. He denounced the Ku Klux Klan and had his house stoned for it. He angered the church establishment enough that he finally had to leave Southwestern in 1925 for the new school in Lubbock, Texas Tech, as chairman of the history department.[3] Here, he was briefly active again in the scholarship society.

In Lubbock Granbery joined an organized socialist alliance and soon found himself in hot water again. Though the school's president defended him, the trustees fired him in 1932, citing economy as their reason. Students and faculty staged several rallies in his defense, but to no avail. After a visit to Brazil, Granbery returned to Southwestern to work for a pittance.[4] A new president, pro-athletics and anti-academics, arrived in 1935 and fired him again three years later. The previous pattern repeated itself. The removal stuck despite protests from students, faculty, and alumni.

After this Granbery left academia and spent his last years as editor of a liberal periodical, *The Emancipator*, published from his home in San Antonio. He died in 1953.

NOTES

[1] Jones, Ralph Wood, *Southwestern University, 1840-1961* (Austin: Jenkins Publishing Co., 1973), p. 257.

[2] "Granbery, John Cowper," in *Who Was Who In America*, Vol. 3 (Chicago: A.N. Marquis Co., 1960), p. 339.

[3] Sudo-Shimamura, Takako, "John C. Granbery: Three Academic Freedom Controversies in the Life of a Social Gospeler in Texas," unpublished M.A. thesis, University of Texas at Austin, 1971, passim.

[4] Southwestern was twice placed on probation by the Southern Association in this period for low faculty salaries.

CHAPTER 3   (1927-34)
THE SCHOLARSHIP SOCIETIES
OF THE SOUTH

Midway through 1927 the Board of Regents of the University of Texas elected Dean Harry Y. Benedict to fill the vacant president's chair at the university. He at once realized that he would no longer be able to fill the role of secretary-treasurer of the Scholarship Societies of the South because of the demands that the new post would surely place on his available time. There were political reasons as well. The president of the University of Texas would be expected to give all his energies to that task. Further, the expanded constituency of the Scholarship Societies of the South would include responsibilities, however limited, outside the state. In addition, the regents might find questionable his focus on what could be construed as a personal obsession not shared by the masses.

The Nolle Era Begins

Accordingly, on August 3 he informed his friend Dean Alfred Nolle of Southwest Texas State that he would have to resign the position he had held for the lifetime of the organization. The task was passed to, or dumped in the lap of, Dean Nolle, the current president of the Scholarship Societies of the South. Nolle made the thirty-mile trip north to Austin to pick up the files of the organization from Dr. Benedict, thus tentatively accepting the resignation. Benedict assured Nolle of his continuing interest in the Scholarship Societies and of his desire to maintain his relationship with the group. For the balance of the year, Nolle, a man of great energy and organizational ability, functioned in the dual role of president and secretary-treasurer.

When the Scholarship Societies of the South convened on the campus of Howard Payne College in Brownwood on February 22, 1928, Benedict's resignation came up officially. The Council accepted it, of course, with reluctance, of course. Benedict, who had intended to be present at the meeting to present his regrets, sent a telegram explaining that "doctor orders me to stay home until entirely well," but vowing not to miss another meeting.[1]

The matter of continuity in the all-important secretary-treasurer's office was settled later in the meeting when the Council elected Dr. Nolle to the position. He thus began a tenure of more than forty years as secretary-treasurer for the organization.

Despite the absence of Dr. Benedict, attendance otherwise was good at Brownwood. Twenty-three schools answered present at the roll call, with only five not represented. Among those in attendance was Dr. O.E. North of Ouachita College in Arkansas, present to plead his case for admission of his school to the society. The charter was granted and North took his seat as an official delegate.

In the late morning, the Council recessed after appointing a record eight committees which were to work during the lunch break and present their findings at the afternoon session. One committee had the charge of finding a more "succinct designation" than "Scholarship Societies of the South." Their report, calling for the use of the term "S.S.S.," was rejected after "warm and lengthy discussion" in favor of the "dignified official title."

Surprising no one, the membership article of the constitution came up for revision again. The debate here focused on the matter of fees to be collected when a student was elected to Junior membership, Senior membership, and Graduate membership. Most students who qualified for Junior membership would expect to meet the requirements (usually top 10 percent of the class) at the next level as well, and the Council doubted the wisdom of charging them the same initiation fee three times running. Accordingly, they imbedded in the constitution what should have been a statutory provision, namely, that a $1.00 fee be assessed for first membership, a fifty cent fee for second membership, and no fee at all for third membership.

The increase was important because, although the society's treasury continued to expand (there was now more than $400 in the bank), a heavier cash drain was expected with the issuance of engraved certificates to new members. In connection with that matter, Dr. Nolle introduced representatives from Star Engraving Company of Houston, who would henceforth provide membership certificates, stationery, keys, and any other organizational paraphernalia.

Since the qualifications for chapter charters were based on purely Texas criteria, the Council decided to change the standard to accept any school which received certification by the "Association of Colleges and Secondary Schools of the Southern States" or similar accrediting organizations. This action opened yet another door leading beyond a merely regional focus for the society.

Some of the newer member schools of the Scholarship Societies of the South raised the question of retroactive membership for students who met the qualifications prior to the school's induction into the Societies. The committee charged with handling this matter made a recommendation that the constitution be amended to allow each school to nominate two former students for honorary membership annually, provided that the nominees for honorary membership had distinguished themselves in postgraduate work. This amendment took effect immediately, when the Council decided unanimously to waive the constitutional requirements for prior notice.

Several of the delegates shared information about the types of programs they were conducting in their respective local chapters. The Council expressed great interest in hearing more about the form that initiation rituals should have. There was at the time no constitutional guidance on this matter, other than that they would not be secret ceremonies.

After offering for several years to host the meeting and having been bypassed in favor of other invitations, Baylor College at Belton received the Council's approval to be the site of the 1929 meeting. The Council charged the executive committee with setting the exact date.

As a last item of business, the Council elected Dr. W.P. Davidson of Southwestern to the post of president. Davidson had been active in the group from the beginning, having participated in both of the 1922 meetings. Miss Bessie Shook from North Texas State became the vice president for the year. Miss Shook would, several years later, take over the job of keeping the minutes of the annual meetings, a task hitherto performed by Dr. Benedict and Prof. Ethel Garrett of Sam Houston State. Dean Nolle accepted election as "permanent" secretary-treasurer. The 1928 meeting concluded with a "colonial supper" provided by the host chapter.[2]

Into The Great Depression

All but three of the chapters showed up for the 1929 meeting, which convened at North Texas State instead of Baylor College, for reasons the minutes do not explain. The dates were February 22 and 23. With the addition of Louisiana College at this session, the organization now had twenty-nine members.

A highlight of the meeting was an address by Dr. Harry Benedict, who was termed "honorary president of the Scholarship Societies of the South." Benedict defended the concept of honor societies, asserting that "education must be competitive. It is morally wrong to give money to teach those who can't or won't study."[3]

A rising force in the Council, Dr. O.T. Gooden from Hendrix College, delivered another address outlining plans of promoting undergraduate scholarship and citing experiments along that line conducted at Swarthmore College and at his own school. This paper evoked a spirited exchange of ideas among the delegates.

Friday evening was the time set this year for the banquet, with entertainment provided by the host chapter. The featured speaker was the outgoing president of the societies, Dr. W.P. Davidson.

Saturday morning, routine business took only a short time. The Council elected its first female president for the 1929-30 term, Prof. Bessie Shook, the host sponsor. Dr. Gooden, whose speech the previous day had stimulated such warm discussion, was chosen vice president to serve alongside Dean Nolle as secretary-treasurer and Prof. Garrett as assistant secretary, a post that appears nowhere in the constitution. The haste of the morning session was occasioned by the scheduled speech by a professor from Southern Methodist University before the entire student body of North Texas State. His topic was "Ye shall know the truth, and the truth shall make you free," and his name was Charles McT. Bishop, "the organizer of the first chapter of the Scholarship Societies at Southwestern University."[4]

Although an invitation from West Texas State was on the floor in 1929, the Council agreed to take the 1930 gathering to East Texas State in Commerce, on the grounds that the location of West Texas State in the Texas Panhandle was too remote from the geographic center of the societies to make it economically feasible to meet there. On the other hand, Commerce, the home of East Texas State, gave easy access to almost all the chapters.

An innovation at this meeting was a presidential report delivered by Prof. Bessie Shook to the representatives from twenty-four chapters. Several addresses and routine business consumed the Friday session, after which the members attended a basketball game at the college gymnasium. The evening banquet featured a men's singing *trio* called "the Four Horsemen of the Puckered Lips." The following morning, February 22, the Council worked on constitutional changes affecting honorary membership for sponsors and the awarding of a society key to the outgoing president, with provision for retroactive awards to all previous occupants of the presidential chair. Dr. O.T. Gooden became the first Council president from outside Texas, with Dean Olsen of Simmons College as his vice president. Dr. Nolle continued as secretary-treasurer.

A familiar face turned up at the 1931 meeting at Baylor College. He was the faculty representative from Texas Tech, Dr. John C. Granbery, Jr. Altogether, eight former presidents of the organization were present. The Friday evening banquet saw the presentation of presidential keys to each of them, in keeping with the decisions reached the previous year.

Almost all the chapters had delegates in attendance. Following the precedent set by Prof. Shook, Council president O.T. Gooden made a "state of the societies" address. He especially emphasized a theme which was dear to him, the expansion of the organization onto other campuses. No new chapters had joined for the previous two years and that was cause for extended organization and increased effort. Considerable discussion ensued, after which the Council adopted a motion to create a committee for the purpose of developing expansion plans, including any constitutional changes that might facilitate the process.

In some ways, however, the society was already growing to an uncomfortable size. The policy of hearing individual reports from each of the chapters was amended so that fifteen chapters would report in 1931 and the remainder in 1932, setting a pattern thereafter of biennial reports from each.

The Council reinstated two chapters which had been suspended for non-attendance at the Council meetings. The constitution provided for such penalty when a chapter missed two consecutive meetings without good cause. Delegations from Ouachita College and Texas A&I were present, making the reinstatement easier. The Council later in the session amended the constitution to provide for a warning to be sent to chapters in danger of suspension for non-attendance.

At the suggestion of Dean Nolle, President Gooden appointed an audit committee for the purpose of verifying the secretary-treasurer's books. A balance of $818 showed that the society's treasury continued to expand under Nolle's stewardship.

The banquet speaker was one of President Gooden's colleagues from Hendrix, a Chaucer scholar named R.L. Campbell. "We found," Miss Shook reported, "that Chaucer was our principal neighbor of the fourteenth century, and that we have borrowed most of our troubles in politics, in sociology, in manners, and in religion from him and his contemporaries."[5] Dr. Benedict's place card for the banquet is among his papers. It includes a drawing of a Chaucerian character and a quotation from the poet and is interlaced with the society's green and blue ribbons.[6]

Bessie Shook this year began a long tenure as recording secretary for the Council. It was not an elective post, but successive presidents appointed Miss Shook to the task for several decades to come. The Council chose Dean Julius Olsen of Simmons College for its next president and Prof. Edna Graham of West Texas State for vice president. President-elect Olsen invited the Council to meet in Abilene in 1932. He was supported by delegates from the other chapters in town, Abilene Christian College and McMurry College, and the Council had little trouble in accepting this bid over two others.[7]

Initiations

The Societies finally resolved the matter of a prescribed initiation ceremony in 1931 by adopting a proposal outlining a general course of action, without specifying the language to be employed. This procedure was undoubtedly based on common practice already in place.

The opening portion of the initiation ceremony centered on a series of questions which were directed at the candidates. The purpose of the questions was to "'stump' the candidate, cause merriment, and generally 'show up' the individual's ignorance."[8] This procedure followed closely along the lines that Southwest Texas State had been using for several years. The campus newspaper reported in 1927 that the chapter met at Dr. Nolle's home for the initiation: "The new members were given a series of tests which they finally passed, and were required to write a theme on their major subject."[9]   The questions at Dr. Nolle's home were similar to the ones listed below, as suggested by the document adopted in 1931. Among were the following:

1. Who is the champion prize fighter of the world?
3. Who is the president of Yale? Harvard? Princeton? University of Texas?
6. Who is the Vice-President of the United States? Secretary of State?
8. What is the area of Texas? Louisiana?
11. What is a "bloc"?
12. Name the chairman of the Senate Foreign Relations Committee.
18. Who invented the incandescent lamp?
20. What man received the latest award of the Nobel Peace Prize? Physics Prize? For what service was the award made?
21. What is a symphony? Sonata?
26. Who is a socialist? A radical? A reactionary?
29. What is the highest waterfall in the world?
31. Who is the author of "Alice in Wonderland"? "Confessions of an Opium Eater"? "Christmas Carol"? "North of Boston"? "Desire under the Elms"? "Cariolanus"?[sic]
39. To what church did Robert E. Lee belong? Woodrow Wilson?
44. If you were to find a coin dated "51 B.C.," what would you do with it?
45. In which Testament, Old or New, is the statement: "Cleanliness is next to Godliness"? In which is the Book of Hezekiah? What form of literature is the Book of Job?
51. What is a condenser?
53. What is the difference between a dinasaurus [sic] and a lizard?
56. What is the didactic meaning of malaria?
59. Who is the president of the Pennsylvania Railroad?
60. Who is editor of the Atlantic Monthly? Saturday Evening Post?

After the candidates were sufficiently humiliated, "the Ritual Proper" could commence. Far more dignified than the preliminary portion would suggest, this element was performed by candlelight. The sponsor (in academic regalia) and the chapter president stood at the front of the room behind the only light, the "candle of knowledge." The initiates, holding unlighted candles, entered by pairs, processing up a center aisle between the old members. Violin and/or piano music played in the background throughout the ceremony. As the first pair approached, the chapter president took the lighted candle in his/her right hand and charged the initiates, "Scholarship is the power of the mind to dispel ignorance and superstition through scientific investigation of truth. By virtue of your scholarship, your leadership, and your character, you have been invited to bring your candle of research and light it by the candle of knowledge of your Alma Mater. In the name of the Scholarship Societies of the South, come, light your candles and make the pledge."

Each pair then lit their candles and repeated the pledge, as follows: "I pledge myself to uphold the purposes of the Scholarship Societies of the South, striving to make its ideals my ideals in scholarship and in service." At this point, one went left and the other right and took their places at the end of the line. When all had completed this act, they stood in a V in front of the sponsor, who led them in repeating the motto, "Ye shall know the truth and the truth shall make you free." Then the sponsor said, "Now that you have received the light of your Alma Mater in reality and in symbol, let us extinguish our symbols and find your places with the members of the _____ Chapter of the Scholarship Societies of the South."

Following this portion of the ceremony, the chapter president read a summary of the nature and aims of the society and made other appropriate remarks. A sponsor gave a short history of the organization and the group was dismissed, with the recommendation that light refreshments be served at this point.[10] Some of the elements of these rituals seem a bit confusing. For example, the initiates were not officially told the purposes of the organization until after they affirmed that they would uphold them. Also, they were told that they had been chosen by virtue of their scholarship, their character, and their leadership, yet nowhere in the society's laws was there any mention of leadership as a criterion for membership. Finally, the pledge commits members to make real the ideals of the society "in service," though there was no explicit mention of that anywhere else either.

The ritual was entirely appropriate to its time. It combined the dignity and symbolism of the candlelight ritual with the rowdiness that must have accompanied the pre-initiation quizzing. In some chapters there were other, more informal, types of activities that could be called "hazing," even among honor society members. One such placed the blindfolded candidate on a plank held by two sturdy members. The plank was lifted off the floor while the members talked to the candidate, all the while bending and then kneeling lower and lower to the floor, giving the candidate the impression he was being lifted high. Then the candidate was ordered to jump! Students of the era considered such pranks great fun.

Reaching Out to the Nation

The coincidence of Washington's birthday with the anniversary of the founding of the honor society finally created a problem in 1932. Dean Julius Olsen of Simmons College, president for the year and also sponsor of the host chapter for the 1932 meeting, wrote President Benedict early in the year, inviting him to come to Abilene to be the guest speaker for the Council meeting.[11] Benedict responded a week later, saying that he was sorry, but the D.A.R. was dedicating a statue of Washington on the university campus that day and he simply had to be present.[12]

Benedict's absence notwithstanding, the meeting took place on schedule. The society welcomed two new chapters, Arkansas State Teachers College and the College of the Ozarks, to membership. The society noted the loss of one chapter. Texas Presbyterian College was a victim of the great depression, and the minutes simply noted that the chapter was "deceased," leaving a total of exactly thirty chapters. The college's records, alumni, and some of its students were transferred to Trinity University.

The weather for the meeting was rainy. The minutes noted that several chapters were absent because "it has been raining for ten days over the entire 'water shed' of the societies." A telegram arrived from the West Texas State delegation on the second day of the meeting saying that they were "waterbound on the plains." Other references were made to Abilene's "weeping weather" and "slippery pavements." President J.W. Hunt of McMurry, who was scheduled to be toastmaster at the banquet, "was mud-bound in San Angelo and could not get to the meeting." These concerns may have been behind a motion to move the date of the Council meeting, a matter that the body finally referred to the executive committee.

Dean Olsen, a physicist, had developed a theme for the meeting. The theme was "Science." President Batsell Baxter of Abilene Christian spoke on the subject of "The Limitation of Biology," stating that while he had taught biology before becoming an administrator, he still noted that science cannot solve "the great mystery of life, why we are here and where we are going." Olsen's presidential address at the banquet was titled "Some Observations of Science."

The Council decided to publish the minutes of the meeting, minutes which hitherto had been kept in the "Minute Book" where only the executive committee had access to them. The Council interpreted the constitution to include persons seeking the Bachelor of Music degree as being eligible for membership. Dr. Rupert N. Richardson, a distinguished Texas historian, spoke at the concluding session on the life of George Washington. With the election of J.M. Bledsoe on East Texas State as president and Dr. John Lord of Texas Christian as vice president, the Council adjourned to meet at Dr. Nolle's school, Southwest Texas State, in 1933.[13]

The theme for the 1933 meeting was "Idealism." Since Dean Nolle was a professor of German, and since one of the principal addresses was by another German scholar, Arkansas State Teachers College sponsor Dr. P.R. Clugston, each chapter answered roll call with a quotation from Goethe. Several responded in the original German, to the delight of Professor Shook, the secretary. (There was, of course, advance warning of this.)

Southwest Texas State hosted the meeting, and although there had been sentiment to change the date, the time was the traditional February 22-23. Since those days fell in the middle of the week, this was a little unusual for the society. In contrast to the previous year, the weather smiled on this gathering. The evening banquet was held at Wimberly, a resort town in the hills west of San Marcos, and the first traces of spring could be seen on the hillsides during the drive.

Dean Olsen proposed that, in addition to publication of the minutes of the meetings, the texts of the speeches also should be put in print. On direction of the Council, President Bledsoe appointed a committee to see to the matter. The result of this action was the publication of a thirty-eight page volume called *Proceedings*. The society published a similar volume under that name annually (except for three years during World War II) through 1956. The following year the sequence continued under the new title, the *Recorder*, which continues to the present day.

Under the heading of new business, Dr. Gooden rose to urge action to expand the society across the Mississippi River. Dean Nolle responded that he was aware of interest outside the three-state area, but he felt the financial condition of the country precluded any immediate results. Many delegates agreed with Gooden, and the Council directed the president to appoint a committee to investigate further. This task fell to the incoming president, Dr. John Lord, who made the appointment as his first act in office.

For the first time, the report of the nominating committee did not receive immediate approval. The committee proposed Dr. John Lord of TCU for president and Prof. Julia Luker of McMurry College for vice president. The routine call for nominations from the floor brought Dr. Lord an opponent in the nomination of Dr. Claud Howard of Southwestern for president. Howard had distinguished himself in debate earlier in the meeting and was about to deliver a brilliant paper of the idealism of Robert Browning as the climax of the meeting. In contrast to modern usage, which grants one vote to the student delegate and one vote to the faculty delegate from each chapter, there was only one vote per chapter. Of the twenty-six chapters present, nineteen voted for Lord and five for Howard. Two chapters did not vote, perhaps indicating that the faculty and student delegates could not agree.

At the conclusion of the meeting, the new president made a Solomon-like appointment of the Committee on Expansion: Dr. Gooden, the advocate of rapid expansion as chair; Dean Nolle, who had his doubts but would be the principal agent of correspondence with any prospective chapters in his post as secretary-treasurer; and the defeated presidential candidate, Dr. Howard. Aside from the appointment of this committee, there was no clue to the great events that were about to engulf the organization in the coming year.

A final note to this meeting shows up in the appendix stating the society's financial standing. In spite of the depression, the organization's treasury continued to grow, now approaching $1,500.

O.T. Gooden was not a man to waste time. He had been pushing expansion for several years and now had the tool in his hands to effect that ambition. As he sent out inquiries to other colleges, he ran across another scholarship society that was forming, with principal focus on the South. Gooden's first contacts with Dr. John L. Lee, Jr., head of Mu Omega Xi, were so promising that the two began to pursue the possibilities of merging their respective societies. When Gooden apprised Dean Nolle, as a member of the expansion committee, of his conversations with Lee, Nolle became concerned. His perusal of the constitution of the rival society disturbed him as much as the possibility that Lee would be the executive secretary of a merged group. In a letter to Dr. Benedict, Nolle included copies of the correspondence on the subject available to him, along with a copy of Mu Omega Xi's proposed constitution. Nolle wanted guidance from the founder of the Scholarship Societies of the South. Upon receipt of Nolle's letter, Benedict responded by telephone, probably agreeing that they should move slowly. In a closing paragraph, Nolle suggested that if the non-Texas schools, like Gooden's, decided to pursue merger, the Texas colleges might reconstitute the Scholarship Societies of Texas. In other words, he proposed secession.[14]

Nolle's concern was unnecessary, for Gooden was growing increasingly disenchanted with Dr. Lee and his organization. In December 1933 he wrote a letter to his colleagues on the expansion committee, Nolle and Howard, and to President Lord, expressing his concerns about Mu Omega Xi: "I am afraid there is not so very much in common between them and us. . . . I do not think he [Dr. Lee] would be a suitable person in such an organization as we have in mind. . . .It seems to me we can lick them to a standstill in the matter of expansion."[15] He continued to urge creation of "a strong fraternity that will develop into a real national body in time and command the respect of all comers." To that end, he enclosed his constitutional proposal, asking them to "criticize it freely."[16]

Gooden's plan included a new, non-parochial name for the organization: "I am suggesting A X, Alpha Chi, the initial letters of the Greek words for Truth and Character for a name." He concluded by appealing for a quick response, since "our time is short."[17] Gooden reiterated these concerns a week later in a letter to Benedict: "The new organization in the South that we have been studying seems to differ too much from ours in spirit and purpose to permit any merger of the two bodies. They have definitely decided against such a policy at this time. The organizer and chief executive officer seems to be singularly lacking in conception of what scholarship is."[18] As an alternative to merger, Gooden again argued for national expansion, and thought a changed structure and name would be necessary to accomplish it. He enclosed a copy of his proposal for a new constitution. In a prophetic vein, he went on: "I think there is a need for a national organization of our type and purpose. I think such an organization is likely to develop in the near future. I am wondering why that organization should not be ours."[19] Since the others on the expansion committee apparently concurred with Gooden's proposals, the document was sent to chapters as the report of the committee. It seems clear that the initiative for these moves lay with Dr. Gooden. Dean Nolle's more cautious approach might well have left the organization a regional body for generations to come. It remained to be seen whether the delegates to the 1934 meeting of the Scholarship Societies of the South would agree. When they convened at Texas State College for Women (formerly College of Industrial Arts) in Denton on February 21, they had in hand copies of a document that would, if adopted, revolutionize their organization.

NOTES

[1] "Minute Book," p. 81; copy of the telegram, dated February 20, 1928 in Benedict Papers at the University of Texas, Box 2B64.

[2] "Minute Book," pp. 77-91.

[3] "Minute Book," p. 99.

[4] "Minute Book," pp. 93-103.

[5] "Minute Book," p. 129.

[6] H.Y. Benedict Papers, U.T. Austin, Box 2B64.

[7] "Minute Book," pp. 121-37.

[8] Pamphlet, "Initiation Ceremonies, Scholarship Societies of the South, Adopted at the Annual Meeting of the Council of the Societies, Baylor College, Belton, Texas," H.Y. Benedict Papers, U.T. Austin, Box 2B64.

[9] Southwest Texas State Teachers College *College Star,* November 23, 1927.

[10] From the 1931 pamphlet, "Initiation Ceremonies... ," Benedict Papers, U.T. Austin, Box 2B64.

[11] Olsen to Benedict, January 1, 1932, Benedict Papers, U.T. Austin, Box 2B64.

[12] Benedict to Olsen, January 8, 1932, Benedict Papers, U.T. Austin, Box 2B64.

[13] *Minutes* of the Eleventh Annual Meeting of the Council of the Scholarship Societies of the South, February 22-23, 1932

[14] Nolle to Benedict, November 20, 1933, with acknowledgment of receipt and note of return phone call, Benedict Papers, U.T. Austin, Box 2B64.

[15] Gooden to "Drs. Lord, Nolle and Howard," December 7, 1933, Benedict Papers, U.T. Austin, Box 2B64.

[16] Ibid.

[17] Ibid.

[18] O.T. Gooden to H.Y. Benedict, December 15, 1933, Benedict Papers, U.T. Austin, Box 2B64.

[19] Ibid.

Focus On ...

ALFRED H. NOLLE

A.H. Nolle was one of the two or three most important figures in the history of Alpha Chi. He came into the organization soon after its founding meeting, representing Southwest Texas State, the school of which he was academic dean. After a one-year term as president of the Scholarship Societies of the South, he succeeded Harry Benedict as the society's secretary-treasurer in 1929 and held the post for the next forty-one years. In a time before the development of an active National Council and additional regions, Nolle single-handedly provided almost all of the continuity of the society, in addition to managing its business affairs. One tribute to him says, "He was at the very center of every decision made by Alpha Chi in its steady rise to a position as an esteemed honor society of national significance."[1]

As secretary-treasurer, Nolle served as the society's financial officer, its principal correspondent, and its editor. When the society developed a scholarship program, it fell to Nolle to manage it. However, he broke one of Benedict's traditions: he avoided taking minutes of meetings, transferring that task to others.

In addition to his Alpha Chi responsibilities, Dean Nolle managed his growing academic program at Southwest Texas State. His Alpha Chi papers take up only a small portion of the files collected under his name at Southwest Texas. He was active in the Association of Texas Colleges, holding all of its principal offices and chairing its Committee on Standards for twenty years. Among his credentials were military service as a major in World War I, membership in Phi Beta Kappa, numerous Kiwanis awards, and a church, St. Marks Episcopal in San Marcos, dedicated in his honor. East Texas Baptist College awarded him an honorary doctorate and a tribute to him was read into the *Congressional Record* by Senator Lyndon B. Johnson.

Nolle's academic field was German, a language he learned as a youth in his native Missouri. He earned two baccalaureate degrees from the University of Missouri, a master's from the University of the South, and took his Ph.D. at the University of Pennsylvania in 1915. He did post-doctoral study in Germany before the United States entered World War I.

He went to Southwest Texas as professor of German after the war, becoming dean in 1922, a position he held until his retirement in 1959. Dr. Nolle died in 1979 at the age of 89.[2]

Alpha Chi honors Dean Nolle's memory and service through the annual scholarship awards named for him and granted to distinguished college juniors.

NOTES

[1] *Recorder*, 1970, p. 5.
[2] *Recorder*, 1979, pp. 3-4.

CHAPTER 4 (1934-37)
ALPHA CHI BEGINS

The thirteenth annual meeting of the Council of the Scholarship Societies convened at 1:30 p.m., February 21, 1934, with Dr. John Lord presiding. Delegations were present from twenty-seven member institutions. After the greetings and approval of the minutes, the president called for committee reports. Two brief routine reports occupied but a few minutes, and then Dr. O.T. Gooden stood to deliver the report of the expansion committee.

He outlined a bold new plan for the structuring of the society beyond the local level. Local chapter organization, he explained, would not be affected, but a major overhaul was in store for what he called the "national body" of the society if the report was adopted. After a careful explanation, and after many questions were asked and answered, former president Earl Huffor moved adoption of the report. Because the Council was not yet satisfied about some of the aspects of the proposal, they passed a motion to table the matter, expecting to resume the debate the next day after more consideration and informal discussion could be given.

When the report was taken from the table the next morning, the Council decided to adopt or reject it in toto, without amendment. However, additional discussion revealed that the only issue of serious contention was the new name. This occasioned substantial debate and was dealt with separately from the main proposal.

The two options were to adopt a Greek letter name or an English name. Gooden, as we have seen, was already urging use of the name "Alpha Chi." A Greek name had been proposed several years earlier, but the Council backed away when Dean Olsen of Simmons College reported that his school's charter prohibited fraternities and sororities on their campus. If the name change was adopted, Olsen said, Simmons "would graciously withdraw from the organization."[1] Subsequently, it dawned on the Council that the organization was not a fraternity or a sorority, but a society. That distinction met the objections raised in the Simmons College charter.

Although the vote centered on "Greek" versus "English" in the abstract, the delegates knew that they were really choosing between "Alpha Chi" and "Shield and Torch."[2] After extended debate, the Council, with each chapter casting one ballot, chose the Greek letter designation. The vote was fifteen to eleven, meaning that it could easily have gone the other way. Once that matter was settled, the Council, with little or no debate, adopted Gooden's suggestion of "Alpha Chi." From that moment, Prof. Shook noted, "the Scholarship Societies of the South became Alpha Chi."[3] Two major items of business remained. The first was the selection of a meeting site for 1935, and the Council agreed to accept the invitation of Ouachita College in Arkadelphia, Arkansas. This action symbolized the new reach of the society, since it meant they would meet outside of Texas for the first time. It also soon caused major difficulties.

The New Structure

Dr. Gooden's vision of a truly national organization began with a structure that he thought would be capable of gathering respect and of mobilizing for a dramatic expansion beyond the current geographic limits. For this purpose there would be two new bodies created from the existing Council of the Scholarship Societies of the South.

The first, called the National Council, was intended to impress prospective schools with the quality of the society. To that end, the Council was to be composed of people with prestigious titles. Gooden had earlier explained to Benedict that the society's only chance for expansion outside its present region was "in securing some outstanding college and university Presidents on a National Council." Further, "the President of the National Council must be a man of influence in untouched territory. The duties of this office need not be many. The name and an occasional letter would be of great help. The main work can be looked after by an Executive Secretary."[4] In earlier correspondence to his colleagues on the expansion committee, he said, "I think if we want to expand, we must go out into new territory and secure some outstanding college Presidents who have influence with their tribe as members of our National Council . . . . Most, if not all, of those to be elected by the Council might be of this sort. We might try Oklahoma, Kansas, Missouri, and some of the other Southern colleges to begin with."[5] The constitution for Alpha Chi provided for an initial election of National Council membership by

the 1934 convention. Thereafter, the National Council would elect at
least six of its own members as terms expired or seats otherwise became
open. The term of office was five years. These persons would hold academic ranks of prestige, either deans or presidents. There was no requirement that their schools have a chapter of Alpha Chi. The remainder, at least six, would be elected from the second successor body, the
Regional Council. As the society expanded, the new Regional Councils
could share in the election of members on the National Council.

The new constitution granted the National Council certain powers
including, among others, the following:

> to elect half its own members;
> to elect its own officers;
> to elect honorary members to the society;
> to share in approval process for new chapter charters;
> to fix duties and expenditures of its officers;
> to fix regional boundaries;
> to interpret the constitution;
> to initiate constitutional changes, subject to ratification by two-thirds
>   of the regions;
> to change initiation fees;
> to hear appeals.

The executive committee of the National Council included the three
national officers: president, vice president, and secretary-treasurer. The
secretary-treasurer was designated as the "executive officer" for the society. The committee also included the executive officers of the regions,
which meant the secretary-treasurers. Under this structure, the last named
officers would be members of the national executive committee but not
of the National Council. The executive committee could:

> make recommendations to the National Council;
> interpret the constitution, subject to appeal to the Council;
> pass on questionable actions of the regions, again subject to appeal;
> carry on the business of the society, subject to review by the Council.

The executive committee became a management team answerable to the
National Council sitting as a board of directors. However, membership
on the National Council proved, in the short run, to be nothing more than
a paper honor.

There was no provision regarding regular meetings for either group, except that the Council met when called into session by the executive committee or by petition of a majority of its members. The following fall the secretary-treasurer had to remind the new president that the constitution left the meeting time up in the air. "I take it that it will prove desirable to have the National Council meeting simultaneously with the Regional Council meeting next February, and that you will at the proper time issue a call for a meeting of the National Council or instruct me as Secretary-Treasurer to do so."[6] The president did not follow through with this notion, and Nolle was left to explain after the 1935 meeting that "the members of the National Council, although all were present at the meeting of the Regional Council except President Whitley, did not hold a separate meeting . . . . The members of the National Council have thus far . . . not exercised the prerogative of electing the six additional members provided for . . . ."[7] Similar comments in the 1936 and 1937 minutes mean that President Benedict never did get around to calling the National Council into session. The Council did not convene for the first time until 1938, after Benedict's death had left the society without a president.

In addition to the National Council, the society would meet as Regional Councils. In the beginning there was only one of these, but the system permitted the creation of additional Regional Councils as circumstances dictated. The Regional Council consisted of a student representative and a faculty representative from each chapter. It elected the same three officers, with the secretary-treasurer as executive officer holding a seat on the national executive committee. The duties of the Regional Councils included:

holding an annual meeting with program and banquet;
ratifying proposed constitutional amendments;
sharing in the acceptance of new chapters within its bounds;
electing its own officers;
adopting its own rules and procedures, as long they were not
contrary to the national constitution.

The regional executive committee could act for the region in the intervals between meetings.

Since the main business of the society for the next two decades consisted mainly of the annual meeting of Region I (to which all chapters initially belonged), the Regional Council was much more important than the National Council. There was an ambiguity present in the conception of the National Council. It was designed on the one hand to be a figure-head, providing, in its membership, the credentials of academic prestige. It did not have to meet except on an irregular basis nor was it necessary for its members to attend the "national" (one region only until 1955) meetings of the society. On the other hand, it held substantial power, including a power which it did not exercise very well, the power to pro-mote expansion.

The records of the annual "national" meetings show that most of the *real* business of Alpha Chi fell to the regional officers. This was in some senses unfortunate, for the region was encouraged to rotate its presidents and vice presidents annually, and to keep its secretary-treasurers in of-fice for lengthy periods. The result was that regional continuity resided in the hands of one person, and the regional secretary-treasurer could frustrate any initiatives he did not agree with. As it happened, the Region routinely elected Dean Nolle to the position, and the National Council just as routinely elected him national secretary-treasurer, thus placing in his hands the role of "executive officer" for both the Regional and the National Councils. Nolle handled these tasks with energy and tact, but the record of very slow growth raises questions about his stewardship of expansion.

The new constitution also removed from the hands of students any voice in their national direction. Heretofore, they could cast a student vote in the Council of the Scholarship Societies of the South, a vote which might or might not be influenced by the vote their faculty repre-sentative had. Now it was to be one vote per chapter, and the faculty vote would prevail if there was disagreement. Further, by shifting some au-thority to the relatively remote National Council, the new constitution concentrated power more heavily in the hands of faculty and administra-tors.

In other respects, things remained much the same. The foreword, or preamble, to the constitution said that Alpha Chi was "dedicated to the stimulation of sound scholarship and devotion to truth wherever such may be found; it is opposed to bigotry, narrowness, and distinction on any basis save that of true genuine worth."

The key resembled the old one. It was a shield with the lamp of knowledge and the raised letters "AX" on the obverse. The reverse side was identical to the old, with the initials of the college, the name of the owner, and the date, February 22, 1922. The motto remained the same as did the colors. Local organization remained untouched, including the overly complicated membership selection criteria. One new element was the introduction of state names and Greek alphabet numbers to designate the chapter nationally. The old chapter names were grandfathered in for local use. The head sponsor continued to be chosen by the president of the institution for a three-year term, but two assistant sponsors could be elected to one-year terms by the chapter membership.[8]

Implementation

After adoption of the constitution, the 1934 session approved the report of a nominating committee proposing the persons who would make up the first National Council of Alpha Chi. The terms of the first group were staggered to allow a well-spaced rotation. Dr. Benedict received the five-year term, with Dr. Lord chosen for four years, Dr. Claud Howard of Southwestern for three years, President S.H. Whitley of East Texas State for two years, Sister M. Clement of Incarnate Word College for one year, and Dr. Nolle for an indefinite term based on his service as regional secretary-treasurer. With the exception of Howard, all these persons held the title of president or dean at their respective schools. In addition, the assembly chose Prof. Edna Graham of West Texas State to be regional president with Prof. C.L. Odom of Centenary as regional vice president. Two prominent names are notably absent. Prof. Bessie Shook, the keeper of the minutes, and Dr. O.T. Gooden, the author of the constitution, did not make the list.

The convention recessed briefly to allow the National Council the opportunity to choose its officers. They reported back that they had chosen Dr. Harry Benedict as the first president of Alpha Chi, with Dean John Lord as vice president, and Dean Alfred Nolle as secretary-treasurer. Benedict's selection was a foregone conclusion. As the only active founder, as the president of the state's largest university, as a figure revered and respected by all, he was the logical choice. Both Gooden and Nolle had urged him to accept the post before the meeting ever began, and he was agreeable, especially since Nolle would bear much of the burden of running the society's day-to-day business.[9]

If the restructuring of the scholarship organization was intended to help in expansion, the short-term effect was not encouraging. At the

Denton meeting Gooden was charged informally with continuing to give thought to the matter. He wrote to President Benedict in the summer that he was confused about his role. He had been trying to work through Dean Nolle, he explained, but Nolle kept putting him off. "I wonder," wrote Gooden, "if he is not favorable to efforts at expansion." Later in the letter, he appealed to Benedict for guidance, without which he was going to discontinue his efforts. He concluded by saying, "I see little hope for us unless we can secure a National Secretary-treasurer that can and will give time to the job."[10] The president sought to soothe the unhappy sponsor, saying, "I do not see how Alpha Chi can do much without a sufficient endowment to provide a permanent Secretary and other expenses. You and Miss Graham and Dr. Nolle and all the rest of us are pretty busy and whatever we do for Alpha Chi has to be done, so to speak, with our left hand and as a 'labor of love.'"[11] The endowment necessary to underwrite the expenses of a national office was not forthcoming for another forty years.

But Gooden was not the only one feeling a lack of direction. Regional President Edna Graham also expressed her frustration in seeking to find out where her responsibilities lay in the matter of expansion. She had written Dean Nolle, she told Benedict, asking for clarification. His response was that she could work as she wished in Texas, Arkansas, and Louisiana, but that expansion outside those states was properly the province of the National Council: "Logically, I believe, the responsibility falls to the lot of the Secretary-Treasurer of the organization." This did not suit Miss Graham much, since she had been actively recruiting in neighboring New Mexico, but without much success. Having clarified the matter, Nolle included another thought which created renewed confusion: "Tentatively, it was agreed, I believe, that Dr. Gooden should act as a sort of co-ordinator of our efforts at expansion. I would suggest that you continue your informal overtures."[12] Blame should not be placed on Dr. Nolle about this; the confusion was the result of a dimly understood new structure and the mixing of formal and informal communications at the Denton meeting. Everyone had much to learn in implementing the operations of the restructured society.

Old Standards, New Symbols

Tangled with the concerns about expansion responsibilities was the matter of society standards. The leadership of the society was already aware that the North Central Association, the accrediting agency that had jurisdiction of the Arkansas colleges, had removed accreditation from Ouachita College two years earlier for athletic violations and weak financial standing. In the spring of 1934, press reports indicated that College of the Ozarks was also going to lose accreditation. When Miss Graham received word of the impending disaffiliation of College of the Ozarks, she wrote to Benedict that she was concerned about the image of Alpha Chi if the two disaccredited schools were allowed to remain in good standing. She asked whether anything should be done immediately or whether they should wait until the 1935 meeting to take steps.[13] Dr. Gooden also expressed concern. He bewailed the state of higher education in Arkansas, with "too many state and too many private colleges." He complained that the organization had allowed the two suspended schools to retain their chapters despite the constitutional provision that called for them to be suspended from Alpha Chi as well. He echoed Prof. Graham's concern, saying, "Unless we act vigorously in such cases we can not expect institutions of standing to have much respect for us."[14] Communications flew back and forth among the leaders of the society throughout the fall. Ouachita, one of the suspended institutions, was the scheduled host of the 1935 meeting. The National Council and the regional officers agreed unanimously among themselves that they could not afford to meet at a suspended chapter. President Benedict offered to host the 1935 meeting at the University of Texas and the Council accepted. Dr. Nolle informed Ouachita's president of the decision and the regional president adjusted her plans accordingly.[15] The 1935 meeting convened on February 21 in Austin. Dr. Nolle called it the first annual meeting of Region I and the fourteenth annual meeting of the National Council.[16] This mixed nomenclature indicated that there was still some confusion in people's minds about the new structure because the first thirteen annual meetings were called meetings of "the Council," without the word "National," an entirely different body from the current "National Council." In fact, the "National Council" did not meet at all in 1935.

Because of the late change of plans, the delegates faced some difficulties in finding lodging. Nolle sent a letter to the chapters less than two weeks prior to the meeting, noting that the state legislature was in session and, accordingly, the hotels in Austin were all booked. He suggested that they might try to find rooms in nearby towns if they planned to stay overnight.[17] Subsequently, Nolle was able to provide a list of private homes, fraternity houses, and dormitories in Austin where delegates might be able to find a bed.

The shape of meetings to come revealed itself early, because Prof. Graham, the regional president, presided throughout the business sessions. She asked Miss Shook to continue her accustomed role as recording secretary, the same task she had performed for the former "Council." National President Benedict made an appearance, but only in the role of host.

Several significant reports headed the first business session. A committee on ritual noted progress on ascertaining the desires of the membership and asked that a successor body be appointed to continue their work. Dr. Gooden reported that Alpha Chi was investigating the possibility of membership in the Association of College Honor Societies. Such an affiliation would represent a major step toward the kind of prestige the organization was seeking, but it did not occur for another two decades.

During the year the chapters had received notice that the society wanted to have an official song, and that entries were solicited. Dr. Autrey Nell Wiley of Texas State College for Women announced that her committee had chosen an entry written by J. Morey Brandstetter, former president of the chapter at Southwest Texas State, as the winner. Set to the tune of "Amici" (the widely employed melody of the Cornell University alma mater), it went:

Hail to thee, we sing together,
Hail to Alpha Chi.
Faithful to thine inspiration,
Truth we glorify.
Keep us loyal, lead us onward,
Ever to be free,
Strong in strength of truest honor,
Long we sing to thee.

Sing with valiant lifting spirit,
Songs of living flame,
Songs that warm the heart with courage,
Lofty is thy name.

Bravely meeting every challenge,
With a lusty cry,
Truth is joy and Truth is changeless,
Hail to Alpha Chi.[18]

Dr. Wiley announced a second place winner entitled "To Alpha Chi" with words by Addie Millican and music by Helen Owens, both of North Texas State. The text of this entry said:

To scholarship and service, too,
We have pledged our loyalty;
To know the truth that makes us free
Our aim shall ever be.

In blue and green our colors wave:
An inspiration true
To those whose loyalty is pledged
Dear Alpha Chi, to you.[19]

The plaques that are now presented to each new chapter had their origin at this meeting. In a "debate . . . that taxed the parliamentary powers of the whole Council," the body decided to provide for each chapter, at the expense of the national treasury, "a 10-inch shield," emblematic of chapter membership in Alpha Chi. The group also awarded a special copy of the shield to President Benedict.[20]

The matter of the two disaccredited chapters was finally dispensed with by officially suspending them—on a temporary basis. Neither had sent a delegation, presumably in anticipation of this action. With one exception, all other chapters were present. It may be noted here that the Regional Council was legislating for the whole organization, serving de facto in much the manner of the National Convention under a subsequent Alpha Chi constitution.

The Regional Council concluded by electing its officers for the coming year. They were P.R. Clugston of Arkansas State Teachers College as president and Clyde T. Reed of Texas A&I as vice president. Sister Mary Clement's tenure on the National Council expired and she did not stand for reelection. In her place, the council elected Dr. O.T. Gooden. With thanks to the University of Texas and her Phi Beta Kappa chapter for hosting them, the council adjourned. In expressing official gratitude later, Nolle told Benedict that "the universal verdict is that you entertained us most royally on your campus and that the meeting of the Council was a fine success."[21] This judgment meant that the transition had been completed to the new format, and while some issues remained unresolved, Alpha Chi was now fully under way.

Papers and Presentations

The society's decision to print the text of the speeches allows a glimpse into the mindset of the faculty of the 1930s. The speeches reveal a world of intellect and classical allusion that was quite different from that of a later era. Regardless of the discipline of their authors, faculty speeches display references to a wide array of scholarly sources. Seldom were the speeches narrowly focused on the author's special field of study.

The theme proposed to the 1934 presenters was "Internationalism." The papers demonstrate an awareness of the problems of the world of the age. John Lord's presidential address that year was entitled "World Peace." He argued that peace could not come through "mechanism" alone, the organization of international peace-keeping bodies. Nor could world peace come through philosophies, like internationalism and pacifism. Finally, world peace would not come through "international culture," by which he meant exchange of cultural ideas via travel, art, and education. Lord summarized by saying, "We may conclude that the world will not drift into peace." It would take an international effort to support peace through the actions of all the world's peoples, not of governments.

Bessie Shook's essay on "Noah's Children" was a study of race, and was a mixture of very limited knowledge (she accepted the theory that the "Amerinds" came from Atlantis) and generous intuition. Her argument, which ranged widely over space and time, concluded:

> Do not misunderstand me. I am not standing for a mixture of races. I believe each color should remain pure, and I would be the last here to sanction miscegenation. But I would also be the last one here to say that any **one** of the colors should inherit the earth. . . . Are Shem [yellow races] and Ham [black races] a menace? Viewed in one way, I would say they are. But are they a greater menace than the sons of Japhet [white races]? . . . Noah's son Japhet has caused practically all the wars of recorded history, and if his civilization is finally overthrown and he goes down in deathless night, the fault, dear Brutus, will be in ourselves, not in our stars nor in the sons of Shem and Ham. [22]

Dr. Rebecca Smith of TCU argued in her paper that internationalism was the result of the reaching out of minds to one another, across barriers of borders, time, and prejudice: "It is my contention that no factor has been so continuously effective in enriching the concept of internationalism as the eager desire of intellectuals to share and spread their thoughts and creations. Scholarship, art, music, science have always been international in spirit, whatever materials they have used."[23]

In 1935 the theme was "Democracy," and President Edna Graham used that term as vehicle to call for educational reform. Arguing that education was not democratic enough because of the stultifying effects of the lecture-grade system, she pointed to several experiments in higher education that promised to create true democracy, with teacher and student as co-workers rather than as adversaries. Among her models were the University of Minnesota, Rollins College in Florida, Swarthmore, and the University of Chicago.

Because the 1935 meeting was at the University of Texas, the society invited a U.T. history professor, J. Evetts Haley, to be its guest speaker. Haley's comments were the antithesis of the cool, detached speeches of the other academics. He took the occasion of Washington's birthday to announce the downfall of Washington's republic, "now apparently little cherished by the mass of the people and repudiated in deed, action and in word by their brain-trust leaders, soft, sophisticated, supercilious mediocrities." The tirade went downhill from there, denouncing the New Deal and all that it stood for. The blame, Haley charged, could be laid at the doorstep of the very educational democracy that Miss Graham had just finished praising. He continued, saying "the apathy of the people generally is terrifying, but the stolid indifference of the highly educated is disgraceful. Education once indicated mental excellence, attainment, and discipline. Democratically, fatuously, we have struck down these standards until education largely means the passing of four frivolous years in college, and a degree is about as much distinction to a man as dewclaws to a cow."[24] Despite the intemperance of this address, Haley was again on the regional program in 1937 at Canyon, Texas, discussing "Some Aspects of Staked Plains Culture," a safer topic. "Mr. Haley is a forceful speaker," Secretary Shook noted, "and in this particular field he is at home; for these reasons he was able to delight his audience."[25] Apparently Miss Shook was somewhat less than thrilled to hear the fiery west Texan again, but fair-minded enough to grant that he carried his audience.

Another straw in the wind was the address titled "Women in Our Democracy" by Prof. Julia Luker of McMurry College. She praised the rise of women to positions of leadership, citing Secretary of Labor Frances Perkins, Senator Hattie Caraway, first lady Eleanor Roosevelt, ambassador Ruth Bryan Owen, and others. She suggested that while women are no longer given credit for having superior intuition, they "do exercise in their political reasoning a divining facility for which the psychologists will have to find a new name."[26] She concluded that the fact that America still seemed morally rudderless "should impel women to justify the efforts of their pioneers in the quest for power. 'For the justification of power is its use to wise and beneficent ends.'"[27]

These and other addresses during the period showed that Alpha Chi was not removed from the events of the day, either in the latest developments in scholarship or in awareness of contemporary world events. The faculty persons who delivered them were citizens of academia and of their world.

Beginning to Mature

Incarnate Word College in San Antonio hosted the 1936 meeting of the society. President Benedict sent his regrets, noting that the University of Texas was the site for a joint meeting of the Mississippi Valley Historical Association (predecessor of the Association of American Historians) and the Texas State Historical Association and that his presence was required in Austin for that event.[28] The meeting, set in April, was later than usual. The 1935 session requested that the regional officers set the date late enough in the spring for the delegates to enjoy the wild flowers and other beauties of spring in the region.[29]

Three committee reports took a very brief time when regional president Clugston called the meeting to order at 1:15 p.m. April 16. One reported that it recommended no changes in the regional bylaws. A second said that the publication of an Alpha Chi magazine, as requested by the last meeting, was not possible at this time. A Committee on Ritual proposed a slightly different initiation ceremony, but recommended that chapters be allowed to do their own or to omit a ritual altogether.

A roll call revealed that only two chapters were absent. With twenty-six present and two suspended, the number shows that no new chapter had joined since the name Alpha Chi was adopted. Dr. Claud Howard noted that Alpha Chi was now listed in national publications and said that that fact accounted for letters of inquiry coming in, one from as far away as Georgia.

The most intriguing matter before the assembly came as an initiative from Alpha Chi alumni in the San Antonio area who were looking for official organization and recognition under the aegis of the society's constitution. Dr. Nolle introduced Mrs. Grace Carter Keeling, an Alpha Chi alumna and guidance counselor at San Antonio's Poe Junior High School. She announced that alums in the San Antonio area, some remote from the schools that elected them to membership, had joined into an informal "San Antonio Alumnus Chapter" with regular meetings and programs. "It is [our] belief," she continued, "that election to Alpha Chi is not a finished honor, but that it is a challenge to carry on the ideals, attitudes, and purposes of the fraternity." Mrs. Keeling had written Dr. Benedict soon after the society's 1935 gathering, asking for his advice about how they should carry on their program while awaiting the Council's decision. The San Antonio group had a dinner meeting scheduled a few days later and she was eager to have some word of support from him.[30] Mrs. Keeling presented a petition from her group to the 1936 meeting, calling for the creation of a recognized alumni structure for the purposes of developing scholarships, sponsoring cultural programs, emphasizing scholarship through some program of recognition of ranking students in the local high schools, and maintaining the ideals of Alpha Chi. A motion to amend the constitution to provide for alumni chapters received the usual action, referral to a committee for report the following year.[31]

The nominating committee report recommended the election of Miss Julia Luker of McMurry College as president, with R.A. Mills of Texas Tech as vice president. Dr. C.L. Odom from Centenary replaced President Whitley on the National Council. With that, the meeting adjourned.

In November the chapters received a letter from Miss Luker, advising them that the next meeting would be on the campus of West Texas State Teachers College at Canyon on April 30-May 1, 1937. The thrust of her note was to invite submission of papers from active members, alumni members, and interested faculty for presentation at the meeting. At least two would be selected for publication in the proceedings. Up until this time, speakers and performers at the annual meetings were drawn almost exclusively from the ranks of sponsors. The meetings were not yet a forum for the display of student scholarship. Though the competition for these presentation opportunities was stiff, the student now at least had a chance to demonstrate his or her talent.[32] The meeting in Canyon made the delegates travel to the far northwestern corner of the Alpha Chi's current area. Perhaps the remoteness and the financial pinch led to one of the weakest turnouts in years, with eight chapters absent. Another notable absence was Harry Benedict, who missed only his third meeting since the inception of the organization. He sent his regrets through Dr. Nolle, but expressed his continued interest in the society.

This meeting saw the appearance of the first new chapter since the society became "Alpha Chi." It was the Texas School of Mines (now University of Texas at El Paso). This was appropriate, given the western motif apparent throughout the proceedings. An afternoon outing took the delegates to the edge of the Palo Duro Canyon, where "four picturesque students, in big hats, gay shirts, and trousers tucked into sure-enough boots" entertained and served light refreshments.[33] At the business session, the society handled the matter of alumni chapters by passing a resolution saying any local chapter could organize an alumni chapter if it saw fit. In an attempt to prod the National Council into action, host sponsor Edna Graham moved that the National Council "meet at the time and place of the Regional meeting in order to take care of any business that might come before it." A substitute motion passed softening this to an invitation only.[34] The Regional Council elected new officers, promoting R.A. Mills of Texas Tech to president and naming J.H. Wisely from Stephen F. Austin State to be vice president. Dean Julius Olsen of Hardin-Simmons University replaced Claud Howard on the National Council. The 1937 meeting was a happy one, and no one knew that the society was about to lose its president and principal founder.

End of the Benedict Era

About a week after the Council adjourned, Harry Benedict, "in the midst of the discharge of his official duties," passed away.[35] In his tribute to the departed president, Alfred Nolle said that Benedict epitomized in his life the ideals of Alpha Chi, truth and character. There was no reason but love of scholarship why Benedict should have concerned himself with organizing a society for the other campuses of this state, Nolle continued, since he had nothing to gain from it.

Harry Benedict was one of the founders, perhaps *the* principal founder, of the organization. Alpha Chi had reason to consider itself orphaned by his death. The society immediately created a scholarship award in his honor and left the office of president vacant for several years for lack of another of his stature to fill it. The fact that Alpha Chi could continue to function quite well without a national president revealed just how little responsibility the National Council and the national president had. But Benedict's importance was such that the society was substantially diminished by his passing.

NOTES

[1] *Recorder*, Autumn 1958, p. 4

[2] O.T. Gooden to H.Y. Benedict, February 9, 1934, Benedict Papers, U.T. Austin, Box 2B64

[3] *Proceedings*, 1934, p. 4.

[4] O.T. Gooden to H.Y. Benedict, February 9, 1934, Benedict Papers, U.T. Austin, Box 2B64.

[5] O.T. Gooden to "Drs. Lord, Nolle, and Howard," December 7, 1933, Benedict Papers, U.T. Austin, Box 2B64.

[6] A.H. Nolle to H.Y. Benedict, December 12, 1934, Benedict Papers, U.T. Austin, Box 2B64

[7] *Proceedings*, 1935, p. 2.

[8] The Gooden proposal in typescript, complete except for the organizational name, is found in the Benedict Papers, attached to Gooden's letter of December 17, 1933.

[9] O.T. Gooden to H.Y. Benedict, February 9, 1934; A.H. Nolle to H.Y. Benedict, February 14, 1934; Benedict Papers, U.T. Austin, Box 2B64.

[10] O.T. Gooden to H.Y. Benedict, August 20, 1934, Benedict Papers, U.T. Austin, Box 2B64.

[11] H.Y. Benedict to O.T. Gooden, August 24, 1934, Benedict Papers, U.T. Austin, Box 2B64.

[12] Quoted in letter, Edna Graham to H.Y. Benedict, June 19, 1934, Benedict Papers, U.T. Austin, Box 2B64.

[13] Edna Graham to H.Y. Benedict, June 19, 1934, Benedict Papers, U.T. Austin, Box 2B64.

[14] O.T. Gooden to H.Y. Benedict, August 20, 1934, Benedict Papers, U.T. Austin, Box 2B64.

[15] A.H. Nolle to H.Y. Benedict, December 12, 1934, Benedict Papers, U.T. Austin, Box 2B64.

[16] *Proceedings*, 1935, p. 2.

[17] A.H. Nolle to the chapters of Alpha Chi, February 8, 1935, Benedict Papers, U.T. Austin, Box 2B64.

[18] *Proceedings*, 1935, p. 12.

[19] Ibid.

[20] Ibid., p. 5.

[21] A.H. Nolle to H.Y. Benedict, April 16, 1935, Benedict Papers, U.T. Austin, Box 2B64.

[22] *Proceedings*, 1934, p. 16.

[23] *Proceedings*, 1934, p. 20.

[24] *Proceedings*, 1935, p. 24.

[25] *Proceedings*, 1937, p. 6.

[26] Ibid., p. 26.

[27] Ibid., p. 30.

[28] Telegram, H.Y. Benedict to A.H. Nolle, April 16, 1936, Benedict Papers, U.T. Austin, Box 2B64.

[29] *Proceedings*, 1935, p. 6.

[30] Grace C. Keeling to H.Y. Benedict, April 26, 1935, Benedict Papers, U.T. Austin, Box 2B64.

[31] *Proceedings*, 1936, pp. 4-5, 10-12.

[32] Julia Luker to the Faculty Advisors and Presidents of Alpha Chi, November 30, 1936, Benedict Papers, U.T. Austin, Box 2B64.

[33] *Proceedings*, 1937, p. 6.

[34] *Proceedings*, 1937, p. 7.

[35] *Proceedings*, 1937, pp. 2-3.

Focus On . . .

HARRY YANDELL BENEDICT

Harry Benedict was born in Louisville, Kentucky, shortly after the Civil War ended. The family moved to Texas, where Harry entered the state university as a student of mathematics. He received his B.S. degree in 1892 and a master's degree a year later. For the next two years, he studied astronomy at the University of Virginia, before completing his formal education at Harvard with a Ph.D. in 1898.

After a short stay at Vanderbilt University, he returned to his alma mater as a professor. His talent and integrity allowed him a quick rise through the academic ranks. In 1911 he became dean of the College of Arts and Sciences, serving in that capacity until 1927, when he was elected to the presidency of the University of Texas.[1] As president, he supervised the construction of the institution's most distinctive landmark, the building called "the Tower." Intended to house administrative offices and the university library, it served as the focal point around which the school subsequently developed. Over its entrance was graven one of Benedict's favorite Bible verses: "Ye shall know the truth and the truth shall make you free."

Dr. Benedict may fairly be called the founder of Alpha Chi. It was on his initiative, along with John Granbery's, that the Southwestern Scholarship Society idea was expanded to take in most of the colleges of the state. Benedict managed the affairs of the new Scholarship Societies of Texas through its early years, serving as secretary-treasurer from 1922 to 1927. The press of his new duties as university president forced him to resign the secretary-treasurer post in 1927, but he continued active in the affairs of the organization, attending as many of its annual meetings as he could and sending his regrets when he could not. When a new constitution established a new name for the society and new role for its leadership in 1934, Harry Benedict was the logical person to be named president of Alpha Chi. He served in that capacity until his death on May 10, 1937, at the age of 67.[2]

Benedict's contributions to his university are honored in a campus building bearing his name. His contributions to Alpha Chi are honored in the scholarship program known as the "Harry Yandell Benedict Memorial Fellowships." His impact on both organizations stretches far beyond these memorials.

NOTES

[1] "Benedict, Harry Yandell," in *Who Was Who in America*, Vol. 1 (Chicago: A.N. Marquis Company, 1942), p. 32.

[2] "Harry Yandell Benedict," in *Proceedings*, 1937, pp. 4-5.

CHAPTER 5 (1937-49)
INTERREGNUM

The Vacant Chair

Partly, it was a tribute to the irreplaceable man. And partly, it was a sign that the job had little significance. Whatever the reason, when the members of the National Council finally met in 1938 to elect new officers, they left the presidential slot empty. When the process was complete, they were exactly where they had been before. John Lord, reelected to another five-year term on the Council, was also reelected vice president. Alfred H. Nolle was reelected secretary-treasurer. And the president's post remained open, "pending the election at a later date of a President to succeed the late Dr. H.Y. Benedict."[1] In the meantime, Dr. Lord would shoulder the usual responsibilities of the presidential office. Though no reason for this unusual course of action was offered in the record, it seems likely that they were holding the vacancy in hopes of securing someone of Benedict's stature to undertake what was essentially a figurehead role. The original concept of the National Council proposed that it be partially filled with college presidents and deans, and that the Council's prestige would then attract new chapters. But, as Nolle reiterated, "the members of the National Council have thus far not exercised the prerogative of electing the six additional members."[2]

The May 1938 meeting assembled at Arkansas State Teachers College in Conway, thus taking it out of the state of Texas for the first time. The presence of a new chapter represented the expansion of the society into a fourth state. It was Oklahoma Alpha, Northeastern Teachers College at Tahlequah. Dr. Nolle reminded the gathering that responsibility for accepting new chapters was now vested in the national executive committee by action of the last regional council meeting. A delegation from College of the Ozarks attended as visitors, with the word that they were in the process of resolving their accreditation problems and expected to meet the requirements for good standing before long.

Charles L. Odom of Centenary, a member of the National Council,

57

moved that students "be given more participation of the program." This simple act, which occasioned only brief discussion, proved to be a turning point in the form of the meetings from that time on. Heretofore, regional council meetings had been the occasion for faculty and administrators to deliver the fruits of their studies, and while these were interesting and informative, even brilliant, they made the meetings an all-faculty enterprise. Now came the opportunity to make the annual meetings a forum for student scholarship and, beginning in 1941, student presentations became a staple of the annual meetings.

A second step in the direction of making Alpha Chi more student oriented was the establishment of the Harry Yandell Benedict Memorial Scholarship. The assembly appropriated the sum of $100 to be awarded each year for ten years to one worthy senior annually. The basis for the award was "high scholarship in his or her undergraduate course, all-around ability as a leader and as a campus personality, intention to engage in purposeful graduate studies, and such other qualifications as the Committee on Awards may determine."[3] They authorized the regional president to appoint a committee to administer the award. The first Benedict Scholarship went to Arthur L. Cunkle, who received his B.A. from Arkansas State Teachers College in 1938 and enrolled in the University of Kansas to study economics in the fall.[4] Cunkle expressed his gratitude to the Council in a letter that was read to the 1939 meeting.

The meeting elected Bessie Shook to fill out Benedict's term on the National Council and picked C.L. Odom of Centenary and Claud Howard of Southwestern to serve as regional president and vice president, respectively, for the coming year. The financial report revealed that the society now had assets in excess of $4,000, indicating that the society had somehow managed to grow financially even through the worst years of the Great Depression.[5]

The annual meeting in 1939 took the society from one of its northernmost sites to its southernmost chapter at Kingsville, Texas. The central theme for the meeting was "Education and Democracy." The theme was addressed in papers by Dr. J.C. Cross of Texas A&I, Rabbi Ephraim Frisch of San Antonio, and the Rev. William H. Molony from St. Edward's. Howard Wilkinson and Paul Bohmfalk, students from Southwestern, led a panel discussion of the theme. The resolution of the preceding year calling for increased student participation was having some effect.

Odom's presidential address was to have been the centerpiece of the evening banquet, but he was not present at the meeting. Dr. Howard, who presided in Odom's place, read the speech to the banquet. Odom was on leave of absence from his school to complete his doctorate at Columbia University.

There were enough members of the National Council present in Kingsville to hold a rare meeting of that largely honorary group. They convened just long enough to reelect Lord and Nolle to their respective posts. The regional assembly reelected Miss Shook to a full term on the National Council. She was serving the last years of Dr. Benedict's term, which expired with this meeting. The presidential slot remained vacant.

A President—For a While

Dr. Claud Howard presided over the 1940 meeting of the Regional Council, this time in his own right as the elected regional president. He was also host sponsor, as the society returned to its birthplace, Southwestern University. The big news of the day was that at last Alpha Chi had a *national* president. Dr. Nolle received word that the University of Texas had a new chief executive officer, President Homer P. Rainey. Nolle approached him about accepting presidency of Alpha Chi as well, though the university still had no chapter of Alpha Chi. When Nolle polled the other five members of the National Council by mail, they agreed to the election of Dr. Rainey, and Nolle secured his acceptance, effective as of the April 1940 meeting of the society.

Rainey's name on Alpha Chi's list of officers was about the only connection the busy man ever had with the organization. He signed the certificates given to new members, but otherwise never attended a meeting of the Regional Council and never called a meeting of the National Council. He lent his name to the enterprise, but little else. The name was valuable, nevertheless. Rainey, a native Texan, held a degree from Austin College. Though he matriculated there before the founding of the Scholarship Societies of Texas, his alma mater was an Alpha Chi school. After earning a Ph.D. and Phi Beta Kappa honors from the University of Chicago, he was a college professor and then president of Franklin College in Indiana and Bucknell University in Pennsylvania. Prior to his acceptance of the presidency in Austin in 1939, he served several years as director of the American Youth Commission. He was clearly the man of stature and influence that the society wanted as its titular leader. By training and experience, he was an American university scholar in the classic mold.

That kind of background did not necessarily prepare him for what he faced in Austin. He engaged from early in his tenure in a running verbal battle with conservative members of the University of Texas Board of Regents. Issues of academic freedom were in the forefront of American collegiate thinking. It was in 1940 that the American Association of University Professors published its definitive statement regarding academic freedom. Rainey's background guaranteed that he would be in sympathy with it. When the Regents fired several faculty members over Rainey's protests in 1944, the battle was joined.

After repeated and heated confrontations, the Regents met in executive session in Houston in October 1944 and fired Rainey. Though there were loud and public protests by students, faculty, and alumni, the dismissal was not reversed. Phi Beta Kappa sent investigators to Austin and condemned the Board for its actions. The Southern Association placed the University on probation. The American Association of University Professors censured the school and kept it on the censured list for nine years. But Rainey stayed fired.

After failing to secure redress from any other source, Rainey took his case to the people of Texas in 1946, running for governor himself. In a field of thirteen candidates, he finished second, placing him in a runoff for the Democratic nomination with Beauford Jester. At that time, the Democratic nomination was tantamount to election in Texas. But Jester won, and Rainey left to become president of Stephens College in Missouri.

Some time in all this fuss, Rainey ceased to be president of Alpha Chi. Obviously, his usefulness to the organization was ended, but it is likely that he resigned because of all the other things on his mind. Once again, Alpha Chi had no national president.[6]

Hiatus: The War Years

The 1940 meeting hosted twenty-seven of the chapters. Dr. C.M. Bishop, the founder of the Southwestern Scholarship Society a quarter century before, was present and spoke to the society, expressing his pleasure at its development and service. The presence of Dr. Bishop was balanced by the absence of Dr. Nolle, who missed a meeting of the society for the first time. He was in Atlanta for a meeting of the Southern Association of Colleges and Schools.

The program for the meeting consisted of papers from faculty members of the society and choral numbers from the Southwestern chorus. There was no program participation by Alpha Chi student delegates. Very little business of significance came before the body. They elected Dr. Paul Witt of Abilene Christian College as president of the region for the coming year with Prof. J.H. Wisely from Stephen F. Austin as his vice president. In accepting election, Dr. Witt vowed to pursue an aggressive approach to expansion. This became his theme through his year in office and for many years while he served on the National Council.

With war raging in Europe and Asia, the theme of the 1941 meeting at Nacogdoches, Texas, was "Scholarship and Americanity," reflecting the isolationist mood of many Americans of the time, a mood that was rapidly shifting even as the group met in March. But the major importance of this meeting lay in the opening statement by Paul Witt, the regional president:

> President Witt made a short talk in which he said his message to the Council was the boys and girls who were appearing on the printed program of the meeting. He had built the program around student participation in the meeting, and both the afternoon and the morning programs were largely the work of student delegates.[7]

The programs bore out Dr. Witt's words. The afternoon session featured eight presentations, five of which were musical. Two more students performed musical selections at the evening banquet and another four presented musical performances in the morning. Altogether, ten chapters had students participating in the presentations.

The Council was so pleased with the results of this experiment that it decided to continue the emphasis. A possible problem in screening what might and what might not be included in the 1942 program was resolved when incoming President Autrey Nell Wiley of Texas State College for Women appointed separate "program adjudicator" committees to screen presentations in the arts, the languages, the sciences, and the social sciences.

Dr. Witt also had the opportunity to deliver the traditional president's speech. His topic was "The Spirit of Americanity." "The president's address was so excellent," Miss Shook noted, "that even the English teachers who were present forgave him for coining the word AMERICANITY."[8]

Dr. Nolle asked and received permission to include in the *Proceedings* a letter to sponsors outlining the need for accuracy and consistency in the reporting of newly inducted members to the national office. "In some instances," he complained, "the names of the members were not even spelled alike in different sections of the same set of records."[9] By the time the next meeting convened at Our Lady of the Lake College in March 1942, the United States was fully involved in the worldwide war. Faculty members spoke on the topics of "The Chapters in the Emergency" and "The Chapters in Their First Year of War." Dr. John McMahon, president of Our Lady of the Lake (later vice president of the National Council, 1954-66 and president 1966-67) addressed the delegates on the subject of "Post-War World Reconstruction." In an obvious reference to the national crisis, the Regional Council resolved that "during these strenuous days, when there is a tendency for scholarship to suffer, all Alpha Chi chapters should be unduly alert [sic] to maintain their usual high standards."[10]

Firmly establishing the tradition of student presentations as the centerpiece of the meeting, the 1942 meeting heard nine papers and performances by students. These more than filled the program, since, in an innovation, each had a faculty discussant to follow up. One of the papers, by Joe Stephens of Centenary, on "Wartime Humor: The Comics" and another, by Constance Jones of Incarnate Word College, on "The Photelometer in Wartime" revealed an awareness of the current world crisis. Seven students from five chapters displayed examples of their art, in an exhibit coordinated by Dr. Mattie Swayne of West Texas State.

Voices from the past appeared at this meeting also. Dr. John Granbery, the first president of the Scholarship Societies of Texas, and Prof. W.P. Davidson, who was present at both of the 1922 meetings, appeared before the assembly and expressed their pride in what the society had become. The most significant item of business, aside from the elections of new officers, was a motion by Dr. Nolle that he be allowed to use society funds to help with travel expenses for the chapters most distant from the meeting sites. The motion was approved without further detail. The society had nearly $7,000 in its treasury at the time.

There was something tentative about the plans for the 1943 meeting.

The Council accepted an invitation from St. Edward's University to meet on their campus, but there was an unusual motion to the effect that the National Council would set the time, something either it or the national executive committee had done routinely in the past, without the need for a motion. Before adjourning, the Regional Council elected its officers for the coming year, choosing Prof. J.H. Wisely from Stephen F. Austin State Teachers College for president and Prof. L.H. Bally of Northeastern State College for vice president. These men, both of them, turned out to be among the more significant regional officers chosen since 1934.[11] This was the last meeting of the Regional Council until 1946. By the end of 1943, wartime travel restrictions made it difficult for persons to go very far from home. After consulting with the chapters via mail, President Wisely canceled the 1943 meeting. In 1944 and 1945, the same restrictions applied, in addition to an appeal from the government not to schedule conventions for the duration. The work of the National Council went on by correspondence, and the work of the chapters went on locally unabated, but with some changes.[12]

For the first twenty years of its existence, Alpha Chi annually initiated more female members than male. This trend flew in the face of national statistics that showed that male graduates outnumbered female graduates by a margin of roughly three to two over the past twenty years. But during the war that ratio was reversed and a preponderance of male graduates did not occur until 1947 and 1948, when the flood of veterans returned to fill the halls of academe.[13] In most colleges, Alpha Chi became almost exclusively a female domain. Since overall student enrollments dropped during the war, the numbers inducted into Alpha Chi also dropped.

The regional officers elected in 1942 continued to serve in their positions throughout the war. President Wisely kept in touch with the other leaders of the society, but in May 1945 he unexpectedly passed away. Vice President Bally assumed the duties of the presidency and prepared for the 1946 meeting. There was some difficulty finding a site for the meeting, since the colleges were in the midst of coping with the beginnings of a flood of returning servicemen, and no school could be found that was willing to serve as host. Eventually, Dr. Nolle invited the meeting to come to Southwest Texas State and the college managed somehow to host the meeting.

1946-48: Reconversion

The theme of the first postwar conference of Alpha Chi was "With Victory: Responsibility." Several items of business demanded immediate attention. One was the selection of leadership. After the greetings the first item of business was a motion to elect Dr. Bally president for the remainder of the session. Twenty-four chapters were in attendance to hear tributes to Prof. Wisely and to "Those Who Served." The war was much in people's minds.

In addition, there had been no elections to the National Council for four years, and thus the terms of the majority of the Council members had expired. One term extended through 1947 and two expired with the 1946 meeting, but one of those was no longer at an Alpha Chi school and was therefore not active in the society. The assembly voted to extend the National Council terms that had expired during the war for another five years each, and elected Dr. Autrey Nell Wiley to fill the one remaining vacancy. Dr. Paul J. Schwab of Trinity University became the next regional president, working with Dr. Charles G. Smith of Baylor as his vice president. The search continued to find a national president to succeed Dr. Rainey, who "is no longer in school work."[14]

The Regional Council resolved the matter of travel assistance for distant delegates by agreeing to pay them three cents per mile for every mile they had to travel beyond a three hundred mile radius of the convention site. Committees which had been more or less dormant during the war years were reactivated, with Dr. Paul Witt of Abilene Christian in charge of expansion, Dr. Schwab in charge of ritual revision, and Dr. J.R. Manning of Texas A&I responsible for alumni affairs.

Student presentations included the usual mix of musical performances, together with papers on timely issues, such as "The Role of Art in the Rehabilitation of War Veterans," "Control of the Atom," and a poignant call, "What I Can Do to Help Improve Race Relations" by Grace Watanabe, a Japanese-American student from Hardin-Simmons. Watanbe's appeal was a call to be inclusive of all races and ethnic groups, a call that did not single out her own ethnic heritage.[15] In his presidential address, Dr. Bally also denounced the racism that had emerged in American life during the war, singling out attacks made on Jews and Japanese-Americans.[16] It was perhaps not yet safe, on the edge of the American South, to question racial prejudice toward blacks.

Alpha Chi went to the campus of Sam Houston State Teachers College in Huntsville for the 1947 meeting. The National Council had still not met and there was as yet no successor to President Rainey. Dr. John Lord, the vice president, still fulfilled that function, which consisted mainly of affixing his name to the certificates of membership.

Most of the student papers focused on the conference theme: "Religion in Education in a Centrifugal Society." There were nearly twenty student presentations, many still of the musical variety.

Plans were made to renew the Benedict Scholarship, which was not awarded during the war years, and President Schwab appointed a committee to look into it. Likewise, the expansion committee was itself expanded to by two members to better facilitate the work. Since there was some interest in revising the constitution, the assembly directed Dr. Schwab to appoint such a committee, specifically mentioning that Dr. O.T. Gooden, "one of the writers of the original constitution," should be included.

Dr. J.R. Manning of Texas A&I became the next president with Dr. Mattie Swayne Mack of West Texas State as vice president. When no chapter came forward to invite the Council to its campus for 1948, site selection was left to the regional executive committee.

The theme selected for the 1948 meeting was "Our Contribution—Present and Future of the United Nations Organization." The scheduled site was Denton, home of North Texas State Teachers College. A number of students had prepared papers to be delivered at the meeting, and Dr. Autrey Nell Wiley had prepared a keynote address.

However, the meeting was called off because of bad weather. The region huddled under an unprecedented downpour of rain that "made travel on the highways unsafe." Although the scheduled date, March 12-13, was not so late in the school year (which normally ended around June 1) that rescheduling was deemed impractical, the crowded calendars of the various schools contributed to a decision to cancel rather than postpone. Dr. Manning reported that he had consulted with the regional executive committee and "a number of past presidents of the Council before making the decision." Dr. Nolle published several of the submitted papers in the *Proceedings*, which appeared on schedule. The officers, as had been the case during the wartime hiatus, continued for another year.[17]

Alpha Chi struggled through the decade prior to 1949, missing three regional meetings because of the war and one because of the weather. The society had had practically no leadership from the National Council and went for long periods with no president at all. Alpha Chi had not added a single new chapter since 1937 and was stalled completely on the matter of expansion. Nevertheless, this was not all lost time. The shift of focus from faculty papers to student presentations at the meetings clearly was an improvement from the point of view of student involvement. Attendance at the regional meetings that were held was consistently strong, with representation from over three-fourths of the chapters at virtually every one. The local chapters continued to work and to induct members. And a new era was about to dawn for Alpha Chi, beginning with the 1949 convention.

NOTES

[1] *Proceedings*, 1938, p. 2.

[2] Ibid.

[3] *Proceedings*, 1938, p. 5.

[4] *Proceedings*, 1938, p. 2.

[5] *Proceedings*, 1938, pp. 6, 9.

[6] The Rainey firing made the national news. Major articles appeared in *Time*, November 13, 1944, pp. 54-56 and *Newsweek*, November 13, 1944, pp. 84-85. Rainey's side of the affair is told in the autobiographical *The Tower and the Dome: A Free University vs. Political Control* (Boulder, Colorado: Pruett Publishing Co., 1971). Another commentary which sided with Rainey is Alice Carol Cox, "The Rainey Affair: A History of the Academic Freedom Controversy at the University of Texas, 1938-1946," a Ph.D. dissertation at the University of Denver, 1970. The distinguished historian Henry Nash Smith, then a professor at Texas, produced a paper titled "The Controversy at the University of Texas, 1939-1945: A Documentary History" which was published by The Student Committee for Academic Freedom of the University of Texas Students' Association and read at a rally on campus in August, 1945. I found a copy, not at Austin, but at Texas Tech. Most of Rainey's papers are at the University of Missouri, but there are some at U.T. Austin, particularly in Box 2.325/A89C.

[7] *Proceedings*, 1941, p. 3.

[8] *Proceedings*, 1941, p. 5.

[9] *Proceedings*, 1941, p. 12.

[10] *Proceedings*, 1942, p. 7.

[11] *Proceedings*, 1942, pp. 3-7.

[12] *Proceedings*, 1946, p. 3.

[13] *Historical Statistics of the United States* (Washington: U.S. Government Printing Office, 1975), Series H-753 and H-754.
[14] *Proceedings*, 1946, p. 8.
[15] *Proceedings*, 1946, pp. 40-43.
[16] Ibid., pp. 17-20.
[17] *Proceedings*, 1948, p. 2.

Focus On . . .

CHAPTER NAMES

Long before the affixing of Greek letters to the chapter names, the society felt the need to find some way of distinguishing them as individuals. Accordingly, they were allowed to adopt any local designation they wished. In 1932 these included:

James A. Garfield	Abilene Christian College
P.R. Clugston	Arkansas State Teachers College
Davis Foute Eagleton	Austin College
Alpha Pi Omega	Baylor College
Kappa Epsilon	Baylor University
Eta Sigma Chi	Centenary College
F.M. Bralley	College of Industrial Arts
Alpha Beta Phi	College of the Ozarks
R.B. Binnion	East Texas State Teachers College
Mu Sigma Chi	Hendrix College
Lincoln	Howard Payne College
O.A. Brownson	Incarnate Word College
Gamma Tau Alpha	Louisiana College
James Winford Hunt	McMurry College
W.H. Bruce	North Texas State Teachers College
Ouachita	Ouachita College
Moye	Our Lady of the Lake College
Woodrow Wilson	Sam Houston State Teachers College
Julius Olsen	Simmons College
Nolle	Southwest Tex. State Teachers College
Southwestern	Southwestern University
A.W. Birdwell	Stephen F. Austin State Teachers Coll.

Sorin	St. Edward's University
Sul Ross	Sul Ross State Teachers College
T.C.U.	Texas Christian University
R.B. Cousins	Texas College of Arts and Industries
Southern	Texas Technological College
Texas Woman's College	Texas Woman's College
Hornbeak	Trinity University
Lloyd Green Allen	West Texas State Teachers College

Each of the names had "Scholarship Society" appended after it except for one, which reversed the order by calling itself the "Scholarship Society of Texas Woman's College." Some names (Nolle, Hornbeak, Julius Olsen) honored past or current sponsors, while others (Lincoln, Woodrow Wilson, James A. Garfield) honored American presidents and some (James Winford Hunt, W.H. Bruce) bore the names of college presidents. Several (Sul Ross, Southwestern, Ouachita among them) simply took the name of the institution. Six adopted Greek letters for their chapter titles.

Even many years later, the National Council of Alpha Chi allowed new chapters to adopt local names that maintained the tradition of a predecessor local scholarship society.

CHAPTER 6 (1949-56)
REVITALIZATION

A Working National Council

Of the several turning points in the story of Alpha Chi, 1949 may fairly be said to be one of the most important. From the tragedy of the death early in the year of Dean John Lord, the long-time acting president of the National Council, came a redefinition and activation of that hitherto moribund institution.

For years the society was held captive to the idea that the National Council should be filled with president and deans, persons of significant academic prestige and esteem. From 1934 on, the prime function of the National Council under this constitution was to give Alpha Chi a national reputation. The society's claim to stature was pinned to the coattails of a distinguished set of figurehead leaders, leavened by a working group of less well-known faculty sponsors. Benedict and Rainey, and, to a lesser degree, Lord in his role as dean of Texas Christian University's graduate school, provided that kind of cachet. Now they were gone, and no one within the ranks of the society could claim that level of national status.

Thus, Alpha Chi turned to the concept of a working National Council. They abandoned the idea of a National Council of presidents and deans, a membership with little to do but lend their names and prestige to the society's letterhead. By changing the constituency and role of the National Council, the society could in time achieve its dream of national stature on its own merits.

The Regional Council met at Incarnate Word College in San Antonio in 1949. In an irregular move, it elected a new vice president for the National Council from the floor, although the constitution provided for that election to be done only by the National Council itself. The meeting chose Dr. T.E. Ferguson of Stephen F. Austin State Teachers College to serve as a member of the National Council and to be its vice president. Ferguson had never held membership in the National Council nor had he served as a regional officer.

Prof. Alma Lueders from Southwest Texas State next read a letter from her dean, Dr. Nolle, who was absent from the meeting. Nolle recommended that a national president be elected, and Prof. Lueders nominated Dr. Paul Schwab of Trinity University for the post. There were no further nominations, and Schwab accepted the position that he would hold for the next seventeen years. Schwab had been active in the organization since before the war. He took over the sponsorship of a chapter with a poor record of attendance and made it an active participant in the organization. Though he had never served on the National Council before, he had a strong record as regional president in 1946-47. Considering the record of lethargy over the preceding years, lack of service on the National Council was probably more of an asset than a liability.

Schwab wasted in no time in moving the National Council to action. He called a meeting of the group to convene immediately after the adjournment of the convention. Though only three other members were present, the Council created a number of new policies for itself. With expansion of the society imminent, the Council decided that new chapter installations would be handled personally by a representative of the group. The expenses involved in travel to new chapter installations would be borne by the society. They adopted other procedures to make the new chapter installation dignified and professional.

Later in the year Schwab summoned the Council together again. Meeting in a hotel in Austin, the National Council had all but one of its members in attendance. As the first order of business, the Council moved to regularize the election of its officers, which, the minutes noted, was an "extra-constitutional" act by the Regional Council. Dr. Huffor, one of the legitimately elected members, presided while the others—L.H. Bally, R.A. Mills, Bessie Shook, and Autrey Nell Wiley—named Schwab and Ferguson to full membership in the Council. Then they confirmed the action of the Region by electing the two men and Nolle to the top three offices. With the absent member Claud Howard, there were now nine members on the Council. Using their prerogative to elect some of their own members, they named Paul Witt and O.T. Gooden to the Council, reserving the twelfth slot for another time. They then sorted out the tenure of the members so as to assure that not all would rotate off at the same time.

Once these matters were settled, the Council turned its attention to the constitution, and passed several changes to be proposed to the Regional Council. One of these removed much of the obfuscated language of the membership article, in favor of a simple standard which said that chapters could elect persons to membership from the ranking 10 percent of the junior and senior classes, provided that the candidates had been at the institution for at least a year. Schools could raise the standards if they wished but could not lower them.

The Council decided to refer questions about alumni chapters to a committee. It resumed the long-neglected practice of electing honorary members by naming two persons to that status. The group approved appropriation of society funds to underwrite their travel expenses for the meeting. The dormant issue of Alpha Chi's relationship to the Association of College Honor Societies came up and Dr. Wiley was charged with looking into the matter. These and other actions set precedents that would be followed by successive councils for years to come.[1]

A National Stage, At Last

The transformation and revitalization of the National Council was not the only exciting development from the 1949 meeting. Dr. Witt's expansion committee had been active and successful. Petitions for membership, the first in a dozen years, came from colleges far removed from the southwestern provenance of Alpha Chi. One of these came, improbably, from a school more than 1,500 miles away, American International College in Springfield, Massachusetts. The second application was Hastings College of Nebraska, not quite so far away but still in a nonadjacent state. Both applications were approved by the Council. Eventually, the National Council commissioned President Schwab to install these chapters. Further, statements of intent to apply came from Hardin College (later Midwestern State University) in Wichita Falls, Texas, and from Marshall College in Huntington, West Virginia.

Further expansion seemed possible among alumni. The Council agreed to grant a charter for an alumni chapter in far south Texas. When the delegate from McMurry College in Abilene, Prof. Julia Luker, also applied for an alumni charter for her school's graduates, the Council realized that they had not given sufficient thought to the formation of alumni chapters, and the whole matter was referred to a committee for additional study.

The student portions of the San Antonio program featured fifteen presentations, several of which were team efforts. Continuing the custom begun in 1941, the *Proceedings* reprinted several of these papers. Dr. Wiley delivered the keynote address on "Expanding Mental Vistas." Twenty-two chapters sent delegations, a weaker turnout than previous years.

North Texas State hosted the 1950 meeting of the Regional Council. New region president Mattie Swayne Mack of West Texas State was in the chair. Twenty-one chapters showed up, but among the missing were the two new chapters from Massachusetts and Nebraska. At that time, when commercial air travel was almost exclusively by propeller-driven aircraft, and before the days of interstate highways, a journey of such length was often a major undertaking.

President Schwab, who made both journeys to install Massachusetts Alpha and Nebraska Alpha, reported on his visits. Dr. Paul Witt, representing the expansion committee, mentioned that several more schools were interested, but that no new chapters would be presented this year.

The students' presentations were as numerous and varied as previous years. Musical presentations again predominated. The principal guest speaker was poet Robert P. Tristram Coffin. The meeting agreed to amend the constitution to include a section allowing for alumni chapters and their governance. Another amendment provided oversight for chapters not within the bounds of a region by placing them under the direct supervision of the National Council.

At the conclusion of the session, the restructured National Council held its second annual meeting. Most of the business was routine housekeeping, except for a provision that specifically recognized the bounds of Region I as being Arkansas, Louisiana, and Texas. This was in obvious preparation for the creation of a Region II at some point in the not-too-distant future.[2] The Council failed to have a quorum for its 1951 meeting and no business could be transacted. By mail ballot, the members subsequently elected Prof. Julia Luker to membership.

The Not-So-Silent Generation

The 1951 meeting of the region gathered at Louisiana College in Pineville. Perhaps the highlight of the meeting was the arrival, a little late, of Dr. Charles Gadaire, representing American International College in Massachusetts. Gadaire reported that he "had experienced his first plane ride in small, somewhat rough airplane and was feeling the results."[3]

The theme of the program was "Scholarship Plus _____." Themes had been suggested for each meeting for the past few years, but the student presentations seemed increasingly to ignore the theme in favor of more personal selections. Certainly this was true of the music, from the beginning, but recently the essays also diverged from it. This theme, however, piqued student interest with papers on Scholarship Plus—Thought, Purpose, Its Application, Brotherhood, Happiness, Understanding, Religion, Art, and the Ideals of Womanhood.

Student interest was up in other ways. This assembly was one of the largest Alpha Chi meetings to date. The attendance roster listed the names of more than eighty persons, even with ten chapters absent. In a question that may have disturbed the peace of the society's leaders, student delegate Bob Messer from Southwestern rose in the business meeting to inquire why students were not given a greater role in the decision-making process of the society. Dr. Schwab responded that students usually attended the meeting only once and therefore could not provide the continuity that faculty leadership could give. The region president for the year, Dr. Otto O. Watts from Hardin-Simmons, suggested that students might be appointed to the regional committees more frequently, and proceeded to name Messer to the audit committee on the spot. Messer's appeal was taken seriously, at least to the extent that student membership on each regional committee became standard from that point on.

Another proposal that may have created some discomfort came from an unidentified delegate who proposed that the annual meeting be held in the fall, when there was less chance of conflict with other activities. After discussion, the assembly agreed to meet, not in the fall, but back in the time slot that had been traditional for many years, namely, the week of February 22.

Two new applicants presented themselves for membership. They were Midwestern University of Texas and Central State College of Edmond, Oklahoma. Because the constitution required that they be accepted by the regional council, neither had representatives at the meeting. Dr. Witt suggested changing the constitution to allow for a mail ballot as new chapters applied, thus speeding the process and retaining interest on the part of the applicants.

Prof. J.E. Caldwell of the host chapter was elected region president for the coming year, with Prof. Myrtle Brown of North Texas State to serve as vice president. Bessie Shook missed her first meeting in years and Dr. Nolle's colleague Prof. Alma Lueders kept the minutes for this meeting.[4]

The organization hosted a record attendance in 1952 at Baylor University in Waco. Twenty-nine chapters responded to the roll call. Dr. Nolle recorded that "the list of visitors from the various chapters is too long to include in these Proceedings, but the attendance both as to delegates and visitors was record breaking."[5] Only five chapters lacked representation at the meeting. The unprecedented number of delegates may in part be attributed to the society's decision at the 1951 meeting to pay delegate travel at three cents per mile for every mile exceeding 150 one way, rather than the previous allocation for of the same for amount for travel in excess of 300 miles.

The theme of the meeting was "Scholarship's Responsibility for Protecting and Promoting Democracy," and ten of the twenty student presentations addressed that topic. The so-called "silent generation" of students continued to press for more responsibility in Alpha Chi. When the all-sponsor nominating committee reported, student delegate Bill Clendenning of North Texas State called for greater student participation. Although this was technically out of order, not being germane to the precise question at hand, President Caldwell allowed the discussion to continue. When he put the question, the assembly adopted the report. Then the president asked for a clarification of the previous concern, which resulted in a motion by student delegate Robert Heslep of Texas Christian, as follows:

> That a committee of five, with a majority of students, be appointed to study the amending of our constitution for the purpose of allowing a slate of student officers and for the purpose of letting the students on this committee serve as a dummy slate of officers; furthermore the report of this committee's amendment to the constitution be presented to the next meeting.[6]

Amended to call for the election of the committee, rather than its appointment, the motion passed and the assembly chose Dr. O.T. Gooden of Hendrix and students Richard Moose of Hendrix, Bill Clendenning of North Texas State, Louise Terry of Texas Wesleyan, and David Cardwell of Southwestern.

The Benedict Scholarship committee recommended that the grant be increased to $200, but that reports from previous recipients be solicited in order to "decide if it is desirable to continue making the award."[7]

Dr. Schwab called the National Council into session in conjunction with the regional conference. They discussed the scope of honorary memberships and the suspension of chapters for non-attendance. They expanded the Council membership to its authorized strength by adding Dr. John McMahon of Our Lady of the Lake to the membership, Dr. Bally of Northeastern Oklahoma having already been added by action of the Regional Council. The Council authorized publication of five hundred copies of a pamphlet on initiation, with three copies to be given to each chapter, with more available for a small price.[8]

In February 1953 the regional meeting returned once again to the campus of Southwestern University. The theme was "Current Challenges to the Idealism of the Student." Twenty-eight chapters attended. "The list of visitors to the meeting is too long to include in these proceedings," Dr. Nolle noted later, "but two chapters deserve special recognition: Southwest Texas State Teachers College had twelve, and Southwestern University had not only its entire chapter of twenty-eight members [including the author of this volume] but many ex-student members who returned for the banquet." Close to one hundred persons attended that meal.[9] President Myrtle Brown led the assembly through the opening greetings and recognized Dean David Harris from Henderson State Teachers College in Arkansas, who came with a petition for membership for his school. The Council, after the reading of the minutes, approved the request. Prof. Brown announced her committee appointments and asked for old business. There being none, she called for any new business and the student initiative of the previous year quickly bubbled up again. Southwestern's Frank Douglass noted that two of the members of the committee had graduated and needed to be replaced. This was done.

The plans for Saturday morning included a number of student presentations. "A Student Forum was scheduled to follow the papers," Miss Shook recorded, "with a panel discussion by four members to be followed by a general discussion, but the panel did not want to discuss the papers; they wanted to talk about something else, and did. They presented a few ideas worth some consideration, and the program went on to its conclusion." It is not hard to read frustration in the secretary's comments.

Immediately following the program, business resumed with a report from David Cardwell, speaking for the committee on student participation. Cardwell proposed the selection of a student program chairman to preside at program presentations, equal representation on all standing committees, a student round table annually, a division of the region into districts with student officers, joint participation between the regional president and his or her chapter in setting up the programs, and a continuation of the committee to discuss further possibilities. With only minor modifications, the Regional Council adopted these proposals.

The president responded by appointing Dr. Gooden and four new students to the ongoing committee. R.G. Dean from Stephen F. Austin won election as student program chairman for the following year. An appeal to have an earlier notice of the annual theme was answered when Sister Margaret Rose of Our Lady of the Lake, the incoming vice president and chair of a committee to select a topic, reported "The Impact of Current Pressures on Traditional Scholarship" to be the 1954 theme.

The National Council did not have a quorum at Georgetown, so they met in Dallas two month later. Two chapters under suspension, notably Ouachita and College of the Ozarks, had cleared up their accreditation problems and needed to be approached about resuming their relationship. St. Edward's had not been attending for several years and also needed to be reactivated. The Council noted that chapter #4, Texas Delta at Texas Presbyterian College, was now defunct because the school had been absorbed by Trinity University. The Council affirmed that the number and the letter designation would never be reassigned.

Exercising its constitutional power to fix the boundaries of regions, the Council agreed to serve notice that Region I would soon be divided in half. The Council approved a motion to augment the expansion committee by several younger members; meantime, each Council member agreed to try to recruit one additional chapter.

The Council accepted most of the proposals from the Regional Convention, modifying the call for parity on standing committees to provide three faculty and three students as voting members and one additional faculty to serve as non-voting chair. Subsequently, the region nominating committee did not comply, stating that it was too difficult to staff such large committees without sure knowledge of who would be attending.

Because expenses for the past year almost equaled income, Dr. Nolle moved that the dues be increased from two dollars to three. After some heated debate, the motion carried.[10] The most dramatic event of the 1954 meeting took place when the closing business meeting was conducted al fresco, in "the Basin" at Big Bend National Park. The host chapter, Sul Ross State Teachers College in remote Alpine, arranged for the entire Saturday to be taken up with a trip to Big Bend. Altogether, some twenty-three chapters attended.

The program committee scheduled the student presentations for Friday, leaving Saturday free for the trip. The elected student presider did not attend, so regional president Troy Crenshaw appointed student Jerry Earnhart of Abilene Christian to preside at the presentations.

The Council elected two relative newcomers, Dr. E. Bruce Thompson of Baylor and Prof. Annie Lee Knox of Texas Wesleyan, to serve as president and vice president for the coming year. The program committee proposed three topics for the following meeting and asked the assembly to choose one. The group picked "The Conflict of Extra-Curricular Activities with the Classroom," a rather more specific focus than previous themes.

Two constitutional amendments received approval. Each gave the students more autonomy. One provided a student and a faculty vote in the Regional Council, replacing the rule that called for voting by chapter. The other accommodated the procedures for amending regional by-laws and the general constitution to allow for vote by delegate rather than by chapter. A redistricting committee, following up on the student resolutions of the previous year, proposed a procedure for planning to develop the district concept further. The Council adopted this idea, ending the "meeting in the Park."

Mitosis

The National Council convened at the Adolphus Hotel in Dallas in April 1954. One item of business, application for membership in the Association of College Honor Societies, passed quickly. A second was the matter of choosing new National Council officers, since the five-year term of the current officers was now expiring. Dr. Schwab was re-elected president and Dr. Nolle secretary-treasurer, but Dr. John McMahon of Our Lady of the Lake was chosen as the new vice president. These three could easily confer during the year, since they lived within sixty miles of one another.

The major item before the Council concerned the division of the society into two regions. The resolution of the previous year to do this was now ready to be accomplished. President Schwab produced maps showing two possible lines of cleavage, one running from northeast to southwest, and the other running from northwest to southeast. The second of these lines seemed best to the Council, so the division was accomplished with the chapters at Canyon, Lubbock, El Paso, Alpine, Kingsville, San Antonio, San Marcos, Austin, Belton, Georgetown, Waco, Brownwood, and Abilene in Region I and all others in Region II, with the understanding that Sam Houston State could opt for either affiliation.

Following up on this decision, the Council decided that all the chapters would meet at Incarnate Word College in San Antonio in 1955 for a joint program, with the understanding that the two regions would separate to organize themselves and plan for meetings the following year, each in its respective bounds. The sequence would then continue indefinitely, with regional meetings in even-numbered years and joint national meetings in odd-numbered years.

With remarkably little discussion the 1955 meeting accepted the proposal for division. A single nominating committee proposed the names of Prof. Gertrude Horgan, vice president of Incarnate Word, for Region I president with Dr. J.R. Manning of Texas A&I as her vice president. The committee named Dr. E.L. Ford from Centenary College to be the first president of Region II, assisted by Prof. Elsie Bodemann of East Texas State as vice president. No nominations came from the floor and the slate was elected. Dr. McMahon moved that the nominating committee report be expanded to include Dean Nolle as Region I secretary-treasurer and this was quickly approved. Later, when the two regions met separately, Region II chose Dr. C.F. Sheley from Stephen F. Austin to be its secretary-treasurer. Invitations for the respective 1956 regional conventions came from Abilene Christian College for Region I and Texas Christian University for Region II.

The student presentations were divided into one group of fine arts presentations (music, art, poetry), and one of papers around the theme of the year, relating to extracurricular activities and their role on campus. The papers, Prof. Shook said, "were fairly balanced for and against extra-curricular activities."[11]

At the close of the meeting, which must have created mixed emotions for many, Alpha Chi moved on to a new format and new relationships.

NOTES

[1] *Proceedings*, 1949, pp. 5, 9-12.
[2] *Proceedings*, 1950, pp. 15-16.
[3] *Proceedings*, 1951, p. 5.
[4] *Proceedings*, 1951, pp. 3-10.
[5] *Proceedings*, 1952, p. 8.
[6] *Proceedings*, 1952, p. 5.
[7] Ibid.
[8] *Proceedings*, 1952, p. 10.
[9] *Proceedings*, 1953, p. 10.
[10] *Proceedings*, 1953, pp. 34-36.
[11] *Proceedings*, 1955, p. 5.

Focus On . . .

PAUL JOSIAH SCHWAB

Paul J. Schwab was the grandson of German immigrants on his father's side and, on his mother's side, a descendant of the English Separatists who came to America in 1620 on the *Mayflower*. He was raised in the midwest as the son of an Evangelical minister.

Schwab began his career in business in Chicago. He saw service in France as an infantry sergeant in World War I. Returning from the service, he completed a college degree at North Central College in Illinois and entered Evangelical Theological Seminary in 1921, graduating two years later with a Bachelor of Divinity degree. He served for several years during and after seminary as a pastor in Illinois.

Schwab came to feel that his real calling lay in teaching, and he earned a master's degree from Northwestern University and his Ph.D. from Yale in the field of religion. He did extensive work in Europe as a Sterling Fellow, collecting materials on the Protestant reformation. In 1928 he took a teaching post in religion at Trinity College, a Presbyterian school in Waxahachie, Texas, becoming dean of the faculty two years later. Trinity moved to San Antonio in 1942, changing its name to Trinity University.

Schwab became the sponsor of the Alpha Chi chapter at Trinity College in 1937 and president of Region I (then the only region) in 1946. His one-year term was so successful that he was elected to the National Council of Alpha Chi in 1949 and immediately chosen president of the society. He held the post for the next seventeen years. That tenure makes him the longest-serving president Alpha Chi has ever had.

Schwab took a National Council that was largely an inactive figurehead group and forged it into an active and progressive force in Alpha Chi. Under his administration the first new chapters outside the southwest came into the society. At the time of his death, still the active president of the society, Alpha Chi had doubled in size, from a small sectional body of thirty-two chapters to a society on the verge of national standing, with sixty-five chapters in twenty states.

Paul Schwab was extremely active in Presbyterian affairs in Texas, as well as in veteran's organizations, scholarly societies, and civic groups. His biographer noted that Schwab's care for students reached into the moral and religious dimensions of their lives: "For him an 'A' student who remains a religiously undependable Aaron Burr—who graduated with highest grades from Princeton—spelled failure."[1] That emphasis, which is not far from Alpha Chi's interest in scholarship undergirded by character, made Schwab an ideal president for the growing organization.

NOTE

[1] Frank R. Neff, Jr., "Paul Josiah Schwab," *Recorder*, Autumn 1966, p. 11.

CHAPTER 7 (1956-66)
A NATIONAL PRESENCE

Regions I and II

Excluding the war years, Alpha Chi scheduled an annual meeting every year of its existence. That sequence ended in 1956, when the society divided into two regional meetings.

Abilene Christian College hosted the meeting of Region I without any of the regional officers present. The president, Gertrude Horgan, had moved from Incarnate Word College to another state and effectively no longer held the post. Vice President J.R. Manning of Texas A&I had illness in his family which kept him at home. Dean Nolle was absent, as was his usual surrogate, Prof. Alma Lueders of Southwest Texas, detained by a death in the family. Accordingly, Dr. Paul Witt, host sponsor and National Councilman, presided at the sessions. Region I was the home region of the president of the National Council, Paul Schwab, and he also was present to give stability to the meeting. Twelve chapters attended and five were absent. Sam Houston State, which had been given the option of Region I or Region II, had chosen Region I, but was not in attendance.

The student programs included the usual mix of musical performances and papers, the papers being organized into a symposium on the theme "Is the Scholar a Specialist?"

Part of the business session was consumed by adjustments required by the split into regions. One such item was the matter of beginning a regional treasury, to which the national organization would give $250 as a start. From these funds the region agreed to support travel expenses according to existing national policies. A constitutional amendment revising the process for accepting new chapters came before the assembly. It called for acceptance of new chapters on a regional basis, with National Council assent and Regional Council assent required, except that the region's executive committee could grant permission in the interval between meetings. Region I voted to approve this amendment.

Region II held its first-ever meeting at Texas Christian University in Fort Worth. Nine chapters showed up, with five missing. After a student musicale, Dr. Wiley of Texas State College for Women led a panel discussion on "Aims and Purposes of Region II."

The theme "Is the Scholar a Specialist?" received treatment here, as it had in Region I. President E. Lee Ford introduced the proposed amendment for accepting new chapters, and Region II approved, but also adopted a motion saying that it preferred to follow only the option that called for a vote by the whole regional meeting, rather than by the executive committee alone.

In following years the two regions held annual meetings. In even-numbered years they met independently at separate sites, and in odd-numbered years they met together in a sort of "national" session. In 1957 the constitution was amended to allow for two-year terms for the regional president and vice president, while preserving the five-year term of the secretary-treasurers. The society obviously felt that, under the new arrangement, continuity in regional programs demanded the longer term.[1] Independent meetings of the two regions were usually less well attended than the national meetings, though all meetings were held on college campuses. Alpha Chi encouraged the regions to hold their independent meetings toward the geographical outer edges so that chapters closer to the center could host the national meetings.

After the "first biennial meeting" of Region I at Abilene in 1956, the regional body moved to El Paso in 1958 for the second meeting, to West Texas State at Canyon in 1960, to Trinity in San Antonio in 1962, Wayland Baptist in Plainview for 1964, and to a relatively new chapter, Texas Lutheran at Seguin, in 1966.

Region II, after the 1956 gathering in Fort Worth, went to Commerce and the campus of East Texas State for 1958, then to Harding College in Searcy, Arkansas, in 1960, back to Fort Worth for the 1962 meeting at Texas Wesleyan, then to Hendrix College at Conway, Arkansas, in 1964, and in 1966 to Ouachita Baptist in Arkadelphia.

Biennial National Meetings

Until 1956 Alpha Chi met annually in what amounted to a national convention, but which was termed the "regional council" and run by that year's Region I president. The "national" officers played very little role in the meeting. Their sphere of activity was strictly confined to the National Council. The 1956 regional meetings, as has been noted, were in different locations, independent of each other. Beginning in 1957 the two came back together to hold the first "biennial national convention," or "the first biennial meeting of Alpha Chi," or "the first biennial meeting of the national organization of Alpha Chi," or "the first biennial national meeting of Alpha Chi." [2] They were not even sure what to call it.

The reason for the confusion lay in the fact that the session was *not constitutional* at all, but merely the result of an *operational* decision of the National Council in 1954 that the two regions, once formed, would meet together every other year. Confusion was apparent even in the enabling action:

> Dr. McMahon moved the Council proceed with the plan of division, creating two regions, each region to continue having an annual meeting, though meeting conjointly biennially for the program. To clarify the motion: all chapters will meet in San Antonio in 1955 for a joint program. At that time division will be perfected and each Region will set up its officers and business arrangements. In 1956 each Region will have its annual Council meeting in its own area, but in 1957 they will meet in the same city, separately for business, but together for program, and thereafter there will be the joint meeting biennially.[3]

The final authority of Alpha Chi was still the twelve-member National Council, not a national convention. In fact, the national meeting should really have been termed "the first biennial joint meeting of Regions I and II of Alpha Chi." In practice, that is much the way it happened in 1957 and continued to happen for another decade. The regional presidents took turns presiding over the joint program meetings. Each regional president also presided at brief separated business sessions of the respective regions. There was no national business transacted, because there was no national entity to transact it except, of course, for the National Council, which had its own meeting at another time and another place.

Our Lady of the Lake College in San Antonio hosted the 1957 meeting(s). Dr. Elsie Bodemann, president of Region II, was the banquet speaker and the Saturday morning keynoter was Dr. H. Howard Hughes of Texas Wesleyan, who would soon be elected president of Region II.

Texas Woman's University in Denton was the site of "the Second Biennial Meeting of Alpha Chi" in April 1959. Its theme was "The Responsibility of the Academically Superior." Thirty chapters sent delegations, including three from "National Council chapters." This time, national President Paul Schwab was in the chair for the opening session, during which he delivered a "presidential address." A highlight of the event was a garden reception on Friday afternoon. Regional presidents Stather Thomas and Dolphus Whitten presided at the other sessions of the meeting, including the banquet, which featured an address by the distinguished author Louis Untermeyer on "What Makes Modern Poetry Modern." Saturday the regions held their separate business meetings after which there was another set of student presentations. Finally, Schwab resumed the chair to preside over a concluding "business session" which featured reports from the regions, a resolutions committee report, and a request for invitations to host the 1961 meeting. Midwestern University and Centenary College extended bids, and it was left to the National Council to decide between them. So no real business was done, except to approve the resolutions.

The 1961 "Thirty-Second Annual Meeting of the Councils of the Societies of Alpha Chi" convened at Shreveport on the campus of Centenary College in April. Dr. Schwab was at home recuperating from a heart attack, so national Vice President John McMahon presided at the opening general meeting. The fifteen numbers on the student programs roughly followed the theme of "Society in Transition." The now-familiar pattern of a banquet with a distinguished guest was followed, with a famous retired professor named Dr. Harden Craig as the featured speaker. The closing business included reports from the regional meetings and from Dr. Witt for the national expansion committee. At a request from the floor, McMahon allowed a time of sharing about local chapter activities. Host sponsor Dr. E. Lee Ford raised the question of holding longer meetings, perhaps two full days instead of two half days. While the body seemed to agree that that was a good idea, no vote could be taken because there was no formal group constituted with power to vote.

Having been bypassed in favor of Centenary two years earlier, Midwestern University was pleased to be able to host the 1963 "national meeting." Very few of the twenty-four student presentations addressed the selected theme, "Motivation in Collegiate and Graduate Education." Dr. Schwab was back in the chair for the opening session to welcome delegates from thirty-six chapters. The first item of business was the induction ceremony for the new members of the Midwestern chapter. Regional officers presided at the remainder of the meetings until the closing session. Featured speakers were Prof. John H. Hallowell of Duke University and Dr. Charles Hounshell from the Woodrow Wilson Foundation. Hounshell's speech was to a concluding luncheon after the adjournment of the final business session.

In 1965 Alpha Chi met in Abilene, Texas, where Hardin-Simmons University hosted the national gathering with assistance from the two other Alpha Chi chapters in the city, Abilene Christian College and McMurry College. More than 150 delegates and visitors from thirty-six chapters were present. Delegates from Georgia, Indiana, Mississippi, Iowa, Tennessee, and Maine were among them. The program followed the traditional lines. The featured speaker was Hardin-Simmons's own Dr. Rupert Richardson, dean of Texas historians. Richardson, Dr. Nolle noted to the assembly, had been a featured speaker at the Scholarship Societies of the South meeting at Hardin-Simmons in 1932. The announced theme for papers was "The Role of the Scholar in a World in Ferment." Twenty-three student presentations constituted the bulk of the program. An innovation at this meeting was a concurrent pair of "round table discussions" for faculty and students, presided over by the two regional presidents, Dr. E.W. Jones of Region I for the faculty and Dr. Woodrow W. Pate of Region II for the students. While the two regions held their individual business meetings, Dr. Schwab convened the "national council chapters" present for informal discussion. Student delegate Mary James of Mississippi College reported to the plenary session on their behalf, saying that they urged the early organization of new regions and continued efforts toward expansion in the northeast.

Expansion

With its eyes fixed on further expansion earlier in this period, the National Council began to concern itself with its competition. Since Phi Beta Kappa, the most famous and oldest general honor society, seemed to be interested only in the most prestigious graduate institutions, it was not considered a rival. However, Phi Kappa Phi, a somewhat older society that inducted both undergraduates and graduates, did seem to be a possible concern. It seemed likely to the Council that there would some day be a union between the two, "but to effect such a merger, we would let Phi Kappa Phi court us."[4] When Nolle attended the Association of College Honor Societies meeting in 1958, he came back with the report that a modus vivendi with Phi Kappa Phi had been worked out under the auspices of a policy proposed by Schwab to the meeting. The policy rejected "one member of the organization supplanting another in the same field (Phi Kappa Phi at Texas Technological College, being an example). . . . With some modifications, [the resolution] was passed unanimously and there will probably be no more rivalry on that score."[5]

Perhaps the most significant step taken by the Council was the authorization of "a broadside to be sent out like the Voice of America to colleges any and everywhere." The Council asked Miss Shook to compose it. From this initiative would come a bountiful harvest of new chapters in the next few years.[6] The appeal would go not only across regional lines, but also across racial lines. The 1955 convention had gone on record with "overwhelming sentiment . . . in favor of admitting . . . chapters [from] 'negro colleges.'"[7]

The society needed expansion. In the twenty-two years since the organization had declared its intentions to become a national body by becoming "Alpha Chi," only eight chapters had been added, in spite of the best postwar efforts of Dr. Witt's expansion committee. Two of those, American International (Massachusetts Alpha) and Hastings (Nebraska Alpha) joined in 1949, but remained anomalies far removed from the neighborhood of the other chapters. Indeed, their very remoteness emphasized the regional nature of Alpha Chi. In seven years no others from their sections joined, and they could not have helped but feel their continued isolation.

A major result of the broadcast appeal was a plethora of new chapters. Between 1957 and 1960 fifteen colleges received membership in Alpha Chi. Included among them were Alpha chapters in South Carolina (Lander College), Georgia (Valdosta State College), Tennessee (Tusculum College), Mississippi (Mississippi College), Utah (Westminster College), Iowa (Wartburg College), and Indiana (Anderson College). With the Massachusetts and Nebraska chapters, there were now seminal chapters in each of what would become the society's seven regions. The others came from the existing bounds of Regions I and II. Chapters outside the existing regions were called "national council chapters" and were the special concern of the national governance structure.[8]

Not all of these chapters came in as a result of Professor Shook's letter. Sometimes the transfer of a society sponsor to a non-Alpha Chi school bore fruit. Indiana Alpha at Anderson College joined as a result of the activities of a new faculty member, Dr. Kenneth Cook, who came there from Hastings College (Nebraska Alpha).[9] Cook, the society's pioneer in Region V, subsequently became president and secretary-treasurer of that region. Sometimes schools encountered Alpha Chi when an alumni member took a teaching job there. Such was the case with East Central State in Oklahoma where Prof. Darrell Terrell, alumnus of Arkansas Gamma at Arkansas State Teachers College, became the first assistant sponsor.[10] In the case of Arkansas Eta at Harding College, which joined in 1957, the initiative came from within the school. Harding's Dean Joseph E. Pryor began looking for a national affiliation for the college's local honor society and selected Alpha Chi, from among several others under consideration, as the one most appropriate to Harding's aims.[11] This relationship became a most fortunate association for Alpha Chi. Many other chapters, seeking to find national affiliation for their local honors groups, subsequently joined as a result of just such a careful search.

Another cause for the rapid development of Alpha Chi in this period may have been its membership in the Association of College Honor Societies, accomplished in 1955.[12] That affiliation granted Alpha Chi a solid credential hitherto lacking and served to give additional exposure for the society to a national collegiate audience. Alpha Chi and the ACHS were a good fit for each other. A year after joining, Paul Schwab, Alpha Chi's delegate to the ACHS meeting, reported to the National Council that the society "was in high favor with the President and members of ACHS."[13] At the 1959 ACHS meeting, Schwab heard a panel that sought to define the characteristics of an ideal college honor society. Almost without exception, Alpha Chi not only met the criteria mentioned by the panel, Schwab said, but he found the standards already embodied, "native to and characteristic of Alpha Chi."[14]

The rapid expansion almost caught the society by surprise. There was considerable confusion about who was the principal contact for interested schools: Dr. Paul Witt, chair of the expansion committee; Dr. Paul Schwab, president of the National Council; or Dean Alfred Nolle, secretary-treasurer of the society. The Council decided in 1956 that Witt should be the principal evangelist for the society, with "Dr. Schwab and

Dr. Nolle to supplement the work done by Witt."[15] The confusion may have returned the following year, when the *Recorder* encouraged potential candidates for admission to approach any of the three.

Witt had considerable help. In 1962 the expansion committee (also known as committee on admissions or membership committee) consisted of nine other persons, including L.H. Bally and Dolphus Whitten for Oklahoma, Kenneth E. Cook for Indiana, E.L. Ford for Louisiana, Ruth D. Harris for Nebraska, Morris A. King for South Carolina, Joseph E. Pryor for Arkansas, and Stather Elliott Thomas for Texas.[16] But the load of new chapter correspondence finally got to be too much for Witt, and he resigned as head of the expansion committee in 1963.[17]

The following year the Executive Committee decided to take over the expansion process on a trial basis, and appropriated $1,500 to undertake a special effort of letter writing and visitation. The plan called for a division of the country into target areas. President Schwab took Louisiana and Mississippi, and Region II secretary-treasurer Joseph Pryor accepted Oklahoma and New Mexico. Dr. Nolle was responsible for Missouri, and Dr. Gadaire of American International was assigned New England. Schwab reported that he had begun his visits, but that did not "present the charms of Alpha Chi" where other societies were already present.[18]

Nearly all of the new chapter installations in this span were handled by the three men who led the expansion project. Of these, Schwab did by far the lion's share, Witt did several, and Nolle the fewest. President Schwab spent a considerable amount of time on the road, installing nearly all the new chapters outside the southwest. In fact, he may have overextended himself. He missed the 1961 national convention because of a heart attack in early March. He retired from active service at Trinity at the end of the semester but, recovering, continued to serve as president of the National Council until his death in 1966.[19] From 1960 to the end of Schwab's life, expansion into new areas continued. Fourteen more chapters were added. Among these were Alpha chapters in North Carolina (Appalachian State), Maine (Nasson College), Ohio (the College of Steubenville), Michigan (Adrian College), Kansas (Sterling College), Kentucky (Murray State University), and South Dakota (Sioux Falls College). President Schwab installed all, or nearly all, of these. By 1963 the executive committee was thinking about creating a Region III in the near future, possibly in the midwest.[20]

The Disaffiliation of TCU

The rapid growth gave Alpha Chi the national presence that it had been wanting, and an approach to genuine prestige. But it did not come soon enough for one chapter, which withdrew in 1964 in quest of an honor society more suitable to its aspirations. This chapter was one of the mainstays of Region II, Texas Christian University. Troy C. Crenshaw of TCU had been regional president in 1954, when there was still only one region. In 1956 he was elected to membership on the National Council.[21] Under Crenshaw the chapter was so active that there was even talk of a TCU alumni chapter in 1956.[22] And when Region II held its first convention ever, TCU was the host chapter in February 1956. At least one TCU alumnus became active in Alpha Chi later, when William Eugene Atkinson, a professor at Tarleton, became Region I secretary-treasurer for two terms.

But Alpha Chi's activity and welcome at Texas Christian began to fade when Crenshaw resigned from the Council and from the sponsor's job because of ill health.[23] His successor, Dr. Landon Colquitt, was equally active for a while, but he too became ill and "the affairs of the Chapter were allowed to drag."[24] Colquitt's illness coincided with a push in Region II to invoke the letter of the law suspending chapters which failed to attend regional conventions two years or more in a row. When the Region II president Richard Yates complained to the National Council about the problem of nonattendance at its meeting of October 21, 1961, the "National Council was gravely concerned and voted unanimously to have the regional presidents contact such chapters, even at some expense, to keep them from becoming delinquent.[25] Yates apparently went straight home and got off a letter to several schools, including TCU. The letter, sent to Colquitt, was passed into the hands of Dr. Winton H. Manning, who had just become the chapter sponsor.[26] Manning was apparently offended by the tone of Yates's note, for his response, while civil, was visibly restrained. After explaining TCU's special problems, he went on to express the opinion that the national organization did not understand TCU's special situation. Pointing out the length and strength of TCU's commitment to Alpha Chi, he said, "It would indeed be tragic, if after this lengthy tradition, the national Council were to act to suspend or void the Charter of the Texas Xi Chapter . . . ."[27] The appeal accomplished its objective, and no action was taken against TCU (which was no means the only, or even gravest, offender).

The seeds of doubt had been planted, however, and the situation rapidly deteriorated. In February 1963 Nolle sent a note to Manning requesting better compliance with Alpha Chi's reporting processes. Dr. Manning was so upset by the letter that he responded to Nolle criticizing the complexity of the paperwork, the apparent unfairness in distributing the *Recorder*, and the slowness of Star Engraving Company (the society's supplier) in forwarding membership certificates. Some of these grievances had been festering for some time. He concluded by resigning as chapter sponsor.

Nolle, in turn, wrote a blistering reply, attempting to refute Manning's complaints item by item and in great detail, calling them "untoward" and "spurious." "In all of the thirty-five years that I have been the Executive Officer of the National Council of Alpha Chi . . . , your letter is the first and only one I have ever received from a Sponsor that finds fault with the policies of the National Council . . and with the manner of their implementation . . . ."[28] Nolle sent Chancellor M.E. Sadler a copy of this letter, and Manning was quick to put in his side of it, concluding, "I think you will agree that an organization which has remained impervious to criticism for that length of time is not in step with progress."[29] Sadler responded immediately, "I hope it may be possible for us to change from Alpha Chi before very long. I have never been very pleased that we were associated with this organization."[30]

James Moudy, then Vice Chancellor for Academic Affairs and later president of TCU, appointed a new sponsor, John T. Everett, Jr., and sent him to the 1963 national convention in Wichita Falls in late March, 1963, with instructions to observe closely and return with an evaluation of the society. Everett reported back in April with a ten-page paper entitled "Impressions Concerning Alpha Chi." It began as a fairly balanced document, citing positive and negative elements. It ended being critical of the society for several reasons. Everett did not like the notion of student presentations at the convention, particularly since there was no time for discussing them. He was disappointed that many Alpha Chi officers, national and regional, were not up for re-election annually. He called this "possible in-group control, especially at the top level. . . . No elections were scheduled for top officers for the meeting at Midwestern, so these gentlemen maintained their positions."[31] He questioned whether TCU should be involved with an organization whose membership came principally from small schools. "It is impossible to overlook the fact that practically all of them are quite small as compared to TCU."[32] Citing the correspondence between Manning and Nolle, he found evidence of "rigidity and lack of vigor," and said the meeting reinforced that impression.[33] Finally, he argued that the chapter at Texas Christian was so inactive as to be virtually meaningless. Everett did not conclude by recommending disaffiliation, but no other course could reasonably result from the tone of his report.

After some consideration the TCU leadership moved in 1964 to disaffiliate. Chancellor Sadler explained to Schwab that the school had been contemplating the action for two years. "TCU has assumed a position of more than regional importance. It is now our desire to affiliate with such national organizations as are best known across the entire country." Pending such affiliation, he said TCU would concentrate on subject matter honors groups and a new Honors Program on campus.[34] Vice Chancellor Moudy told Nolle that what TCU was really after was a chapter of Phi Beta Kappa.[35]

What appeared to have happened here was a combination of events. The threat of suspension came at just the wrong time and tainted the relationship with the new sponsor, Dr. Manning. Subsequent misunderstandings between him and Nolle escalated into hostility. This breakdown in cordiality coincided with the desire of TCU administrators for a more prestigious organization with more of a national reputation. Perhaps this made a separation inevitable, but the problems between the national office and the TCU sponsor precipitated it early.

The affair raised the question of what niche Alpha Chi was to serve. Was the society, as Dr. Everett suggested, a regional body of small schools? If it was, would it remain so? The next few years would provide some clues for answering those questions.

Changing the Guard

The period 1956-66 saw a changeover from the leaders who had governed the society through the postwar years, and the emergence of a new generation of leaders poised to guide Alpha Chi for the next era. President Schwab continued to serve in his position until his death in 1966, a month short of his seventy-second birthday. Though he suffered a heart attack in the spring of 1961 which caused him to miss that year's convention, he recovered sufficiently to reassume the reins of the organization by summer. He continued the heavy load of new chapter installations, but this was tempered by his retirement from active teaching in 1963.

Upon Schwab's death, Vice President John McMahon, president of Our Lady of the Lake College, summoned the National Council into session in Dallas. When the question of succession was raised, Dr. Nolle pointed out that, under the parliamentary authority then in use (Sturgis), a vice president automatically assumed the presidency in case of death of the incumbent. The Council affirmed this by vote, but McMahon announced that he would hold the position only to the end of Schwab's term the following year. He cited the pressure of his duties at his college as reason for not being able to offer himself to Alpha Chi beyond that point. This, however, gave the National Council some breathing space and a chance to decide on the new leadership a year hence.[36] Also leaving the Council by death was Miss Bessie Shook. The first woman president of the society and the longtime recorder of Alpha Chi's minutes, she came on the Council in 1938 as the replacement for Harry Benedict. Shook served on the Council from that time until 1964, when the retired educator's fifth term expired. Nominated for reelection to yet another term, she declined, saying that it was time for someone younger to take her place. Still serving as the Council's recorder, she noted her own protestations in the minutes, and then wrote, "The Council would not have it so, and she was elected to the class of '68, a four-year term."[37] She did not serve out the term, dying in January 1966.[38]

The Council's ranks were depleted by other losses. Dolphus Whitten departed by virtue of leaving Henderson State College for the dean's job at Oklahoma City University, a non-Alpha Chi school. Though the Council ruled he could serve out his term, he left at the end of it.[39] Julia Luker of McMurry, Council member from 1951-56, passed away in 1959 as did Dean Thomas E. Ferguson of Stephen F. Austin, former vice president of the National Council and Council member until 1958.[40] Dr. George Sixbey of Northeast Louisiana State resigned from the Council in 1962 because he moved to another school. Dr. L.H. Bally of Northeastern State College in Oklahoma died in 1963 while serving on the National Council.[41]

Dr. Autrey Nell Wiley of Texas Women's University, member of the National Council since 1946 and founding editor of the *Recorder*, announced in 1966 that she would be giving up the editorship, though not yet leaving the Council. For ten years she edited and produced a very effective publication for the society. Wiley was president over the last regional meeting before World War II.[42] She continued to serve on the National Council until the society's reorganization in 1970.

As these and other pioneers of Alpha Chi left the scene, new faces emerged to replace them. When Harding College of Searcy, Arkansas, joined the society in 1957, its first sponsor was the college's academic dean, Joseph E. Pryor. Pryor, with his tall frame, courtly manner, incisive mind, and perennial bow tie, quickly became a fixture in Region II. Within a very short time, he became secretary-treasurer of the region, filling out the term of Region II's first incumbent in that post, Dr. C.F. Sheley of Stephen F. Austin, who had resigned.[43] The position placed him on the National Council and the national executive committee. Pryor was reelected the following year to a full five-year term. In 1966 President McMahon appointed him to record the minutes of the National Council, a task he was to continue for many years by appointment and by election.[44]

Another rising star was Dr. Edwin W. Gaston, Jr. of Stephen F. Austin. Gaston was an alumnus member of Alpha Chi before he joined the English faculty at Stephen F. Austin. Succeeding Dr. Sheley as sponsor at the school in 1960, he possessed a quiet competence that soon received recognition in his region. They elected him to the National Council for a five-year term in 1962.[45] The following spring he became vice president of the region and succeeded to the presidency of Region II in 1965. He became an increasing force in the discussions in the National Council. He further achieved prominence by serving as host sponsor for the joint meeting of the two regions in March, 1967. A month later he found himself nominated to be president of the entire organization.

Dr. Jess G. Carnes was a colleague of Dr. Schwab at Trinity University. He became head sponsor in 1959. At the 1961 regional meeting, he chaired the resolutions committee, made his report, sat down, and heard the nominating committee place his name before the meeting for a two-year term as president. His warm smile and gentle demeanor combined with a talent for hard work and won him much admiration. Carnes was named to the National Council for the first time in April 1967. The presence of Dr. Schwab, also from Trinity, made it awkward to elect him sooner. It is a sign of the high esteem in which he was held that, before

Carnes had even attended his first meeting, his name was presented by the Council's nominating committee for the post of national president.[46]

Alpha Chi and Its Times

The society did not exist in a vacuum, and the events of the era occasionally evoked a comment in the official records. At the 1957 convention, for example, Prof. H. Howard Hughes of Texas Wesleyan expressed the opinion that the popular image of scholarship was improving. He cited the example of the current national hero, Prof. Charles Van Doren of Columbia University, who was astounding the nation with his phenomenal memory and erudition by his weekly performances on a prime time television game show called "21": "It has been observed editorially here and there over the nation that Charles Van Doren may be instrumental in making the love of knowledge and scholarly pursuits something to be desired and respected rather than scorned and ridiculed."[47] Unfortunately, it soon became public knowledge that Van Doren had been cheating and the whole incident had rather the opposite effect than Hughes was supposing.

Prof. Richard E. Yates, president of Region II, delivered his valedictory address to the regional convention in 1962 on "A New Frontier in an Old Section." The frontier for the South, he said, was race relations. In tracing the history of slavery and its successor, racial segregation, he urged the delegates to use their brains: "I do not cry aloud for reform and change. They are not produced by crying aloud. I urge, instead, the more productive employment of study and reflection. The truth will not make us free unless we know the truth; and knowing the truth will not make us free, unless we reflect on it and understand it." In urging the study of the race problem of the South, he noted that the issue involved "a multiplicity of inter-related factors, which compels the student to give attention to history, political science, law, economics, sociology, psychology, and religion—to name only the most obvious of the disciplines. . . ." His awareness of the struggles then going on was obvious in the content of the speech.[48]

The Autumn 1963 issue of the *Recorder* was dedicated to Lyndon B. Johnson, President of the United States. Johnson, a graduate of Southwest Texas State Teachers College, was a former student and current friend of Dr. Nolle. In 1959 Senator Johnson introduced a tribute to Nolle in the *Congressional Record* on the occasion of the teacher's imminent retirement as Dean at Southwest Texas.[49] Perhaps this was in response to Nolle's having secured Johnson an honorary membership in Alpha Chi, as one of twenty-two such memberships granted by the National Council in May 1959.[50] Johnson's succession to the presidency on the death of President John Kennedy evoked within a week letters of support and assurances of their prayers from both Nolle and Schwab.[51] A full color portrait of LBJ (the only color ever introduced into the pages of the *Recorder*) was a feature, and the cover called the issue "the Lyndon B. Johnson Number."

Disturbances on college campuses, in urban ghettoes, in cultural change, and in a distant war received their share of discussion. Region II's theme for 1966 was "Toward the Mending of Fragmented Man and Society." Several student papers addressed the theme, as did the presidential address of Dr. Edwin Gaston. Gaston spoke of alienation of God from man and man from society: "The complexities of twentieth century life make the gulfs appear . . . wider than ever before. Seemingly, never has the distance been greater from Main Street to the East of Eden, from Wall Street to the tenant farm, and from the LBJ Ranch to the Ho Chi Minh Trail."[52] Gaston said there could probably be no absolute answers to society's alienations, but that patches could be put on the rents in the social fabric. He called for an application of the mind that would marshal evidence before developing a point of view, rather than the other way around, as seemed so often the case. The speech showed the scholar wrestling with the problems of his day.

Later in the year Region I President Robert M. Platt of McMurry College addressed the Hardin-Simmons school assembly on the subject "Discontent on the American College Campus." Quoting popular music of the day (Bob Dylan's "The Times, They Are A'Changin'," Jan and Dean's "The Eve of Destruction," and the Beatles' "Nowhere Man"), Platt called upon society to listen to the voices of young prophets in order to overcome the "generation gap." He concluded, "If there is any place in America where the generational gap can be bridged, it should be the Christian college or university. But it will take much grace and much patience and much forgiveness to overcome the mutual distrust our stereotypes have perpetuated."[53]

Clearly, the membership of the society was well aware of events in the world around it. Yet it was not often on the campus of Alpha Chi schools that the greatest unrest occurred, and many of them were relatively sheltered by size and location from the crisis, for a while at least.

Governance

It was the task of the National Council to make the basic decisions for the operations of the society. Often these were routine matters like electing qualified nominees to honorary membership or determining the size of scholarships. The Council was also responsible for filling vacancies among its own ranks, when they occurred because of death, resignation, or term expiration. Matters of somewhat greater moment also came before the members of the leadership group at their annual meetings.

The Council usually held its annual meeting in a hotel rather than on a college campus. The preferred site was the Baker Hotel in Dallas, and the time was usually early May, but an occasional fall meeting also had to be scheduled. The organization underwrote the expenses of the members to the Council meetings, and beginning in 1962 also met their expenses to the biennial joint meetings in the odd-numbered years.[54] The Council took responsibility for handling the financial management of the society. It audited the financial reports of the secretary-treasurer with audit committees drawn from its own membership. It set the fiscal year and appropriated society funds for conventions. It fixed dues, subject to contitutional limits, and set in motion raises in the constitutional limits when the times seemed to dictate such a course.

In 1960 the Council secured a copyright for the name and the seal of the society and arranged for it to be chartered by the state of Texas, with Dr. Nolle as the principal agent of record and San Marcos as the seat of the charter.[55] After Dr. Nolle retired at Southwest Texas State, it appeared there might be a problem with securing him office space for his Alpha Chi operations. But the school's president provided space to the society without charge in 1962, thus providing a considerable savings to the society in terms of money and convenience.[56] The society also moved to establish an archive by accepting the offer of the "mother chapter" at Southwestern of a room to house Alpha Chi records.[57]

Constitutional amendments usually originated in the National Council and had to have a two-thirds approval of that body and a similar consent from the regions to go into effect. Several amendments came before the Council during the period. They effected no particularly significant changes, but were rather a matter of fine-tuning and adapting to slightly changed circumstances.

The Council administered the society's scholarship program. In 1956 it agreed to enlarge the Benedict Scholarship stipend from $100 to $200 and to grant one in each of the regions for 1957-58. Some schools, like Hastings and American International, were now defined as being outside the bounds of Region II and were designated "national chapters." For the time being they would be incorporated in one or the other of the existing regions for scholarship competition purposes.[58] Soon, however, the National Council began to offer a scholarship of $100 to "a student in one of the chapters under National jurisdiction."[59]

Another concern was the matter of honorary memberships. After granting two and denying another, the Council realized that it needed some kind of standard procedure. Pending development of a broader policy, they agreed that chapter sponsors who had served a minimum of three years and were recommended by their chapter could be elected. Further, the Council would provide the veteran sponsors certficates authenticating their membership.[60]

Service on the National Council required the ability to sit through long discussions. Council members understood that the things that they were debating were important, even if only to individuals here and there through the society. Council members did not begrudge the time and effort required for that kind of service.

Local Chapter Activities

The first biennial meeting of Region II in 1956 produced an insight into local chapter activities, as individuals shared their school's procedures. Texas Wesleyan noted that they invited all the freshmen to their initiation in March, hoping to inspire them to work toward qualifying for membership. Texas Christian University said they took the fall honor roll of freshman students and contacted them with information about Alpha Chi, also seeking to encourage them to aspire to membership. The Centenary chapter awarded a prize to the ranking freshman and sponsored outstanding scholars to speak to the student body. East Texas State reached out even earlier, sponsoring programs for high school seniors that encouraged them to work hard in college. North Texas State advertised their chapter with posters reading, "Do you want in Alpha

Chi?....Make some good grades!" Henderson State provided a tutorial program and TCU's athletic department paid an Alpha Chi senior "to tutor the football team." TSCW participated in the Honors Day program each year. Students and faculty were still discussing when "attendants . . . appeared at the door with the harp, upon which Kathryn Rapp (TCU) was to play."[61]

These and similar activities characterized the real work of Alpha Chi, which took place at the grass roots. Except for the advantages to be gained in attendance at conventions, the "upper echelon" work of the society was undertaken to enable local chapters to do their jobs. The society not only wanted to recognize and honor outstanding scholarship; it also wanted to make that scholarship effective for good in the lives of the members, on the campuses, and in the world beyond.

NOTES

[1] These conclusions are inferred from the fact that they began the two-year terms in 1957. Miss Shook's national minutes for 1957 unaccountably and uncharacteristically omit any mention of such a decision, but it must have been done at that time. The official records of the two regions likewise did not allude to electing their leadership to two-year terms because their minutes for 1957 were not published at all in the official journal. Since the constitution, as amended to April 1, 1956, provided for one-year terms, and since two-year terms were the norm by 1958, the 1957 national meeting *must* have ratified the amendment, to take effect immediately. Probably the omissions are attributable to the shift from *Proceedings* edited by Dr. Nolle to *Recorder* edited by Dr. Wiley. The 1957 *Recorder* was the first issue of that new journal, and the one where the 1957 regional minutes should have appeared.

[2] *Recorder*, Autumn 1957, pp. 1, 3, 34.

[3] *Proceedings*, 1954, p. 24.

[4] *Proceedings*, 1956, p. 53.

[5] *Recorder*, Spring 1958, p. 35.

[6] *Proceedings*, 1956, p. 56.

[7] *Proceedings*, 1955, p. 7.

[8] *Recorder*, Autumn 1959, p. 3.

[9] *Recorder*, Autumn 1959, p. 4.

[10] *Recorder*, Autumn 1961/Spring 1962, p. 48.

[11] Telephone interview with Joseph E. Pryor, January 11, 1997.

[12] *Proceedings*, 1955, p. 27.

[13] *Proceedings*, 1956, p. 53.

[14] *Recorder*, Autumn 1959, p. 4.

[15] *Proceedings*, 1956, p. 56.

[16] Letterhead, Paul C. Witt to Winton H. Manning, February 3, 1962, in Alpha Chi file at Texas Christian University archive.

[17] *Recorder*, 1963, p. 35.

[18] *Recorder*, 1964, p. 44.

[19] *Recorder*, Spring 1961, p. 10.

[20] *Recorder*, Spring 1963, p. 23.

[21] Paul Schwab to T.C. Crenshaw, April 23, 1956, Alpha Chi File, TCU.

[22] T. C. Crenshaw to Elsie Bodemann, vice president of Region II, October 24, 1955, Alpha Chi File, TCU.

[23] *Recorder*, Autumn 1957, p. 37.

[24] Winton H. Manning to Richard E. Yates, president of Region II, October 27, 1961, Alpha Chi file, TCU.

[25] *Recorder*, Autumn 1961/Spring 1962, p. 41.

[26] Paul Schwab to Winton H. Manning, October 4, 1961, Alpha Chi File, TCU.

[27] Manning to Yates, October 27, 1961, Alpha Chi file, TCU.

[28] Nolle to Manning, March 1, 1963, Alpha Chi file, TCU.

[29] Manning to Sadler, March 4, 1963, Alpha Chi file, TCU.

[30] Sadler to Manning, March 5, 1963, Alpha Chi file, TCU.

[31] John T. Everett, Jr., "Impressions Concerning Alpha Chi," p. 6, Alpha Chi file, TCU.

[32] Ibid., p. 5.

[33] Ibid., p. 6.

[34] Sadler to Schwab, July 8, 1964, Alpha Chi file, TCU.

[35] Moudy to Nolle, August 20, 1964, Alpha Chi file, TCU.

[36] *Recorder,* Autumn 1966, p. 13.

[37] *Recorder*, Spring 1964,, p. 46.

[38] *Recorder*, Spring 1966, p. 3.

[39] *Recorder*, Spring 1958, p. 35.

[40] *Recorder*, Autumn 1959, p. 37.

[41] *Recorder*, Spring 1964, p. 45.

[42] *Recorder*, Spring 1967/Autumn 1967, p. 5.

[43] *Recorder*, Autumn 1959, p. 21.

[44] *Recorder*, Autumn 1966, p. 17.

[45] *Recorder*, Autumn 1961/Spring 1962, p. 29.

[46] *Recorder*, Spring 1967/Fall 1967, p. 48.

[47] *Recorder*, Autumn 1957, pp. 15-16.

[48] *Recorder,* Autumn 1961/Spring 1962, pp. 30-37.

[49] *Recorder*, Autumn 1963, p. 8.

[50] *Recorder*, Autumn 1959, p. 36.

[51] *Recorder*, Autumn 1963, p. 2.
[52] *Recorder*, Spring 1966, p. 25.
[53] *Recorder*, Autumn 1966, p. 21.
[54] *Recorder*, Autumn 1962, p. 29.
[55] *Recorder*, Autumn 1960, p. 2.
[56] *Recorder*, Spring 1963, p. 23; Spring 1960, p. 37.
[57] *Recorder*, Spring 1960, p. 38.
[58] *Proceedings*, 1956, p. 55.
[59] *Recorder*, 1960, p. 39.
[60] *Proceedings*, 1956, p. 55.
[61] *Proceedings*, 1956, pp. 51-52.

Focus On . . .

BESSIE SHOOK

Bessie Shook, longtime professor of English at North Texas State, was the most significant woman of the early history of Alpha Chi. She was the first woman to serve as president of the society. In 1929 the Scholarship Societies of the South elected her to the office of president for a one-year term. She was the only woman to hold the top leadership post in the society until Dr. Gayle White became president in 1987. More significantly for Alpha Chi, she was the minutes secretary of the regional meetings from 1934 until the regions divided, and then of the national meetings. She kept the minutes of the National Council from the time she took Harry Benedict's seat on the Council in 1938 to her death in 1966.[1]

A Phi Beta Kappa graduate of the University of Texas, Shook became faculty sponsor at North Texas State in 1924. In 1928 her abilities earned her election to the vice presidency of the society.

In Alpha Chi, in addition to her authorship of the minutes, she also undertook to write a major ritual revision which was adopted in 1936. When Alpha Chi decided to write the first of several letters inviting applications from colleges and universities outside its region, the National Council turned to Prof. Shook for the text. From that letter came the beginning of the great growth of the society in the 1960s and 1970s.

Miss Shook may have been the person most concerned with preserving the history of the society. On several occasions she went on record as urging preservation of Alpha Chi's story. This book is the first major response to that call.

In 1965 Alpha Chi elected Bessie Shook to honorary membership, a distinction that was not much dispensed in that time. Dr. Autrey Nell Wiley, her cross-town neighbor at Texas Woman's University in Denton, said of her in an article celebrating Shook's contributions to Alpha Chi: "She has walked proudly with her colleagues through every stage of service in the history of Alpha Chi: from campus to state to region to nation."[2]

NOTES

[1] *Recorder*, Spring 1966, p. 3.
[2] *Recorder*, Spring 1965, pp. 4-5.

CHAPTER 8 (1967-70)
NEW ENERGY, NEW DIRECTIONS

A New Leadership Team

When the National Council gathered at the Baker Hotel in April 1967, it had before it the issue of leadership. President McMahon made it clear at the previous meeting that he would not serve as an officer, though he would agree to continue on the Council. McMahon appointed a nominating committee, consisting of himself, Alfred Nolle, and Region 1 secretary-treasurer Otto Watts of Hardin-Simmons, to make several recommendations to the 1967 meeting. Five Council vacancies had to be filled and a new president and vice president nominated. On behalf of the committee, Watts proposed the name of Trinity's Dr. Jess Carnes for president. Though Carnes had no experience on the Council, he was well-liked and respected, and inherited the mantle of the deceased Schwab as the sponsor at Trinity. Immediately after this nomination was announced and other nominations requested, Council member Woodrow Pate of Centenary proposed the name of Edwin Gaston. As it turned out, neither of these nominations was a surprise. Council members had suggested both men to the nominating committee. The committee secured an agreement from each that he would serve if elected, before settling on only one name to present to the Council. Without further ado, the Council voted by secret ballot and elected Gaston. Pate moved the election of Carnes for vice president by acclamation, and the Council approved. These two novices, along with the veteran Nolle, composed the new leadership team.[1]

Two years later Dr. Nolle decided to retire and served notice that he wished to be replaced as national secretary-treasurer by January 1, 1970. The Council accepted his resignation with many expressions of esteem and immediately elected the man who was by that time the obvious choice, Dean Joseph E. Pryor of Harding College.[2] Pryor, whose tasks already included the traditional dean's chores, was also Harding's athletic representative, sponsor of her prize-winning yearbook, chair of most of the faculty committees on his campus, and active participant in the regional accrediting agency. With Gaston and Carnes, Pryor led the society into its greatest period of geographic and institutional growth.

Gaston immediately began to charge the society with new energy. His dual priorities, he announced in an open letter published in the 1967 *Recorder*, were the expansion of Alpha Chi by the addition of new chapters, and the organization of new regions for the benefit of the new chapters and the existing "national" chapters as yet unaffiliated with a region. To that end, he and Dr. Pryor were preparing a letter to prospective member schools. He also sought to recruit neighboring Alpha Chi schools, supplementing the national letter with his own personalized, localized encouragement.[3]

Gaston's presidential letter a year later reported the results of the growth initiative, twenty-seven new chapters in two years. The installation of those new chapters, he noted, was a major task that had been shared by himself and several members of the National Council. Gaston also commissioned several other chapter sponsors to share in the undertaking. The president announced plans for the 1969 national meeting, which would gather on the campus of East Central State College in Ada, Oklahoma. He further announced that, in contrast to previous years, there would be no theme for papers to address. Gaston noted that time constraints would prevent the acceptance of more than one paper and "one other type of presentation" from a given chapter.

Carnes also became very busy very quickly. At the 1967 executive committee meeting, he accepted the editorship of the *Recorder*, a vacancy created when Dr. Wiley decided to resign her post. Although he was serving as vice president, the editor's responsibility was not part of the job description. The heavy workload associated with producing the *Recorder* twice a year was over and above his vice presidential responsibilities, and earned him "an editorial fee" of $150. Because of the timing of the resignation and the appointment of a successor, only one "dual" issue came out in 1967.

Meetings and Councils

The biennial joint meeting of the two regions assembled at Stephen F. Austin State College in March 1967. The host sponsor was also the president of Region II, Dr. Edwin Gaston. John McMahon presided over his only national meeting as president of the society, though he had been in the chair in 1961 when President Schwab was ill. The theme for the students papers, if they wished to address it, was "The Search for Truth." Thirty-five chapters sent representatives, most of them from the host region.

The distinguished guest speaker was Dr. Hans Rosenhaupt of the Woodrow Wilson Foundation, an organization which assisted aspiring students to prepare for careers in college teaching. He noted that, over the years, 132 Woodrow Wilson Fellows had come from schools that currently had Alpha Chi chapters.

After the banquet President McMahon led a discussion among the sponsors concerning ways of improving local chapter operations. A similar discussion for students was going on in a neighboring room, under the guidance of Dean Joseph Pryor.

In many ways this was a typical meeting. There were fifteen program numbers presented by student delegates. Both regions held their separate business meetings and chose new officers. From opening invocation to final gavel, the meeting extended over a twenty-two hour period on Friday and Saturday. The longer meeting that students had occasionally requested in past years was not yet realized.[4] Region I went back to Canyon in the Texas Panhandle, the home of West Texas State University and the site of the 1960 regional meeting. Eleven student numbers were on the program. Two events highlighted the meeting. One was an afternoon trip to the Palo Duro Canyon, during which the delegates rode on a narrow gauge train in the park. The Friday evening program featured a readers theatre production of Stephen Vincent Benet's "They Burned the Books," performed by West Texas State students. Despite the outstanding entertainment, only eighteen delegates, aside from the host chapter, were in attendance.[5]

Region II's agenda was much more crowded. Nearly thirty students made presentations out of the eighteen schools represented. They met at the College of the Ozarks at Clarksville in west central Arkansas. The meeting was entertained by presentations by the college choir and by two one-act plays. President James Atteberry led a faculty discussion while Dean Pryor led a student session, as he had done the previous year at Nacogdoches. Region II chose not to have a theme, and Atteberry attributed the large number and high quality of the papers presented to the absence of thematic limitations on subject matter.[6]

The 1969 assembly turned out to be the last joint meeting of the two regions, ending a tradition begun in 1955. Meeting at Ada, Oklahoma, on the campus of East Central State College, the meeting attracted about 150 delegates and visitors. Time allowed only nineteen student presentations. The principal address was made by a colleague of President Gaston, Texas folklorist Francis E. Abernethy of Stephen F. Austin. After the adjournment of the formal evening session, Abernethy brought out his guitar and led a spirited folk song sing-along with the delegates. Region II had twenty-two of its twenty-five chapters represented at the meeting. Region I's longtime secretary-treasurer, Dr. Otto Watts, turned over his post because of a new constitutional provision limiting reelections. The Region chose the retiring region president, Wendell Cain of West Texas State, to succeed him. Both regions conducted only routine business and were through in less than an hour.

The 1970 meetings of the regions convened at Southwestern University and Texas Wesleyan University in the spring. Both meetings were well attended, and for once, Region I had more student presentations than Region II. Routine business was the order of the day, except for debate and ratification of a major constitutional revision that would change the face of the society and make the 1971 meeting a true *national* gathering.[7]

The Crossroads

The May 3, 1969, gathering of the National Council was the most important meeting that the Council ever had, before or since. It made several major decisions, any one of which would have been the landmark legislation of a previous meeting. The decisions reached by the eleven men gathered in Room 4 of the Baker Hotel in Dallas changed the course of the society forever.

The conferees were Dr. James Atteberry of Harding College, president of Region II; Dr. Wendell Cain of West Texas State, president of Region I; Dr. Jess G. Carnes of Trinity University, vice president of the Council; Dean F. Burr Clifford of Southwestern University, elected by Region I; Dean Charles Gadaire of American International College; Dr. Edwin W. Gaston, Jr. of Stephen F. Austin State College, president of the Council; Dr. John L. McMahon, president of Our Lady of the Lake College and immediate past president of the Council; Dr. Alfred H. Nolle,

now retired from Southwest Texas State College and longtime secretary-treasurer of Alpha Chi; Dr. Woodrow W. Pate of Centenary College, elected by Region II; Dean Joseph E. Pryor of Harding College,
secretary-treasurer of Region II; and Dr. Otto O. Watts of Hardin-
Simmons University, secretary-treasurer of Region I. The lone female
member of the Council, Dr. Autrey Nell Wiley of Texas Woman's University, was at home receiving recognition as a distinguished alumna of
her school.

This group heard Dr. Gaston report that Alpha Chi had grown to
ninety-three chapters; changed the publication schedule of the *Recorder*;
shifted two chapters to different regions; established the tentative boundaries for the creation of three new regions; received Dr. Nolle's resignation as secretary-treasurer after forty-plus years in that post; and approved
the draft of a major constitutional restructuring.

The Proposed Constitution

Dr. Woodrow Pate was the principal author of the constitutional revision. He embodied in it much from the existing pattern, some new
guidelines conforming to what the society was already doing, and major
innovations for the governance of Alpha Chi.

By far the most significant of the new provisions was Article IV,
which created a new structure, the National Convention. Pate envisioned
the biennial National Convention as the final authority for the society.
Composed of one faculty and one student voting member from each chapter, it was a delegated body which nevertheless represented the grassroots
of Alpha Chi. The officers of the National Council were the officers of
the National Convention. Among its powers was the right to elect a majority of the members to the National Council. This article took the existing biennial joint meeting of Regions I and II and gave it official standing and extensive power.

Under the provisions of the new Article V, the National Council
would be composed of at least eight members elected by the Convention, plus the regional secretary-treasurers. The intent was to keep a majority of the Council answerable to the National Convention for election
and re-election, thus emphasizing the importance of the Convention.
Nominations for membership would come from the Council itself, but
the option of nominations from the floor of the Convention made it al-

ways possible for the Convention to elect whomever it pleased, regardless of the Council's guidance. (Through 1995 the Convention has elected a floor nominee only twice, in 1971 and 1973.) Each Council member served a term of four years, which coincided with the term length of regional secretary-treasurers. One section provided for a limit of twelve consecutive years of service.[8] Otherwise, the new Council functioned very much as the old one did. However, it gained an additional duty in that it would be the sole agency for approving new chapters, a power heretofore shared with the respective regions. Constitutional amendments had to receive approval of two-thirds of the Council before being passed on to the Convention. The new Council received the power to set the fee structure of the society as it saw fit, whereas fees had previously been specifically defined in the provisions of the constitution, requiring an amendment in order to raise them.

The concept of the National Council as established here broke forever from the idea set forth in 1934 that the Council should include prestigious academics who might not have to do much but lend their name. That notion had long since been outgrown in practice, but the provision that the Council should elect most of its own members remained as something of an anachronism. The membership structure proposed in this draft set up a Council composed of ordinary sponsors whose academic reputations might be smaller but whose availability to work might be greater. Further, the Council would answer directly to the whole body of the society as Alpha Chi expressed the corporate will through the National Convention.

The proposal reduced the size of the national executive committee by deleting regional secretary-treasurers from membership. With the creation of new regions, the size of the committee would quickly have become unwieldy and expensive if left as it was.

The regional meetings picked up a new nomenclature, now being termed "regional conventions" rather than "regional councils." They now became biennial, alternating years with the national conventions. The draft constitution provided that additional "interim business meetings" might be held, if needed, at the time and site of the national convention.

The new constitution specified the duties of the regional officers in some detail, as it did also for the national officers. At both levels the previous designation of the secretary-treasurer as the executive officer was changed to give that authority to the president. At both levels the president was charged with "calling" the meeting. At both levels the vice president took over the duty of program chair, a task previously assigned to the president.

At the local level the new constitution improved clarity and flexibility. No longer would the local committee structure be specified in the constitution. The new arrangement prescribed no quorum limits, leaving that matter to each chapter to decide for itself. The long-standing confusion about membership was clarified in a stroke, by doing away with the concept of annual elections to "junior membership," "senior membership," and "alumni membership." While persons could be elected to membership as juniors, seniors, or upon graduation, they were simply called "active members" and the one election granted permanent membership.

Pate's draft received "thorough discussion" from the Council, including several suggested changes. They directed Pate to incorporate the ideas into a new draft, which would then be circulated by mail. Minor fine-tuning was entrusted to the executive committee. If members still had serious objections after that, a special meeting of the Council would thrash them out in January 1970. The goal was to submit the proposal to Regions I and II at their spring 1970 meetings, with an eye to completing the process at that time, in order to place it into full effect in time for the 1971 national meeting.[9]

In fact, considerable correspondence was required to perfect the draft. By mail "the members of the National Council went through the Constitution section by section, resolving the points of difference and making improvements in the wording." Once this was accomplished to everyone's satisfaction, the executive committee met on January 16, 1970, and finalized the document for ratification by the regions.[10] Region II met at Texas Wesleyan in Fort Worth in March and, on motion by Dr. Pate in his role as chapter sponsor, approved the proposal unanimously. Region I met the following month at Southwestern. There the proposed constitution also received the needed ratification, but the assembly made its approval contingent on a change in the document. Based on the successful experience at their college with student members on faculty committees, the delegates from McMurry College proposed that students be included in the membership of the National Council.[11] The precise form of that representation was left open, though the author of the motion had in mind electing a student from and by each region each year.[12] The inclusion of a student voice in the governing body of the society affirmed Alpha Chi's claim that it was, first and foremost, an organization for students. Further, students had been routinely serving on regional committees for years. In an age of student upheaval and resentment against adult authority, the inclusion of students also forestalled any possible charges of a generation gap in Alpha Chi by making student representatives party to the decision-making process.

This unexpected development precipitated an extended discussion at the National Council meeting the following month. Eventually, Dr. Carnes moved, with a second from the constitution's author, Dr. Pate, that the Council accept the amendment. Although there was one dissenting vote, the Council passed the change by the required two-thirds and submitted the amendment to the chapters by mail. The amendment received the necessary approval and the new constitution, dated June 1, 1970, was printed and distributed.

The Council took the rather amorphous suggestion from Region I, put it in proper language, and gave it definite shape. The group settled on language calling for the election of five students to the National Council. These were to be elected at the National Convention to two-year terms, thus preserving, and extending, the principle that a majority of the National Council should be elected by the National Convention. The number five coincided with the number of regions that would be functioning by the time of the national convention, but the provision rather clearly did not envision the student Council members as conforming to any particular regional distribution.

A Profusion of New Chapters

Alpha Chi added thirty new chapters to its rolls in the three-year span between the National Council meetings of 1967 and 1970. These were scattered all over the country. Even the existing regions experienced growth, with Region I adding two important new chapters at Angelo State and Tarleton State, both recently risen from the junior college ranks. Region II had only one new chapter, but it was a very large one, the University of Texas at Arlington.

Outside the established regions, nine schools from the southeastern part of the United States received Alpha Chi chapters. Three of these were in North Carolina, a state that would soon boast more chapters of

Alpha Chi than any state except Texas. These were East Carolina State, Atlantic Christian, and Elon College. Three more came from Tennessee: Lincoln Memorial University, Carson-Newman College, and Tennessee Wesleyan. Also joining were Talladega College in Alabama, the University of Tampa in Florida, and Berry College in Georgia. Joined with the other schools already present in the area, these constituted the core of a new regional conference, to be called Region III.

What was soon to become Region IV in the plains states took in five new schools. The University of Southern Colorado had been on again, off again for several years, but finally came aboard in 1968. Originally assigned to Region I, it soon found its natural cluster with the other plains schools. Others included William Woods College in Missouri, St. Mary of the Plains in Kansas, St. Ambrose in Iowa, and the College of St. Scholastica in Minnesota.

The midwest added six chapters. These became part of the proposed new Region V. Two, Nazareth and Kentucky Wesleyan, were in Kentucky. Davis and Elkins College and Concord College were located in West Virginia. Olivet College of Michigan and Eureka College of Illinois rounded out the group.

Other schools that were added to the list in the west and the northeast had no immediate prospects of being joined with a regional body, but seven new chapters came from those two sections. Three were in California, including Pepperdine University, which quickly became the bulwark of Alpha Chi in the west, along with Azusa Pacific and California Baptist. Fort Wright State College became Washington Alpha. In the northeast, the University of Maine at Farmington, Ricker College of Maine, and the University of New Haven were the additions. Though that area, which was to become Region VI in 1972, now is densely packed with Alpha Chi schools, all three of these chapters are defunct.

While this wave of new chapters was very welcome, the colleges had a wide range of commitment to the society. Some became very important to Alpha Chi, providing faculty and student National Council members, scholarship winners, and a winner of the best chapter award. But nine of the thirty are no longer active, for a variety of reasons. Four of the schools have closed, one has switched to Phi Kappa Phi, and others have simply lost interest.

President Gaston assigned the task of installing these new chapters to several designated representatives of the society. Among those participating as installing officers were Dean Autrey Nell Wiley, Dean Joseph Pryor, President Gaston, Dr. Charles Gadaire, Dr. James Atteberry, Dr. Woodrow Pate, Dr. John G. Barden, Dr. Loyd D. Frashier, Vice President Carnes, Dr. Wendell Cain, Prof. Agnes Renner, and perhaps others. Barden, Renner, and Frashier were not members of the Council, at least at that time. Gaston took a considerable part of this responsibility upon himself

New Regions

By the time the new constitution went into effect, there *were*, in fact, five regions. Looking ahead, the executive committee in 1968 discussed plans for regional expansion, and came up with a proposal to present to the 1969 National Council meeting. Under the plan Region I would expand to take in the entire west, including the Rocky Mountain states. Region II would expand north to encompass the Mississippi Valley and the northern plains. A new Region III would include the southeast and the Ohio Valley, and a new Region IV would take in New England and the Middle Atlantic areas. When this was presented to the Council, there was obvious doubt. The Council agreed that they wished to create new regions, but not the ones suggested.

Woodrow Pate had a counter-proposal, which he had already distributed by mail in advance of the meeting. He argued that Regions I and II should be left intact, with the possible addition of the school at Pueblo, Colorado, to Region I. Under the Pate plan, the new Region III included all schools in Alabama, Tennessee, Georgia, North Carolina, South Carolina, and Florida. Schools in the plains states from Kansas northward would be the new Region IV. Finally, Pate suggested a new Region V for schools in Kentucky, Indiana, Ohio, Michigan, and West Virginia. New England and the west would remain unorganized for the time being. At some point Mississippi was removed from Region II and added to Region III. Obviously, some states were omitted, because Alpha Chi did not have chapters there yet. These states, it could be assumed, would be added to the existing regions as new Alpha chapters came along. A motion to adopt this plan prevailed.

Once the dimensions of the new regions were established, the next problem was the organization of the new structures. A motion to send a National Council member to each regional meeting was approved. The

National Council agreed to underwrite the expenses of the organizational meetings out of national funds, and the usual rebate to regions from national initiation fees would begin January 1, 1970.[13]

The executive committee appointed the representatives to the new regions from its own ranks at its meeting in July. President Gaston agreed to supervise the establishment of Region III, Vice President Carnes took Region V, and Secretary-Treasurer-elect Pryor undertook Region IV. Each had the task of selecting a time, sending out invitations to the appropriate chapters, and choosing a hotel/motel site in a central location in the region.[14] Region IV was the first to meet. Dr. Pryor assembled them in Omaha on February 21. Eight chapters sent delegations. They chose Dr. John O. Chellevold of Wartburg College in Iowa as the first president of the region, with Dr. Kenneth Smith of Sterling College in Kansas as vice president. A little later that year, Smith moved and had to resign. The national executive committee recommended that he not be replaced at once, but that the region could meet to elect a successor to fill out the term when the chapters met for the national convention in 1971. However, the region did not assemble in 1971, and so the position remained vacant. Westmar College's Dr. James Divelbiss, a future national president, received a four-year term as regional secretary-treasurer.

The other regions organized in April. Region V, under Jess Carnes, met in Cincinnati on April 11. The seven chapters present at that meeting picked Dr. Dan Scully from Adrian College in Michigan to be president. Prof. Ralph Cornell of Huntington College was vice president, and Dr. James Parr from Kentucky's Murray State became secretary-treasurer. Soon afterward, Parr took another position outside the region and the national executive committee recommended that he be replaced by another Murray State professor, Clell Peterson.

Nine chapters met with Dr. Gaston at the Downtowner Hotel in Atlanta in late April to establish Region III. They chose Dr. Susan Logan from Appalachian State to head the regional officers, with Dr. Leonard Rowlett from Lincoln Memorial University in Tennessee as regional vice president and Carson-Newman College's Dr. Ben Philbeck as secretary-treasurer.[15]

With five regions up and running, new national leadership, and a new constitutional structure, the society was now ready for major development. Another symbol of that change appeared at once. On the recommendation of the National Council the executive committee arranged for the first meeting of the new national convention to be in Memphis, Tennessee, and *not* on a college campus.

NOTES

[1] *Recorder*, Spring/Autumn 1967, p. 49.

[2] *Recorder*, Spring 1969, p. 18.

[3] *Recorder*, 1967, pp. 7-8.

[4] *Recorder*, Spring/Autumn 1967, pp. 15-18.

[5] *Recorder*, Spring 1968, pp. 6-7.

[6] *Recorder*, Spring 1968, pp. 11-16.

[7] *Recorder*, 1970, pp. 22-37.

[8] "Proposed Alpha Chi Constitution," a mimeographed draft submitted to the chapters prior to the Regional meetings of spring 1970.

[9] *Recorder*, Spring 1969, p. 17.

[10] *Recorder*, 1970, p. 10.

[11] *Recorder*, 1970, pp. 26-27.

[12] Annotated draft of the "Proposed Alpha Chi Constitution," as approved by the National Council January 16, 1970, and circulated to the chapters.

[13] *Recorder*, Spring 1969, pp. 16-17.

[14] *Recorder*, 1970, p. 7.

[15] *Recorder*, 1970, pp. 11-12; telephone interview with Edwin Gaston, January 16, 1997.

Focus On . . .

EDWIN W. GASTON, JR.

A popular saying about children whose characters resembled that of their parents went "the acorn never falls far from the tree." Such could be said about Edwin Gaston. Born and raised in Nacogdoches, Texas, he attended Stephen F. Austin State Teachers College and received his baccalaureate degree from the college in his home town. Later, he returned to be chairman of the English department and dean of the graduate school. As an undergraduate at Stephen F. Austin, he won election to Alpha Chi in

1947, so that his later affiliation with the society was a home-coming. He was the first Alpha Chi alumnus to be president of the society. Exactly three years younger than the society, his birthday was February 22!

However, Gaston's career was anything but provincial. During World War II Gaston saw service in the Marine Corps in the battles for Leyte and Guam as a forward observer for 155 mm artillery. The bulk of his undergraduate career was paid for by the G.I. Bill. Gaining an M.A. degree from his alma mater, he took his Ph.D. in English from Texas Tech University, at the time also an Alpha Chi school. After some time as a reporter and publicist, he taught at Tech before returning to Stephen F. Austin. A specialist in regional letters, he wrote a book entitled *The Early Novel in the Southwest* to go with numerous published articles. Gaston held a Fulbright professorship in Finland in 1964-65.[1]

After several years as chapter sponsor and regional officer, Gaston was remarkably well suited to the task of president of Alpha Chi. Elected national president in 1967, he gave the society the real push it needed to become a national presence. Under his stewardship the society more than doubled its size, growing from 70 chapters to nearly 200 and from two regions to six. Though he was still relatively young and could have served another term, Gaston in 1979 honored the intent of the 1970 constitution and stepped down after twelve years as president. His contributions earned him a prominent place in the pantheon of significant Alpha Chi leaders.

NOTE

[1] *Recorder*, 1967, p. 6; telephone interview, January 16, 1997.

CHAPTER 9 (1970-79)
NEW SIZE, NEW SHAPE

Change, major change, appeared in the offing for Alpha Chi as the 1970s began. With a new constitution and twice as many chapters, the society was called to make significant adaptations. Most of the changes turned out well, but there was also a price to be paid. Whether caused by the enormous growth or by the times, Alpha Chi lost a considerable amount of its internal discipline. The society with fifty or sixty chapters fiercely insisted that they all had to attend the regional meetings regularly, and it suspended them when they failed to do so. The threat of such action was an immediate cause of Texas Christian University's decision to withdraw from Alpha Chi in the 1960s. Region II, which maintained its standards more rigidly than Region I, usually had a higher percentage of attendance at its meetings. Its attempts to enforce the constitutional requirements led to recurring discussions in the National Council, to which appeals were directed. While the requirement remained in the new constitution, the new regional organizations never developed the same kind of tradition. The National Council of the 1970s continued to discuss how to encourage attendance, but they never invoked the suspension clause. Indeed, their disciplinary concerns lay more in the area of simply getting the chapters to induct and report their new members each year.

The Regions

There were many more positive than negative aspects to the rapid growth of Alpha Chi. Just as Regions I and II had had distinct organizational cultures through the 1960s, so the new regions developed their special identities and cultures. Representatives from the older areas of the conservative southwest, for example, were startled to discover that the northeastern regional convention one year had a wine-and-cheese reception for their faculty and student delegates.

The southeastern region convention, which soon was larger than the two older regions, staunchly resisted any suggestions that they might consider dividing into two regions. Though the size of their gatherings militated against the kind of intimacy that was the tradition at regional meetings, they liked it that way. Region III also established a tradition of holding its meetings in easily accessible Atlanta. Rather than meet on a college campus each biennium, they held their assemblies at hotels in the city. Thus, the distinctiveness of these newly emerging bodies leavened the whole and strengthened the diversity of the society.

After the organizational meetings of 1970, the new regions next had occasion to meet each other face to face as a sidelight of the first National Convention in 1971. The new constitution provided that "an interim business session may be held at the National Convention."[1] The older regions continued this tradition, based on their previous experience with annual meetings, and two of the three new regions took the opportunity in 1971. Region III extended its organizational process. President Susan Logan appointed several committees and the twelve chapters present discussed tentative arrangements for their 1972 convention. Region V's meeting consisted of the president, Daniel Scully; the secretary-treasurer, Clell Peterson; and the region's senior sponsor, Kenneth Cook. They discussed plans for the 1972 meeting and Dr. Cook invited the region to meet with him at Anderson College.[2] Region IV opted not to meet.

Regions I and II had more business to transact. The three younger regions had elected their first officers in 1970. The officer rotation schedules for the two older regions, however, called for an election in 1971. Region I chose Norman Spellmann of Southwestern (whose father had been one of the original members of the Southwestern Scholarship Society in 1915) and Robert Fain of Tarleton State as their president and vice president. Secretary-treasurer Wendell Cain was in the middle of his four-year term. Region II picked Lee Morgan of Centenary and William W. Trigg of Arkansas Polytechnic to lead the region for the next two years. Dean Bailey McBride of Oklahoma Christian College continued into his second year as secretary-treasurer. He had been chosen in 1970 to fill out Dean Pryor's term when Pryor resigned to accept the post of national secretary-treasurer. Both of the older regions also made plans for the 1972 meetings.[3]

Soon after the 1971 convention, the national officers met to plan for the future. President Gaston, noting the increasing number of chapters in the northeastern United States, recommended that Alpha Chi proceed to

PIONEERS

Dean Harry Yandell Benedict

Dean Alfred H. Nolle

Dr. John L. McMahon

Professor Bessie Shook

LEADERS

Dr. Autrey Nell Wiley

Dr. Edwin W. Gaston, Jr.

*Dr. Paul J. Schwab (fourth from left) at the 1957 chapter inauguration of
South Carolina Alpha, Lander College*

LEADERS

Dr. Edwin Gaston, Dr. James Divelbiss, Dr. Joseph Pryor, and Dr. Bailey McBride

Dr. Jess Carnes

Dr. James Divelbiss

Sr. Teresa Brady and Dr. Jorge Gonzalez

Dr. Patricia Williams

LEADERS

Dr. Joseph E. Pryor, Dr. Barbara Clark, Dr. Dennis Organ, Dr. Gayle White, and Dr. Robert Sledge at 1983 executive committee meeting

Dr. Dennis Organ, Dr. Otis McCowan, Dr. Robert Sledge, Dr. Gayle White, Dr. Walden Freeman, and Dr. Joseph Pryor at 1992 ribbon-cutting for national office

COUNCIL MEMBERS

National Council meeting in Chicago, 1993

CONVENTION SPEAKERS

Robert H. Ferrell, 1987

Robert Muller autographs his book, 1985

Paul Michelson, 1991

Leon Harris, 1995

Sarah Weddington, 1983

Dan Rather, 1993

CONVENTION SCENES

Brescia College wins President's Cup,
Orlando 1991

Registration, San Antonio 1983

Delegate voting, Atlanta 1995

Dr. Joseph E. Pryor (left) presenting the
first Distinguished Alumni Award to
Dr. John White, Williamsburg 1987

Mixer fun,
Atlanta 1995

CHAPTER ACTIVITY

Missouri Kappa inauguration at Hannibal-LaGrange College, 1990

Induction ceremony at Indiana Institute of Technology's Indiana Lambda chapter, 1986

Hawaii Beta members at Hawaii Pacific University welcoming freshmen to campus with a skit on meeting academic potential, 1977

organize them into Region VI at once, and the executive committee agreed.[4] A de facto regional identity of sorts already existed. Dr. Charles Gadaire, the founding sponsor of Massachusetts Alpha chapter in 1949, gathered an informal regional meeting in March 1971 on the campus of North Adams State College, at which time they made plans to gather again the following year at Springfield. President Gaston made arrangements to attend, and thus made the meeting the de jure organizational gathering for the region.

Region VI elected Prof. Frank Flaumenhaft of the University of New Haven as its first president and Fred J. Parent of Nasson College as vice president. The fiscal operations of the region were entrusted to Dr. Edward Davis from American International College, who became secretary-treasurer.[5] Region VI had some difficulty in getting underway. Structurally, a region prospered according to the energy and talent of the secretary-treasurer, and Dr. Davis was having health problems. The region did not meet at the national convention site in 1973, so it was not until 1974 that it met again. American International was again the host school. Unlike the others, who met in the spring, Region VI met that year in October. Dr. Parent was elected president and Dr. Timothy Bergendahl of North Adams State became the vice president. By the following year Davis, widely regarded as the father of Region VI, had passed away and Vice President Bergendahl agreed to take over the secretary-treasurer post. Bergendahl became the real driving force behind the expansion of Alpha Chi in New England.[6] Region VI, being remote from the sites of the national conventions of the 1970s, was sometimes poorly represented. In 1977, there were not enough Region VI delegates in San Antonio for them to convene an official meeting. On the other hand, Region VI began a vibrant regional newsletter under the guidance of Sister Teresa Brady from Pace University at White Plains, New York.[7]

It was not unusual for the new regions to have occasional trouble with their organization. Region V, for example, postponed and ultimately canceled its planned 1974 session at Kentucky Wesleyan because only a few planned to attend, citing among other reasons the gasoline shortage of the era.

The society completed its regional organization of the nation in 1980 with the creation of Region VII. By 1978 the National Council concluded that, although there were still relatively few chapters in the west, the time was ripe to organize Region VII. The bounds of the region were set to include "those chapters that are located west of the continental divide."[8] This meant a shift of region for the chapter at Grand Canyon College in Phoenix, which had been assigned to Region I when it received a charter in 1971. One of the elected members of the National Council was Dr. Loyd Frashier from Pepperdine University in California. He agreed to host the organizational meeting, and Dr. Pryor was dispatched to represent the executive committee at the meeting scheduled for March 1980.

The Students

Alpha Chi did not really feel the stirrings of student unrest of the 1960s until the following decade, and that only in mild form. Some of Alpha Chi's immunity was probably attributable to the relative absence of major universities from its membership roster. President Gaston pointed to this possibility when he reflected on the lack of dissent in Alpha Chi in a letter to Secretary-Treasurer Joseph Pryor. "I suspect that student unrest in the east is beginning to undermine recognition societies. . . . I think . . . that it is serious or at least potentially serious. . . . We still have a good deal of room for growth on the Pacific coast; although I recognize that there, as in the East, student unrest is widespread. But if we concentrate on the small colleges, rather than the large private and state-supported ones, we can probably recruit enough chapters to get a Western Region going in a few years."[9] Another reason for the relative lack of controversy may have been that students were made participants in the structure of the society at all levels. Local chapter officers were students, with assistance from the faculty sponsor mainly at the points of maintaining continuity and reporting new members. Regional and national meetings were built around the student presentations. Often regional and national meetings featured student discussion groups where they could consider the issues of the society apart from much sponsor participation.

The most visible evidence of students having a share of power was their presence as members of the National Council with full voice and vote. The first meeting of Alpha Chi under the new constitution saw the election of the first class of student Council members. The student forum at Memphis included a long discussion of ideas. At that session the students broke up into regional groupings for a time before sharing the ideas with the plenary. A number of the suggestions that emerged were collated and published.[10] The executive committee, meeting later that spring, took due note of the proposals and recommended that the next National Council meeting adopt a number of the ideas expressed.[11] Many of these ideas in fact became the procedure followed at future conventions, including a longer convention, a student mixer early in the schedule, concurrent sessions of student papers, time limits on the presentations, and a keynote address by a speaker with national reputation.

The 1971 student meeting also gave an opportunity for the delegates to get to know each other and to identify persons who might make good National Council members. The convention was due to elect five students at large, without regard to their regional affiliation, to serve a two-year term. There were ten nominations, all made from the floor. The first class to be elected consisted of Joy Crouch from East Central State in Oklahoma, Jackie DeVore from Lander College in South Carolina, John Maple from Oklahoma Christian College, John Ragle from McMurry College in Texas, and Lawrence Rasmussen from Dana College in Nebraska.[12] Ragle emerged as the spokesman for the group, but each participated in Council deliberations and committees. Years later Maple, now a professor himself, served as vice president and president of Region II. Over the years the students seldom found themselves aligned as a group against the faculty members of the Council. Almost always, if there was a close division on an issue, students and faculty could be found in both camps.

At the 1973 national convention in St. Louis, several of the proposed changes were put into effect. The first item on the agenda after registration was a "mixer" on Thursday evening. Since the Memphis meeting had begun late on a Friday morning, this gathering represented a longer convention, as the student caucus had requested, as well as the get-acquainted time that was also proposed at Memphis. The election process for the 1973-75 class of student members was slightly different, as the six regions nominated "favorite sons and daughters" for the five positions. Two additional nominations from the floor completed the slate of candidates. One of those, Sandra DeVries from Houston Baptist College, gained election. The others chosen were Region II's nominee, Swaid N. Swaid of Harding College, Region III's nominee Tara Ann Kelly from George Mason University, Region IV's nominee Connie Tague from Westmar College, and Region V's nominee Ron Thompson from Kentucky Wesleyan.[13]   Regions I and VI were not particularly pleased by this outcome. It may have been some consolation that Region I's unsuccessful nominee, Naomi Shihab, had some of her poetry published in the *Recorder*. She later became a well-known American poet.

From the floor of the Convention came a motion to elect six student members. The unidentified delegate argued that there were six regions now, and that the obvious principle of naming a number of students equal to the number of regions should be followed. President Gaston pointed out that this would require an amendment to the constitution and that amending the constitution required previous notice. John Ragle moved, with a second from Swaid Swaid, that the convention direct the National Council to prepare such an amendment for presentation in 1975, and this was done. A delegate also expressed concern over the constitutional provision that restricted eligibility for election to "any junior undergraduate student" from an Alpha Chi school, arguing that this effectively disenfranchised half of the students.[14] Gaston responded that he did not believe seniors were precluded by this language, but that the framers of that article intended to elect students who would still be undergraduates during most of their tenure as Council members. Dr. Woodrow Pate, who was the principal framer, moved that the convention interpret the constitution strictly, "excluding seniors from consideration." Noting that constitutional interpretation was the prerogative of the National Council, Gaston recessed the Convention long enough to convene the Council, while the assembly watched. The Council vote backed the president's original interpretation and seniors were deemed eligible.[15]

The students were not through. When Gaston declared the Convention back in session, Ragle moved the creation of an Alpha Chi research project funded by the society. The motion proposed creation of a task force of fifteen students under a faculty advisor to hold three-week workshops on a critical current issue, with an eye to publishing their results. This, Ragle said, would help to fulfill Alpha Chi's commitment to make scholarship effective for good. After extensive debate, this motion lost 37-32. Jackie DeVore then moved that the National Council be charged to develop some alternative plan for applying scholarly talent within the organization, and this passed. The Convention saw the need to do something constructive, but did not feel the Ragle proposal was the proper vehicle.

And there was more. The Convention passed another motion calling for students to preside at some of the program sessions. At the 1973 meeting the presiders were all present or past regional officers.[16] In accordance with this resolution, all of the program sessions had student presiders in 1975.

The tone of all these proposals was cordial and non-adversarial. There was not the same mood two years later in Atlanta. The format for student election was roughly the same. The Convention passed the constitutional change allowing election of six students. The six regions plus a caucus of the National Council chapters from the west all named candidates. Region I named two and Region II proposed three candidates, for a total of ten possibilities. In the outcome, one student was elected from each established region except VI, and one from the National Council chapters.

The report of the resolutions committee in Atlanta caused considerable debate. Most such reports are expressions of gratitude to persons who contributed to the meeting and the organization. Three of the seven resolutions proposed by the committee were of that nature and received quick approval. The others were substantive and controversial. One pushed the executive committee to rapid action in the creation of a professional office with a paid executive director and at least one field representative. Another looked to pursuing plans for merger with similar organizations, with an eye to building up the size and funding necessary to underwrite the expenses of a full-time national office. In the same vein, another resolution called for a search of the fund-raising skills on Alpha Chi campuses, in order to find new techniques of funding in an era when the funding of higher education seemed in jeopardy. Finally, the committee proposed the creation of a special task force to consider the impact of grade inflation and non-traditional grading systems "that may tend to distort or even prevent the identification of excellence in scholarship."[17] Another part of the same resolution noted "the possible need to reappraise the lack of specificity in the present moral criteria for membership in Alpha Chi."[18]

The Convention, stimulated by these unaccustomed ideas, engaged in extensive debate, the result of which was a series of motions that addressed the concerns, but not always the content, of the report. The delegates affirmed a continuing quest for financial sources, a study of the feasibility of the field representative, and an exploration of merger, all contingent on adequate funding. The call for a study committee on criteria of membership also met approval.

Then Ann Shuttee, student delegate from Schwab's and Carnes's school, Trinity University, moved that the reference to moral criteria be deleted altogether. This proposal drew extended debate, sometimes pitting representatives from state schools against those from church-related institutions. But there was no absolute division along those lines (Trinity was itself a Presbyterian school), and when the issue was put to a vote, it failed.

Though this had been a testy and chaotic business session up to this point, worse was about to ensue. It did not, however, come as a result of student unrest. The discussion had claimed so much time that the convention exceeded its expected time of adjournment. Representatives of the hotel came forward to demand the immediate dismissal of the meeting, because they had another meeting scheduled for the room and needed to prepare for that. In the midst of balloting for the new members of the Council, student and faculty, the meeting "had to be adjourned abruptly." Before the closing gavel Region IV's President Walden Freeman moved that the ballots be counted later, and that those who had a majority could then be declared elected. If any run-offs were required they could be done by mail ballot from all of the registered official delegates at the Atlanta convention. President Gaston appointed Dr. James Divelbiss of Westmar College to be custodian of the ballots. Divelbiss would notify Dr. Pryor's office of the result and Pryor could then announce the result and conduct any necessary additional balloting.

In due course, Divelbiss reported that six students had received the proper number of votes and no runoff was necessary for those positions. In addition, three faculty members, all incumbents, all national officers, received a majority of votes and were elected. In addition to Gaston. Carnes, and Pryor, the fourth faculty position would go to the winner of a runoff between Ben Philbeck of Carson-Newman and Ray Dollar from Sam Houston State. The mail ballot elected Philbeck to complete the National Council roster.

The next two national conventions produced little such commotion and settled down into a routine. The restructuring of the National Council was not quite complete, however. In the 1976 National Council meeting, sentiment emerged for the election of the student delegates by the regions at the time of the regional conventions. After due deliberation, including the objection that this would violate the constitutional principle that Council membership should be elected primarily by the National Convention, Dr. Bergendahl moved that there be seven students on the Council, one elected by each established region at its independent meeting and one more elected by the National Council chapters at the time of the national convention. Further, the students thus elected would be considered members of the respective regional executive committees.[19] Upon ratification of the proposal by the 1977 convention, the matter of implementation next came up, since the current students had been elected to two-year terms, which were then expiring. The terms of the incumbent student members of the National Council were extended by one year, to conclude at the meeting of the regions in 1978. The National Council chapters met to elect their member for 1977-79 and chose Donna Nelson from Pepperdine. It happened that Greg Milliron, one the incumbents whose term had just been extended, was also from Pepperdine. Thus, for one Council meeting, that school had two student members on the National Council. Since the Pepperdine sponsor, Dr. Loyd Frashier, was an elected faculty member of the National Council, the west coast chapter briefly had one-seventh of the votes.

Nelson, the only novice student member in 1977, was the only veteran student member in 1978, when she was joined by six students who were representing their respective regions: Angela Kreidel of Abilene Christian in I, Rebecca Risinger of Sam Houston State in II, Marc Niemoller of Greensboro College in III, Brian Proctor of Westmar College in IV, Phil Burkett of Huntington College in V, and Ivana Tallerico of Pace University in VI. Kreidel and Tallerico actually served at three Council meetings, since Regions I and VI met late in 1980, during or after the spring National Council meeting, and were thus not able to elect their successors in time for them to attend.

The New National Council

The adoption of the new constitution meant that all the existing terms of the National Council came to an end. Several persons thus found their tenure on the Council prematurely terminated. Among these, Autrey Nell Wiley and John McMahon chose not to run for another term. The retiring Council nominated, under the guidelines of the new constitution, incumbents Charles Gadaire of American International, Jess Carnes of Trinity, Edwin Gaston of Stephen F. Austin State, Woodrow Pate of

Centenary, Joseph Pryor of Harding, and Billy Smith of Hardin-Simmons for the eight positions on the new Council, along with Loyd Frashier of Pepperdine and Susan Logan of Appalachian State. When this slate was presented to the 1971 convention, several other names were proposed from the floor: Lemoine Lewis of Abilene Christian, who had been serving on the Council as president of Region I; Daniel Scully of Adrian College, the first president of the new Region V; and Carl Stockton of Talladega College.

The convention elected all of the proposed slate except Smith, plus Dr. Scully from the floor nominees. Since there were to be two classes of faculty members, serving staggered four-year terms, the successful candidates then drew lots to determine who among them would have to stand for reelection in two years. As a result the class of 1973 was composed of Frashier, Gadaire, Logan, and Scully, with Pate, Pryor, Carnes and Gaston drawing the full terms to expire in 1975. Dr. Susan Logan actually drew a four-year term and Dr. Gaston a two-year term, but Logan exchanged with the president in order to insure his continued leadership over a longer period of time.[20] Contrary to his own new constitution, Dr. Pate then moved that the Convention elect Gaston, Carnes, and Pryor to their national offices. This was done, though the new constitution reserved election of the national officers as a task for the National Council.[21]

These eight faculty, along with the five students elected at the same time, plus the five regional secretary-treasurers, composed the new National Council. This leadership body was somewhat larger than the comparable structures in other honor societies, but it served Alpha Chi well by allowing participation from all constituencies of the society. By the end of the decade, it expanded by four as a result of the organization of two more regions.

The work of the new Council resembled that of the old in most respects. It continued to oversee the financial affairs of the society, most of which were entrusted to the secretary-treasurer. The Council's role lay in giving advice regarding investments, appropriating funds for non-routine tasks, auditing the books, and setting dues structures. A major financial concern, as noted earlier, was the development of the society treasury to the point that its interest could support a full-time national office.

The subject of raising membership fees came up at the first meeting of the new Council. Following the practice of previous National Councils, the body met at the Baker Hotel in Dallas in 1972. A motion to raise the existing membership fee from six dollars to seven received long debate. Eventually it failed.[22] The inflation of the early 1970s soon caused the Council to reconsider and, in 1976, the members increased induction fees to ten dollars per member with only minimal debate.[23]

The National Council also operated the scholarship program of the society, as part of the portfolio of the vice president. Previously, the National Council appropriated funds and selected worthy recipients for the "Benedict Scholarships" in support of graduate work. They had also made available undergraduate scholarships to the chapters outside Regions I and II, each of which had its own scholarship awards. At the 1970 Council meeting, in anticipation of the creation of new regions and in recognition of the services of the recently retired Alfred Nolle, the system was restructured. After announcing the 1970 award to Arthur Shearin of Harding, who later, as a faculty member, would serve as secretary-treasurer of Region II, Carnes moved that the Benedict award be called the "H.Y. Benedict Fellowship" and the undergraduate award, open now to students from any chapter, would become the "Alfred H. Nolle Scholarship."[24] In 1971 the Council expanded the number of recipients to two for each award annually[25] and in 1972 increased them again to three each.[26] Despite a temporary trial of four recipients each for 1979 only, the Council returned to three in 1980.[27] As the number of applicants and the size of the awards grew over the years, the work load became too heavy for one selection committee. The executive committee decided in 1974 to choose two committees, one for the Benedict Fellowships and one for the Nolle Scholarships, each composed of two faculty and one student from the National Council.[28]

It was the task of the National Council to make nominations to the Convention for its own faculty members. Normally, these amounted to about eight nominees, or double the number of vacancies. The constitution enjoined the Council to "be cognizant of the need for representation on the Council from the established Regions and from the areas where National Council chapters are located."[29] Normally the electees came from this list. However, in 1971, Dr. Dan Scully of Adrian College was elected after nomination from the floor, and in 1973 Dr. Robert Sledge of McMurry College won election from the floor. Most times, though, there were no other nominations than those put forward by the Council.

The Council was scrupulous to abide by the need to achieve regional diversity, even though this representation was already present in the participation of the secretary-treasurers and would soon be even more present when the regions started electing their own student representatives.

As in the case of other organizations, incumbency had considerable value. However, sometimes a valuable Council member who had given full service and commitment got lost in the convention shuffle and failed of reelection. This was almost always disappointing to the candidate and to the other members of the Council who served with him or her. The fact that the ranks of Alpha Chi sponsors were filled with talented and dedicated persons, and that the successor was able to serve effectively, did little to ease the disappointment. Election to the Council depended on many factors, including the candidates' credentials, their visibility at key moments, their having unusual qualifications, their support from their own regions, and sometimes their physical appearance. (The parade of candidates before the convention came to be known unofficially as "the beauty contest.") There was no visible electioneering and only rarely so much as a rudimentary word-of-mouth campaign. Usually information about the candidate was gleaned from short biographical statements and from questions like, "What do you know about this person?" or "Who are you going to vote for?"

In 1977 a vacancy caused by the resignation of Ben Philbeck in the middle of his term caused the election of five persons. The nominating report proposed that the four persons with the highest number of votes be elected to four-year terms and the fifth highest recipient take the two-year term. That year Prof. Howard Griffin was chosen to fill out Philbeck's term.

Above the National Council level, leadership was vested in the executive committee. At the scheduled time of the first meeting of the new executive committee, Dr. Gaston was unable to attend due to illness in the family. Since a two-person meeting was not really appropriate, Gaston appointed Region IV Secretary-Treasurer James Divelbiss to sit in for him.[30]

This proved to be a prophetic substitution. In 1975 Carnes, in anticipation of his impending retirement, asked not to be reelected to the vice presidency, though he was willing to serve four more years on the Council. In his place the Council chose Divelbiss. From 1971 to 1979 the executive committee included Gaston, Carnes or Divelbiss, and Pryor.

The election of Divelbiss created some confusion. His membership on the National Council was based on his role as secretary-treasurer of Region IV, to which he had already been reelected to serve until 1979. Divelbiss continued to serve in the dual role until 1978, when he finally turned over his regional responsibilities to Dr. Walden Freeman of William Woods College. However, that would have meant that his term on the National Council expired a year short of the end of his vice presidential term. In anticipation of such an eventuality, the National Council made an official interpretation of the constitution at its 1977 meeting, providing that a term as national officer took precedence over the Council term. Thus Divelbiss, and any others in similar situation, would serve out the vice presidential term, even if he earlier ended the term that placed him on the Council.[31]

By 1978 President Gaston let it be known that he did not plan to seek reelection in 1979. He would at that point have completed twelve years as president, and felt that was enough. Further, he had become dean of the graduate school at Stephen F. Austin in 1976, and those duties weighed more heavily. Dr. Carnes likewise intended to retire from the Council. Further, a month before Gaston's last day as president, Alfred Nolle died. A new era thus approached for the society.

It was the task of the 1979-80 Council, a mix of old and new members, to elect the national officers for 1979-83. After adjournment of the convention in 1979, Gaston presided for the last time to supervise the election of his successor. There were two nominees, Vice President James Divelbiss and Region II Secretary-Treasurer Bailey McBride, dean of Oklahoma Christian College. Divelbiss was elected and McBride was promptly chosen without opposition to be vice president. Some measure of continuity was provided by the reelection of Joseph E. Pryor to the post of national secretary-treasurer. But the Council felt a little bereft, and elected Gaston to continue for two more years with voice but without vote "to give advice to the council."[32]

In 1975 the National Convention amended the constitution to provide for an editor of publications, who would take over the role that Carnes had been filling for eight years. The new editor would meet with the executive committee as a member without vote. He would be subject to annual reelection.[33] Dr. Pryor recommended that a member of the English department at Harding, Dr. Dennis M. Organ, would be a good candidate for the job. A rare fall meeting of the Council that year elected

Organ to the post, and he went to work immediately, putting out the 1976 edition of the *Recorder*.[34] The fall meeting was necessitated by the confusion surrounding the end of the Atlanta convention. At that point, no one knew who the members of the Council were, and that could not be determined in time to organize a meeting before the end of the spring semester.

Under Organ the *Recorder* took on a new form. Through 1975 the cover of the publication stated the title and the volume with a big "AX" as the dominant feature. The 1976 edition and succeeding volumes featured a monochrome work of student art, with the other information present in a subordinate aspect. Inside, Organ reversed the previous format which led off with the official proceedings of the conventions and councils, and left the student papers to the second half. Now the presentations would be first.

The "Newsletter" also changed. Begun in 1970 as the "Supplement" to the *Recorder*, it was primarily a small, typewritten sheet that gave out vital information in advance of meetings and reported events sooner than they could be distributed by the *Recorder*. The Council changed the name to the "Newsletter" in 1972, but Carnes had trouble filling its pages, because he was unable to get much cooperation from the chapters in reporting their activities. In fact, there was so little that Carnes did not publish an edition in 1973.[35] With more time and funding, Organ produced a series of attractive periodicals, published semi-annually. They featured photography, feature stories, significant information about Alpha Chi activities, presidential opinion columns, and, beginning with the December 1978 issue, pictures and biographies of National Council members.

Editor Organ was also charged with publication of a faculty handbook. The need for such a guide had been felt around the society for a number of years before the National Council approved a motion to have the editor study the possibilities and, if feasible, publish it.[36] At the 1979 Council meeting, Organ reported that the handbook was in the works for the coming summer.[37] The project was completed in the fall of 1979 and a copy sent to every sponsor.[38]

The Chapters

Expansion continued to be the Alpha Chi theme in the 1970s as it had been for the few years before. The society added fourteen new chapters in 1971, seven in 1972, and a record sixteen in 1973. After a relative lull with only four new chapters in 1974, Alpha Chi added seventeen in 1975, another record; 1976 was hardly a letdown with thirteen, with four again in 1977 and thirteen in 1978. The decade concluded with the addition of nine chapters in 1979. While there were some losses as well, the society, which had installed chapter #100 in 1970, almost doubled its size in one decade, adding chapter #200 early in 1980.

The new chapters added to the diversity of the society. Some were traditionally black schools, like Bethune-Cookman (#183), Shaw University (#128) North Carolina A&T (#131), and Johnson C. Smith University (#159). Some were large state schools like George Mason University (#121), Arizona State (#197), and Illinois State (#173). Some were denominational schools: Brigham Young of Hawaii (#101—Latter Day Saints), Houston Baptist (#119 - Baptist), Bridgewater College (#132 —Church of the Brethren), Brescia College (#137—Roman Catholic), and Kansas Wesleyan (#172—Methodist). Some were in the far south like the University of the Americas (#106) in Mexico and the University of Texas at Brownsville (#186). Some were far to the north like Lake Superior State in Michigan (#130). They represented forty-two states and the District of Columbia, plus, of course, Mexico.

The number of members was impressive too. Dr. Pryor summarized the decade for the executive committee in 1979, reporting the annual number of student inductions:

1970	4,222
1971	4,198
1972	4,538
1973	5,166
1974	5,517
1975	5,862
1976	5,737
1977	6,904
1978	6,180.[39]

The mailouts to college and university presidents continued to be a fruitful avenue of approach. In addressing these letters, Alpha Chi was careful not to approach schools that had chapters of Phi Kappa Phi or Phi Beta Kappa. There had been for many years an agreement between Alpha Chi and Phi Kappa Phi that neither would recruit at the other's schools. This agreement had been negotiated in the late 1950s under the guidance of the Association of College Honor Societies. However, at least one school had been lost to Phi Kappa Phi and another was toying with the idea of switching in 1973. Dr. Pryor wrote to the president of the rival organization to inquire if Phi Kappa Phi still accepted the 1958 agreement.[40] The response was reported to the Council at the 1974 meeting, and it sounded suspiciously like an unfriendly takeover was afoot. The men who negotiated the original agreement were long since gone from the leadership of the respective societies, and Dr. Pryor (himself elected to membership in Phi Kappa Phi as a student) reported that "the current president of Phi Kappa Phi had written that Phi Kappa Phi now planned to follow an independent course establishing chapters of Phi Kappa Phi on any campus where there was mutual agreement between the university and Phi Kappa Phi for establishing a chapter, irrespective of whether a chapter of Alpha Chi existed there."[41] Upon hearing Pryor's report, the National Council promptly resolved to follow a similar strategy. Nevertheless, the mailouts scrupulously avoided Phi Kappa Phi schools.[42] (As recently as 1996, Alpha Chi lost Elon College to Phi Kappa Phi at the instance of the Alpha Chi sponsor there. In the few cases where this has happened, the initiative seems to have been local. There is no evidence that Phi Kappa Phi, its stated policy to the contrary notwithstanding, has attempted to subvert Alpha Chi chapters.)

There had been discussion early in the decade of the possibility of a merger between Alpha Chi and one or two similar societies. This idea was discussed at the 1975 convention, for example.[43] After some further investigation, the executive committee recommended that no further consideration be given to the possibility.[44]

With expansion proceeding at such a rapid pace, such matters should have been of little concern. What was a major concern was the delinquency of chapters. Not only were some not attending conventions as the constitution required, but they were not even reporting members. This pattern pointed up the great fact that underlay the success of Alpha Chi: the local chapter, where the influence of the society was greatest on the greatest number, was only as effective as the chapter sponsor. If the sponsor was committed, active, and ingenious, the chapter flourished. If the sponsor was indifferent, inactive, or unimaginative, the chapter floundered. While most of the sponsors fell into the former category, there were enough of the latter to cause concern. The National Council, the executive committee, and the regional conventions spent countless hours seeking solutions.

Caught up in the numbers race, and also unwilling to deprive students of the opportunities they had earned, no Alpha Chi agency was eager to invoke the constitutional penalty of suspension. To the contrary, extraordinary efforts were undertaken to restore delinquent chapters, and sometimes a dormant chapter could be revived.

To enhance the appeal of the society, the National Council made provisions to allow the "grandfathering" of graduated members of a local honor society recently affiliated with Alpha Chi by allowing them to be inducted retroactively.[45] Likewise, the definition of the term "regular student" in the constitution's eligibility requirements was left to the local chapter. This issue was a sign of the times. More and more students were matriculating through college at the rate of a few courses a year. Should they be counted in competition with more traditional students? The Council left the answer to the chapters. This stance was not the evasion of a tough question on the Council's part, but rather represented a desire to take into account the wide variations of college life on the campuses.[46]

The Council addressed the matter of faculty participation in local chapters by proposing an amendment to the constitution that would allow faculty alumni members to vote and hold office in the local chapter of the school where they were employed.[47]

These adjustments must be considered part of the adaptation of the society to its increasing size. Alpha Chi at the end of the decade was substantially different from what it had been in 1970. This was apparent in the changing shape of the national convention.

The Conventions

The first of the new style conventions met at Memphis in 1971. It was the first true national convention, the first general meeting outside the bounds of the original four states, the first to elect National Council members, the first to pass any kind of substantive legislation, and the first national meeting not held on a college campus.

The site was the Holiday Inn-Holiday City in Memphis. This institution was more than a working motel; it was also the headquarters and training center for the whole Holiday Inn chain. The convention began with a business session at 10 a.m. on Friday, March 19. Nearly 200 delegates answered roll call. Student presentations began in the afternoon and continued again the next morning. The Friday evening banquet featured entertainment by the "Belles and Beaux" singing group from Harding College. After the banquet the convention divided into discussion groups, with the faculty meeting chaired by President Edwin Gaston and the student assembly chaired by Prof. Robert Sledge from McMurry College, who was believed to have some rapport with the students. The concluding business session Saturday morning included committee reports, region reports, reports from the previous night's discussion groups, and election of eight faculty and five student members to compose the bulk of the new National Council. Dr. Nolle, recently retired as national secretary-treasurer, addressed the convention while the ballots were being tabulated.[48]

The 1973 convention, modified along the lines suggested by the students in 1971, looked even more like subsequent ones. The meeting began with a structured student mixer on Thursday evening, March 22. The site was the Hilton Hotel near the St. Louis airport. Business began at 8:30 Friday morning with routine organizational matters. At 9 a.m. the student presentations began. This time these were scheduled in three concurrent sections, concluding about an hour later. After a break a second set of concurrent presentations took the convention to a lunch break, which was unstructured. Regional meetings led off the afternoon, after which the delegates boarded Gray Line buses for a guided tour through St. Louis, including a stop at the famous Shaw Arboretum.

The evening banquet featured Dr. Walter H. Judd, sometime missionary to China, sometime United States congressman from Minnesota, and well-known leader of conservative causes. Yet another set of student papers and presentations took up the first part of Saturday morning, and the convention concluded with another business session. Sixty-four chapters sent representatives to St. Louis and sixty-one students demonstrated the fruits of their studies. An unusually high number of the student presentations took the form of original poetry.[49]

The Atlanta American Motor Hotel in downtown Atlanta was the scene of the memorable 1975 convention. A total of 231 delegates from sixty-nine chapters were in attendance. The business meetings were so crowded that it was difficult to ascertain who were authorized voting delegates and who were not. To resolve this issue, each voting delegate received a large colored card at registration, and votes were counted by cards raised. Two guest speakers graced the Alpha Chi podium at this meeting. Reg Murphy was the editor of the Atlanta *Constitution*, and the victim of a recent kidnapping. He spoke proudly about his city as the banquet speaker on Thursday night. After the banquet the five student members of the National Council led a student mixer.

An innovation Friday morning was the serving of a continental breakfast paid for by the National Council. There were five concurrent sessions of student papers after the breakfast with a student presiding at each. ABC television anchorman Howard K. Smith was the featured speaker in the late morning, addressing the topic "Changing Challenge to America." Friday afternoon began with regional meetings as before, followed by a bus tour of Atlanta. The evening was left free. Saturday began with another continental breakfast and five sections of student presentations.

The meeting concluded with the business meeting. So many topics were raised for discussion that the convention could not adjourn at the agreed-upon time. The hotel management insisted that the delegates leave before the final business of electing National Council members was completed. After the adjournment a brief ad hoc meeting of the incumbent Council in one of the foyers completed a truly chaotic meeting.[50] When the delegates tried to drive away from the hotel, they found themselves stalled by a Dogwood Festival parade that blocked the street in front of the hotel.

For 1977 Alpha Chi returned to Texas, to the St. Anthony Hotel in downtown San Antonio. At this meeting the Council began the tradition of guaranteeing "quad rates" for delegates who wished to get the best possible price by staying four to a room. The Council subsequently undertook responsibility for helping students find roommates to take advantage of the quad rates.[51] The convention pattern was well-established by now, beginning with a buffet banquet at 7 p.m. on Thursday, March 19. The banquet speaker was CBS television newsman Charles Kuralt, who spoke on "America Behind the Headlines," a foreshadowing of his "On The Road" program of later years when he gained his greatest renown. After the address President Gaston held a business session. The roll call showed 253 delegates from seventy-eight chapters in attendance. Several constitutional amendments were presented and passed after to-ken discussion. Nominees for five faculty positions on the National Council were announced. No nominations were forthcoming from the floor. The evening concluded with a student mixer led by the three host chapters (Trinity, Incarnate Word, Our Lady of the Lake) while the faculty met with President Gaston.

Friday morning featured a continental breakfast, four concurrent student sections, and an address from Edwin Gaston on "The American Spirit and the Changing Work Ethic," which was subsequently published in the *Recorder*. A Gray Line tour of San Antonio in the afternoon included the Alamo and the old market, in addition to other attractions. Saturday's session began with a continental breakfast and student presentations and concluded with a business session. The report of Dr. Susan Logan's resolutions committee triggered debate as it had in Atlanta. All the proposed resolutions passed, some unanimously, and one by the margin of 44 to 35. Other routine business allowed the convention to conclude in good order.[52]

Alpha Chi was about to discover that New Orleans is the most attractive meeting spot for its delegates. The 1979 convention met at the Grand Hotel on Canal Street with a record number of participants: 424 delegates represented 108 chapters from thirty-one states, according to Secretary-Treasurer Joe Pryor's count. The evening session was supposed to feature Dr. Daniel J. Boorstin, noted historian and legal scholar, then serving as the Librarian of Congress. At almost the last moment, Boorstin was forced to cancel because his presence was required at congressional hearings in Washington. Dr. Gaston pressed into service his friend and colleague Dr. Francis E. Abernethy, executive secretary of the Texas Folklore Society. He illustrated his topic "Folk Music on the American Frontier," by singing and playing selections on his guitar. Abernethy had been the main speaker at the national convention in 1969, and was well received. The Louisiana College chapter hosted the student mixer after the business session.

Next day the convention began with student presentations. The student performances were grouped into three sets of seven concurrent sections each through the convention, with additional art displays available the whole time. Altogether, the program contained 106 presentations. A bus tour took delegates through the French Quarter, along the levees, and into one of New Orleans' unique cemeteries.

At the business session on the last day, only one unexpected event occurred. During a discussion of potential convention cities, student delegate Eileen Grigg of Pace University moved that the National Council consider restricting the choice of the 1981 convention site to a state that had ratified the then-pending Equal Rights Amendment. This was not strictly a student concern, since the second to the motion came from Council member Dr. Barbara Clark. "After a period of vigorous discussion," Dr. Pryor recorded, "the motion failed on a hand vote of official delegates."[53]

Though it brought up nothing controversial, the resolutions committee had its hands full with the retirement of President Edwin Gaston and former Vice President Jess Carnes, and the recent death of Dr. Nolle. Thanks also went to Dr. Pryor in two separate resolutions and to his wife, Mrs. Bessie Mae Pryor, who worked so graciously and efficiently at the registration process. In an unusual display of gratitude, the convention granted her honorary membership in recognition of her service. After giving Gaston and Carnes plaques in recognition of their contributions to the development of Alpha Chi, the convention adjourned, closing the Gaston era.[54]

NOTES

[1] Article VIII, Section 2.

[2] *Recorder*, 1971, pp. 23-25.

[3] *Recorder*, 1971, pp. 18-22.

[4] *Recorder*, 1971, pp. 11-12.

[5] *Recorder*, 1972, p. 4 and inside front cover.

[6] Telephone interview with Edwin W. Gaston, Jr., January 18, 1997; *Recorder*, 1974, p. 42; *Recorder*, 1975, p. 32.

[7] *Recorder*, 1976, p. 70.

[8] *Recorder*, 1978, p. 71.

[9] Gaston to Pryor, December 2, 1971, Alpha Chi Archives, Southwestern University, Box 7, Mars Hill file.

[10] *Recorder*, 1971, pp. 7, 10.

[11] *Recorder*, 1971, p. 13.

[12] *Recorder*, 1971, p. 8.

[13] *Recorder*, 1973, pp. 17-18.

[14] *Recorder*, 1981, p. 68.

[15] *Recorder*, 1973, pp. 17-18.

[16] *Recorder*, 1973, p. 18.

[17] *Recorder*, 1975, p. 15.

[18] Ibid.
[19] *Recorder*, 1976, pp. 70-72.
[20] *Recorder*, 1981, p. 68.
[21] *Recorder*, 1971, p. 8.
[22] *Recorder*, 1972, p. 6.
[23] *Recorder*, 1976, p. 7.
[24] *Recorder*, 1970, pp. 13-14.
[25] *Recorder*, 1971, pp. 82-83.
[26] *Recorder*, 1972, pp. 7-8.
[27] *Recorder*, 1979, p. 69.
[28] *Recorder*, 1974, p. 16.
[29] Article V, Section 3, Subsection e.
[30] *Recorder*, 1971, p. 11.
[31] *Recorder*, 1977, p. 75.
[32] *Recorder,* 1979, p. 61.
[33] *Recorder*, 1975, p. 16.
[34] *Recorder*, 1976, pp. 3-7, 70.
[35] Dittoed letter, Jess Carnes to "Sponsors, Alpha Chi Chapters," April 3, 1974.
[36] *Recorder,* 1977, p. 74.
[37] *Recorder*, 1979, p. 68.
[38] *Recorder*, 1980, p. 66.
[39] *Recorder*, 1979, pp. 73-74.
[40] *Recorder*, 1973, p. 32.
[41] *Recorder*, 1974, p. 7.
[42] *Recorder*, 1976, p. 77.
[43] *Recorder*, 1975, pp. 14-15.
[44] *Recorder*, 1976, p. 76.
[45] *Recorder*, 1977, p. 74.
[46] Ibid.
[47] *Recorder*, 1976, p. 77.
[48] *Recorder*, 1971, pp. 4-9.
[49] *Recorder*, 1973, pp. 4-22.
[50] *Recorder*, 1975, pp. 2-16.
[51] *Recorder*, 1977, pp. 75-76.
[52] *Recorder*, 1977, pp. 69-73.
[53] *Recorder*, 1979, pp. 60-61.
[54] *Recorder*, 1979, pp. 57-66.

THE DIVERSITY OF ALPHA CHI

While it is impossible to gather statistical data reflecting the ethnic diversity and the international background of Alpha Chi members, some students, such as scholarship winners and National Council members, can be identified in terms of that diversity.

From those groups, consider the following:

Allen E. Schmidt, 1957 Benedict Scholarship winner from Hardin-Simmons University, Canada

Jereldine Cross, 1962 Benedict Scholarship winner from Wayland Baptist College, Native American

Swaid N. Swaid, 1973-75 National Council Member from Harding College, Middle East

Marc Niemoller,1978-80 National Council Member from Greensboro College, Germany

Ivana Tallerico, 1978-80 National Council Member from Pace University, Italy

Ninu Satinder Sethi, 1979-80 National Council Member from Pepperdine University, born in India and raised in Japan

Chilufya Konie, 1980-82 National Council Member from Pace University at White Plains, Zambia

Opoku Boahene, 1984-86 National Council Member from East Central Oklahoma State University, Ghana

Shelley Slinn Neilson, 1984-86 National Council Member from Columbia Christian College, Canada

Ting Sun, 1986 Nolle Scholarship winner from Austin College, China

Chumei Wong, 1986 Nolle Scholarship alternate from Pace University in New York City, China

Craig A. Bell, 1986-88 National Council Member from Johnson C. Smith University, African-American

Luigina Cavaggioni, 1990 Nolle Scholarship winner from Marymount Manhattan College, Italy

Heather R. Hattori, 1990-92 National Council Member from Stephen F. Austin University, Japanese-American

Peung Vongs, 1990-92 National Council Member from College of White Plains of Pace University, Vietnamese-American

Anna M. Gotangco, 1990-92 National Council Member from Columbia College, Philippine-American

Yuri Zats, 1991 Benedict Fellowship winner from Menlo College, born in U.S.S.R.

Leroy Transfield, 1992-94 National Council Member from Brigham Young University—Hawaii, New Zealand

Manish Mamnani, 1993 Benedict Fellowship winner from New Mexico State University, India

Devesh Raj, 1994-96 National Council Member from Angelo State University, India

Michael Galkovsky, 1996-98 National Council Member from Freed-Hardeman University, Ukraine.

CHAPTER 10 (1979-87)
STEADY ON COURSE

The period following the retirement of Edwin Gaston was in most respects a time for moving forward along the lines of development already laid down. Where one man had served as president for the previous twelve years, three persons would hold the post in the next twelve, showing that there was no reason to be concerned about the society's direction, even without an experienced hand at the helm. Conventions followed the format perfected in the 1970s with little modification in form. The organization of Region VII early in 1980 signaled the end of the creation of new regions and the end of "National Council chapters." The scholarship program of the period also resembled that of the previous decade very closely. The time for innovation in Alpha Chi was not over, but the time for consolidation was clearly at hand.

National Conventions

The national conventions of the next period demonstrated the shift of the center of gravity of the society toward the east and north. Alpha Chi met in 1981 in Nashville, then returned in 1983 to its most frequent past meeting site, San Antonio. The Louisville convention of 1985 represented the farthest north that Alpha Chi had ever gone and its first time in Region V. In 1987 the society met in Williamsburg, Virginia, its easternmost site ever. The success of a meeting was always dependent to some degree on the weather, and venturing farther north for meetings in the late winter and early spring required a bit of faith.

The Nashville convention headquarters was the famous Maxwell House, set on a hill overlooking the Cumberland River a few miles from the downtown area. Scheduled in early April, the convention enjoyed fine spring weather. Attendance was down a little from the New Orleans gathering two years earlier, but was still a strong showing, with a hundred chapters represented among the delegates.

Among the 382 attendees was a bus-load of twenty-nine sponsors and students from Abilene Christian University led by sponsor Dr.

139

Lemoine Lewis, by far the largest chapter delegation ever seen at the recent national conventions. Among them was Lewis's daughter Claudia, a Nolle Scholarship winner of the previous year, and other students who made twenty-one presentations on the program. When President Divelbiss opened the floor for comments at the sponsors' caucus late on the first evening, the first questions were directed at Lewis by faculty members who wanted to know how he had done it.

The speaker for the by-now-traditional opening banquet was Dr. Mack Craig, vice president of David Lipscomb College (Tennessee Kappa chapter) who discussed the cultural and historical features of Nashville, providing an effective introduction for the next afternoon's bus tour of the city and a scholarly counterpoint to all the attention given to the Grand Old Opry by some of the delegates. After the banquet and opening business session, the chapter from Belmont College in Nashville led the student mixer. The bus tour on Friday afternoon took delegates to a number of historic homes and sites in the Nashville area and included a visit to the Parthenon, a full-size reproduction of the ancient structure.

The closing business session included routine reports and resolutions. One resolution encouraged the regions to observe the sixtieth anniversary of the founding of Alpha Chi at their conventions the following spring. The convention passed several constitutional amendments designed to adapt the document to the completion of the organization of regions in all parts of the United States. The provision for National Council chapters remained, but no more would be established in the bounds of the U.S.A.[1] The 1983 convention in San Antonio was a lesson in the finer points of Murphy's Law. Alpha Chi had held a very successful convention in 1977 at the St. Anthony Hotel in the Alamo city. With that happy experience in mind, the society signed a contract with the hotel two years in advance, fixed prices, and set a date in mid-March 1983. However, a major chain purchased the St. Anthony and decided to begin an extensive renovation. This caused some concern among the Alpha Chi leadership, but the hotel assured them that the remodeling would be completed by January 1. That deadline was subsequently pushed back to February 1 and then to March 1.

When Alpha Chi officials visited the site in February, construction was still under way, but they received assurances that the hotel would be ready, even if the hotel management had to rent generators to provide power. But it became apparent in corporate headquarters that, while it might be possible for the hotel to host the meeting, it would be too expensive for them. About two weeks before the convention's scheduled opening, the chain informed Alpha Chi's planners by mail that the St. Anthony had arranged for the convention to be shifted to another, better located hotel, the Hilton Palacio del Rio, on the river adjacent to La Villita. The St. Anthony agreed to foot the bill for any difference in prices.

When the delegates arrived, they discovered that communications between the St. Anthony and the Palacio del Rio had malfunctioned. The society had reserved 190 rooms, many of them scheduled to be occupied by four persons; the Palacio del Rio understood that there would be190 persons, and had set aside rooms accordingly. The result was that the hotel could not house all the delegates, and some had to be farmed out to two other hotels nearby. Nor could the hotel accommodate all of the program numbers, so some of them were sent across the street to the San Antonio Convention Center. Fortunately, the delegates took all this confusion in stride and the convention went off fairly well.[2]

The guest speaker for this occasion was an Alpha Chi alumna, Sarah Weddington, recently a top-level White House advisor for the Carter administration. Weddington was greeted at the podium by two guests. One was former Alpha Chi vice president Dr. Jess Carnes, now retired and living in San Antonio. The other was her brother, John Ragle, a member of the first class of student National Council members. When Dr. Pryor called the roll after the banquet and speech, 117 chapters responded, with a little more than four hundred delegates present. The student members of the National Council led the mixer late in the evening.

After student presentations Friday morning and a business session, the convention adjourned for lunch, to return in early afternoon for the bus tour of some of the city's landmarks. The tour included brief stops at the Alamo, the Institute of Texan Cultures, the Governor's Palace and El Mercado, the old town market. Saturday morning held more student presentations and a concluding business session.[3]

The 1985 convention met at Louisville's Hyatt Regency Hotel in late March 1985. The delegates shared the hotel with the Georgetown University basketball team, which was playing in the national championships at Lexington that weekend. Attendance was down somewhat, with only 368 present. The banquet speaker was Dr. Robert Muller, assistant secretary general of the United Nations. Following the banquet, the student members of the National Council led a student mixer while the sponsors broke into three groups. Dr. Charles Oliver of Arkansas College led one discussion on the special interests of small chapters while Dr. Kyle Sessions of Illinois State University led a counterpart meeting for large chapters. The third section focused on new chapters, with Dr. Myrna Hammons of Northeastern Oklahoma State presiding.

The first Friday morning session featured seven concurrent student sections of about five papers each. After a break the entire convention assembled for a section of eight musical presentations. The morning concluded with regional meetings and a brief plenary business session. The tour of Louisville took in Churchill Downs, the Louisville Slugger baseball factory across the Ohio River, and other sights.

Saturday's schedule included the usual continental breakfast and a set of ten concurrent sections of presentations, followed by another set of six concurrent sections. A business session concluded the meeting. In it the convention approved several constitutional amendments aimed at clarifying language and specifically allowing the use of local chapter names of historic value in addition to the state-Greek letter denominator used by the national organization. The convention also approved the reincorporation of the society to conform to tax laws, with the seat to be at Georgetown, Texas. At the conclusion the president installed four newly elected National Council members, using a selection from the new book of rituals that had just been approved.[4]

In 1987 the National Council took a chance with the weather at Williamsburg, Virginia. The price of the accommodations was considerably lower if the convention could be held in the late winter rather than in the spring. Though the temperatures were relatively cool, no bad weather encumbered the delegates' visits to Colonial Williamsburg and the gamble succeeded. The main convention hotel was the Fort Magruder Inn, built on the site of a Civil War fortification of the same name, less than a mile from the historic district. All of the meetings were held in the building, but it could not accommodate all the delegates and they were spread among the Fort Magruder and two other nearby lodgings.

In keeping with the history emphasis of the site, the banquet speaker was Dr. Robert M. Ferrell of the University of Indiana, who discussed the subject of one of his biographies, President Harry S Truman. The opening session also featured the presentation of a president's gavel by Dr. Norman Spellmann of Southwestern, the society's archivist. The gavel was made from wood salvaged from a renovation of the Administration Building at Southwestern where the first meeting of the society was held in 1922.

In order to free up time for the special program the next day, the schedule called for two sets of student papers, each with eight concurrent sections, that same evening. There was no mixer, since the papers did not conclude until 11 p.m. And early (7:45 a.m.) the next morning, the convention reassembled for the showing of an orientation film aimed at introducing the delegates to Colonial Williamsburg. This was followed by a business session to elect new National Council members, and then the delegates were provided with tickets for admission into the historic district and released to begin an all-day visit to the sights. Another set of student papers kicked off the Friday evening schedule at 7:30 while the National Council was meeting in another part of the building. The concluding meeting Friday was a performing arts session with sixteen presentations, again concluding at 11 p.m.

Next morning, delegates who skipped breakfast got to sleep a little later, since another set of seven student papers began the day at 8:30 a.m. The regions met at 10 a.m. and the final business session concluded at 12:30 p.m. after a very busy three days. The convention was the largest yet, with more than five hundred present from 129 chapters. These numbers, along with 166 student presentations, easily surpassed all previous records for Alpha Chi conventions.[5]

Leadership Changes

This period of Alpha Chi's history began with a changeover of officers. When Dr. Gaston retired as president in 1979, his replacement was Dr. James Divelbiss from Westmar College in Iowa, the incumbent vice president. The National Council elected a new vice president, Dean Bailey B. McBride from Oklahoma Christian College. The two men came to the National Council through the same route, by election as regional secretary-treasurer. Divelbiss was secretary-treasurer of Region IV when he came on the Council, and continued to hold that post and the national vice presidency for a while. In 1979 he was elected by the National Convention as an at-large member of the Council. McBride had been secretary-treasurer of Region II since 1969 when he succeeded Dr. Joseph Pryor of Harding College in that post. He continued to serve in the dual capacity after 1979, as Divelbiss had done before him. Since Dr. Pryor had come on to the Council via the regional secretary-treasurer's post as well, and was reelected to another term as national secretary-treasurer in 1979, all three national officers had that in common.

They had something else in common, too. Their membership on the Council dated to before 1971, when the new constitution went into effect. That meant that all three would have to rotate off the Council in 1983, when the constitution's twelve-year limit for continuous National Council service would come into play. Alpha Chi would thus leave 1983 with a completely new set of national officers.

McBride saw this and began to think of ways to maintain continuity. His solution was to resign after two years, so that a new vice president could be elected and serve at least two years on the Executive Committee before, possibly, inheriting the presidency with some experience. McBride's resignation was also prompted by an increase in his duties at his college. He made his intentions known well in advance of the 1981 convention, for which he was the planner. Again, as he offered his resignation, he gave his rationale. He said "that continuity of leadership and vision was needed to insure the continued growth of Alpha Chi over the next ten years."[6] When the National Council met at the close of the last convention business session at Nashville, the Council was prepared to deal with the matter by electing Dr. Robert W. Sledge to complete McBride's term. There was some sentiment at the time to make the election a four-year term, thus staggering the presidential and vice presidential tenures, but the Council finally decided on a two-year term that would put both offices up for election in 1985 and place Sledge in a position to be chosen president.[7] The problem was that Sledge had been on the Council since 1973, and normally, his service on the Council would end in 1985, but the Council had previously interpreted the constitution to say that the tenure of the national office had precedence over term limits. Under this interpretation, he would serve as president until the expiration of the presidential term in 1987, though his Council term would end in 1985.

Alpha Chi had already signed a contract with the St. Anthony Hotel at that point, so Sledge had responsibility for planning the 1985 convention there. At the end of that meeting, McBride's plan came to fruition with the election of Sledge to a four-year term as president and the selection of Dean Gayle Webb White, of the School of Business at Southern

Arkansas, as vice president for a similar tenure. McBride was the one who placed her name in nomination, too.

A second solution to the problem of continuity came via constitutional revision. For many years, Alpha Chi had been seeking some way of securing a professional national office. All of the work of handling Alpha Chi records had been accomplished by Dean Pryor alongside his very full duties at Harding. Aided only by part-time paid secretaries, and with a great deal of assistance from his wife, Bessie Mae Pryor, the Harding dean had run a skilled operation, handling Alpha Chi's growing registration lists, correspondence with local chapters, and the society's increasingly complex financial operations.[8] The limitations of available funds made it impossible for the society to afford a paid operation—until the 1980s. At that point, with the increasing size of Alpha Chi's operations, what had been desirable became necessary, and what had been impossible became feasible.

Recognizing that no volunteer would be able to pick up the task when Pryor had to lay it down in 1983, the Council decided to establish a paid national office. President Divelbiss urged the 1982 National Council meeting to propose amendments to the constitution setting up the job. "[Divelbiss] stated that for about a decade the Executive Committee had seen the approaching need for an executive director, on at least a part-time basis, and that investments had been methodically increased to provide sufficient annual income for such an undertaking."[9] The Council, after making suggestions about the constitutional changes required, approved the general idea, leaving precise wording to the executive committee. The executive committee perfected the language and the proposal came before the convention in 1983.

After the convention approved the changes, the Council met to implement the decision. Dr. Pryor, who was retiring from the Harding administration, might be available to continue to run the Alpha Chi business in a paid part-time role, if he was willing. When the Council discovered that he was willing, it met in executive session and named Joseph E. Pryor as Alpha Chi's first executive director.[10] Pryor's duties would continue to be just about what they had been before, except that the post was relieved of the responsibility of taking minutes at meetings.

The constitutional reorganization affected other national offices as well. In place of the former post of secretary-treasurer, the new structure included the position of national secretary. The first person elected to this post was Dr. Barbara R. Clark from Oglethorpe University. So, the executive committee after San Antonio included President Sledge, Vice President White, and Secretary Clark as voting members, plus Executive Director Pryor and Editor Dennis Organ as ex officio members without vote. This leadership team guided the direction of Alpha Chi for the succeeding four years.

Some of the duties of the officers were rearranged. The secretary became the administrator of the scholarship program, a task heretofore reserved to the vice president. The secretary also received responsibility for chairing the Council's audit committee, in addition to the usual tasks associated with a secretary's post. The office became the backup for the executive director's position, and vice versa, just as the vice president and president would serve each other's duties in cases of emergency. The increasing size and complexity of national conventions made the vice president's office sufficiently burdensome to relieve it of most other tasks besides convention management.[11] President Divelbiss took over responsibility for the scholarship competition in 1981 so as to free Vice President McBride to concentrate his energies on the convention.[12] This was a far cry from the early 1970s, when Vice President Jess Carnes was editor, convention planner, and scholarship chairman all at once. The change in vice presidential duties showed how far the society had come in the previous few years.

Milestones

The maturing of Alpha Chi as a national organization could be seen in other ways. The San Antonio convention approved another constitutional amendment that created the national office of archivist, to be appointed by the National Council as the executive director and the editor of publications were. Unlike the latter two, this was an unpaid office and did not provide the incumbent with a seat on the executive committee.[13] Several years earlier there had been an offer from Southwestern University to house Alpha Chi archives. At that time the holdings of the society were not so extensive that they needed to be, or could be, moved from the office of the secretary-treasurer. Now they were sufficiently large that an archive could be planned. Lacking a permanent seat for a national office, which would normally be the logical site for such holdings, the executive committee discussed approaching Southwestern again.[14]

Vice President Sledge questioned Southwestern about the idea, and the school was amenable. Temporarily, the school identified a room in one of their turn-of-the-century office buildings as the proper location and a selection of material was deposited there. The Council appointed Dr. Norman Spellmann, the local sponsor, as archivist.[15] Subsequently the university needed the room for other purposes and the materials were placed in an old storage building.[16] Finally they were retrieved from that inadequate location and placed in the special collections section of the school's library under professional supervision.

Alpha Chi's jewelry supplier in 1980 was Star Engraving Company of Houston. The relationship was almost fifty years old and was entirely satisfactory to Alpha Chi. Star had only recently expanded its line of services and begun providing gold Alpha Chi seals to be affixed to diplomas.[17] In 1981 rumors of Star's impending shutdown reached the ears of Dr. Pryor. Upon investigation he found that Star had been purchased by another company and the new parent company had decided that since Star was not making enough profit, they were closing it down. Star provided not only the jewelry for the organization, but also printed the membership certificates and charters, which meant that some new source had to be found quickly.

Dr. Pryor then sought bids from several other suppliers, but reported to the 1981 executive committee meeting that he had not received adequate responses and asked to defer a decision until the end of the summer, when a conference call could allow a choice to be made.[18] Dr. Divelbiss told the 1982 meeting of the Council that the executive committee had decided on Josten's Diploma Company in Minnesota for certificates and Brown's Awards Company from Jonesboro, Arkansas, for jewelry.[19] Brown's was quick to follow up on the contact. Tim and Dianna Brown represented the company at the San Antonio convention with a jewelry and graduation accessories display.[20] The executive committee that summer began to investigate whether Brown's might not be able to provide other materials as well.[21] The Browns were present at Louisville in 1985, with an expanded line of materials, including tee shirts and sun visors as souvenirs of the convention.[22] At the invitation of the executive committee, the company had developed a further line of Alpha Chi accessories. The 1985 National Council affirmed the agreement and Brown's began publishing flyers about their holdings for circulation through the Alpha Chi national office. The first printing in 1986 was for

9,000 copies.[23] This was a major change for the society. Until recent years it had been very careful to preserve the integrity of the Alpha Chi symbols. Members were not supposed to allow anyone else to wear their pins. Jewelry could not be purchased from Star Engraving without a permit signed by the national office certifying that the purchaser was indeed a member. The National Council had recently dropped that requirement. Authorization of tee shirts, sweat shirts, sun visors, and other items of apparel extended still further a new and more relaxed attitude on the part of the organization's leadership. By the time of the 1987 convention, the line included stationery, gummed stickers, backpacks, stoles, and honor cords.[24]

At the 1987 Council meeting, Dr. Jorge Gonzalez and other members raised questions about the relationship with Brown's and asked whether competitive bids ought not to be sought. The matter eventually was referred to the executive committee for whatever action they thought appropriate.[25] When the executive committee met that summer, the matter of supplies came up in another context. Josten's, which had been producing the membership certificates, and which was occasionally slow with deliveries, served notice that they needed to increase the price they charged. Brown's put in a bid to continue the certificate service at the same quality and the same price. It was Gonzalez, now vice president and a member of the executive committee, who moved acceptance of the Brown's bid. The question was resolved, at least for the time being.[26]

Gonzalez earned the gratitude of hundreds of Alpha Chi sponsors by a suggestion he made in 1985. He asked that the president appoint someone to look into the possibility of creating an inexpensive pin to replace the emerald green and sapphire blue ribbons that had been pinned to Alpha Chi inductees for generations. Each sponsor had the task of securing the materials and preparing these.[27] The executive committee looked into the matter and asked Brown's to produce some sample designs. By the time of the 1986 Council meeting, the pins were ready. Shown to the Council, the samples impressed the members sufficiently that they authorized purchase of one of the designs for distribution to the chapters.[28] These proved so popular that the supplier reported in 1988 that they were supplanting the usual jewelry, so that the sale of Alpha Chi keys began to diminish.[29]

Alpha Chi continued its growth during this era, at the same vigorous pace. Chapter #200 was chartered in 1980. In his last official message to the National Council at the 1987 meeting, President Sledge reported the approval of twelve new chapters during the year just past, the last of which, Fresno Pacific College, received the number 285.

Numbers of members also increased. In 1978 the society was inducting more than 6,000 members annually. By 1987 that figure was running in excess of 8,000 annually, and the grand total of members ever inducted was growing toward 200,000.

Organization of the final region needed to encompass the nation occurred in 1980 when Region VII gathered for its first meeting on the campus of Pepperdine University in Malibu, California. Ten chapters attended the organizational meeting. Dr. Joseph Pryor represented the national executive committee for the event. Ninu Sethi of Pepperdine, who was a student National Council member by virtue of her election by the "National Council chapters" at Nashville, helped plan the convention. Student papers and organizational business, the routine matters of a regional convention, were features of Region VII from the start. The first slate of regional officers included Dr. Dale Robertson from Brigham Young University of Hawaii as president, Dr. Bob Gilliam from Pepperdine as vice president, and Dr. Loyd Frashier of Pepperdine, a long time member of the National Council, as secretary-treasurer. Miss Sethi's tenure on the National Council lasted only one year, when the convention elected James Kinsel of Menlo College to a full term of two years, putting Region VII in phase with the other regions.[30]

The amount of work that the National Council had to handle increased with the growing size and complexity of the society. To meet this problem, President Sledge in 1983 appointed Council members to several new committees, which would do some of the preliminary study and deliberation of matters in their respective spheres before bringing their judgments to the main body. In addition to the usual committees, scholarship and audit, he named an awards committee, a development committee, a ritual revision committee, and an honorary membership committee and a convention plans committee. The agenda provided time for these groups to work. The Council did much of its work through these and other committees from that time on.[31]

Alpha Chi was also growing financially. It had to, to accommodate the triple stress of inflation, larger conventions, and a new professional national office. The task of giving preliminary thought to this matter naturally fell to the executive committee, but also to the new development committee. The first step on development came from the executive committee. In 1985 they proposed that the next meeting of the Council raise the student initiation fees by five dollars. Some of the extra funds would be set aside in a permanent endowment fund. The endowment fund could also be the receptacle for special contributions, an eventuality the society had not yet planned for.[32] These recommendations came in 1986 to Dr. Wilmoth Carter's development committee. Carter's committee approved the idea and the Council acted to raise the dues, stipulating that one dollar from each would go to the special fund which could not be touched without consent of a two-thirds vote of the National Convention.[33] By the following year the endowment fund had grown above $3,000 and would continue to rise rapidly after that. Donations from three Council members had increased the total by $500. Meantime, the executive committee devised an investment strategy for other funds that placed some of the society's funds in low-risk stocks and some in no-risk bond issues, in addition to a liquid checking account.[34] This strategy, which was admittedly temporary, was the culmination of several years of discussions about how best to invest Alpha Chi's growing assets. The 1983 executive committee discussions considered the possibility of securing professional investment advice.[35] At the following Council meeting in 1984, Dr. Pryor suggested a particular firm in Atlanta. Dr. Barbara Clark, who was rapidly becoming the Council's best voice on such matters, was delegated to investigate.[36] Her report the following year suggested that the society would be better served by doing their own investing.[37] Though the National Council was groping its way very slowly toward a satisfactory financial policy, the assets of the organization continued to grow. By 1987 they exceeded $285,000, more than a fourth of the way toward the informal goal of one million dollars, a sum that was thought to be the necessary minimum to underwrite the expenses of a full-time national office.

Alpha Chi last revised its Manual of Rituals in 1973. The ritual revision committee appointed in 1984 was charged with updating and expanding it. under the leadership of Dr. Walden Freeman, a new handbook was produced in 1986. The new book modified the existing ritual for new member induction only slightly, making optional a reference to the religious and moral ideals of one's alma mater. The ritual for new officers and new chapters also closely followed the previous forms. The booklet contained new rituals for installing regional officers, National

Council members, and national officers. The concluding sections, a history of the society and a digest of the constitution, were rewritten to complete the revised manual. Some language was changed, looking for gender-neutral terms as much as possible. The installation of new chapters became the inauguration of new chapters. All remained true to the traditions of the society, and most of the original language was retained.[38]

Concern over the continuing validity of Alpha Chi's tax status led in 1984 to investigations about the society's incorporation. The organization wanted to be sure that its tax-exempt umbrella covered the regions and the chapters as well as the national society. Dr. Pryor sought a legal opinion about incorporation in Arkansas and was told that the society would be better advised to update its Texas articles of incorporation.[39] At the instruction of the executive committee, Dr. Sledge investigated the matter with the Texas Secretary of State's office and found that some slight modification needed to be made in the charter. He submitted these to the National Council for approval by mail ballot. With an affirmative vote, the "Restated Articles of Incorporation of Alpha Chi, a Non-Profit Corporation" went to the 1985 convention for approval. When the national convention also approved them unanimously, and the appropriate Texas officials were notified, the process was complete. Dr. Pryor placed the document[40] in Alpha Chi's safety deposit box in Searcy for safekeeping. The charter named Dr. Norman Spellmann and his successors as sponsor at Southwestern University as the agent of record, and designated Georgetown as its seat.[41]

A few years later the society discovered that the Texas Secretary of State's office had indeed filed the document but had proceeded to lose track of it. They sent a letter to Dr. Nolle at San Marcos, based on the previous charter, asking whether Alpha Chi wished to renew its charter. When Dr. Nolle (long deceased) did not respond, the state canceled the charter in 1986. This was discovered in 1992 and rectified.[42]

Recognitions

One of the new committees of 1984 was the awards committee. Armed with a few preliminary suggestions, the committee produced several proposals that aimed to grant a higher degree of public recognition to those who served Alpha Chi with distinction. Chaired by the Region V secretary-treasurer, Sister Mary Lucia Dudzinski of the College of

Mount St. Joseph on the Ohio, it included Dr. Bob Gilliam from Pepperdine University and student Robert Winstead of Berry College.

The committee's first motion was one that could be acted on very quickly. It proposed a service award for faculty sponsors who had served Alpha Chi for ten years or more. With almost no debate, the motion passed.[43] At the national convention the following year, President Sledge presented certificates to forty-seven sponsors. Though no service prior to 1970 was counted, a few of these had more than twenty years of service, including Dr. Pryor and Dr. Kenneth Cook.[44]

The other two proposals required more deliberation and planning. The first was the creation of an award recognizing the outstanding chapter of the society for a given period. This idea was approved in principle by the Council and referred back to the committee for the development of details.[45] In 1985 the plan was complete. Dudzinski's committee proposed to award a "President's Cup," a traveling trophy that would be kept by the winner for the two years between national conventions. With their name engraved on it, and a smaller replica for permanent possession, the chapter would pass it on to the next biennial recipient at the next convention. The committee projected the first award for 1987.

To qualify, a chapter had first to be nominated by its region, and regions could nominate, if they chose, one candidate for every twenty chapters in the region. The final judges, the national awards committee, would base their decisions on materials submitted by the competing chapters. The period under consideration was to be the three years immediately preceding the award. Criteria included convention attendance, student presentations, scholarship applicants, and local chapter activities. The standards would be sent to the chapters as soon as possible, so that they could be planning their applications to the 1986 regional conventions.[46]

Sister Dudzinski rotated off the Council in 1986, and the president assigned Dr. Bob Gilliam to chair the committee, with help from Dr. Otis McCowan, Dr. Paul Michelson, and student delegate Stephanie Netsch. They refined and itemized the criteria still further and announced that the regions had nominated fourteen chapters: Abilene Christian (Region I), Midwestern State (I), East Texas State (II), Harding (II), Berry (III), Freed-Hardeman (III), Greensboro (III), Sioux Falls (IV), Southwest Baptist (IV), Brescia (V), College of White Plains of Pace University (VI), Pace at Pleasantville (VI), Delaware State (VI), and Pepperdine

(VII). These chapters had another year to improve their already outstanding credentials.[47]

The committee met at the 1987 convention at Williamsburg and pored over the submitted materials. In due course they reached their decision, but revealed it to no one until just before the announcement and presentation, when they shared the secret with the president. Not many moments before the convention adjourned, President Sledge asked the nominated chapters to stand and receive the greetings of the convention. Then he invited the winning chapter, College of White Plains of Pace University, to come forward. Led by their sponsor, Sister M. Teresa Brady, who had herself just been elected national secretary-treasurer, several jubilant young women came forward to receive the trophy, which was almost too much for any one of them to lift.[48]

The final proposal from the 1984 awards committee was the creation of an award to honor a distinguished alum of Alpha Chi. This prompted extended discussion in the National Council meeting regarding how many such awards should be made, but it was agreed that it should be presented at the national conventions. Fortified with the Council's approval in principle, the committee proceeded to work out further dimensions of the idea.[49] By the following year the proposal was in final shape. The national office would solicit nominations from the chapters. These portfolios would be given to the awards committee at the Council meetings in even-numbered years (the regional convention years) and the committee would make a selection, subject to final approval by the Council. Up to three candidates might be selected to receive the award. It would be announced immediately, and the recipient(s) invited to attend and address the next national convention.[50]

In 1986 the Council named the first recipient of the award. He was Dr. John Michael White, one of Dr. Pryor's former student at Harding and now distinguished chemist at the University of Texas. Alternates for the award were poet Naomi Shihab Nye, originally at Trinity University, and music professor Virginia Irving of Sam Houston State.[51] This was not White's first notice in Alpha Chi. He received the Region II scholarship in 1959 as he completed his studies at Harding. He was recipient also of a Woodrow Wilson fellowship after an undergraduate career marked by scholarly, athletic, musical, and leadership distinctions.[52]

Dr. White received his award at Williamsburg from the hands of his mentor, Dr. Pryor. His career had taken him to the University of Illinois and Cal Tech, but since 1966 he had been at the University of Texas. He was also a visiting fellow at Los Alamos National Laboratory. His research had resulted in more than 170 articles in refereed journals and he well represented the life-long quest for knowledge that Alpha Chi espoused.[53]

Chapters and Regions

By 1980 all of the regions were established with their own officers, their own traditions, their own structures, their own treasuries. In the case of the five younger regions, however, those treasuries were not sufficiently stocked to allow them to support their chapters as they wished. From the establishment of Regions III, IV, and V, the National Council recognized that it would be a while before they could be self-supporting. Accordingly, the Council made annual provision for national money to be used to support convention attendance by the younger regions and National Council chapters. In the case of all of those except the newest one, the Council began to question how much longer this temporary concession would last. Throughout the early 1980s there was an annual debate in the Council about these subsidies. Normally, this was so frustrating that the Council referred the matter to the executive committee for final disposition for the year.

The subsidies to Region III seemed particularly vulnerable to termination. By 1979 the region was already in a different category. The executive committee that year set its subsidies at a maximum of $50 per official delegate for convention attendance, while IV, V, and VI received up to $100. Region VII, which was planning its initial meeting in 1980, received up to $150 in recognition of its greater distances and its infant treasury. The difference for Region III was that its assets totaled more than $6,000, only slightly less than Region I's $8,000. Region II had a comfortable $18,000 treasury, while the other three ran around $2,000 to $3,000.[54] Region III's representatives argued that the region needed more money because it had so many more chapters than the others.

The following year the executive committee served notice that, in their opinion, "Region III is reaching the maturity status of Regions I and II and . . . this was the last time that Region III should be treated differently from Regions I and II."[55] The committee set the subsidies considerably higher this time since 1981 would be a national convention year, requiring more travel for most. In 1982 the issue came up again, and the Council appropriated the subsidies for the last four regions, but left the decision about III up to the executive committee, which granted III's request to be treated like the other younger regions a little longer.[56]

By 1983 Region V's treasury had grown to near par with III's. The national executive committee, to whom the decision had been referred, as usual, granted up to $90 per official delegate to III and V, up to $120 per official delegate for IV and VI, and up to $180 per official delegate for VII, for attendance at the 1984 regional meetings.[57] The plan for 1987 put the five younger regions back on a par, with each of their official delegates being granted a travel allotment based on the distance they had to come to the convention. When the Council seemed satisfied with this decision, the president "concluded that we have put in abeyance the possibility of discontinuing subsidies in the near future."[58]

A related matter was the formula by which the national treasury rebated a portion of the dues income to the originating region. For many years the Council accomplished this by simply sending back a percentage, based on how many students were inducted in the region. Region II, which had most of the big chapters, was a principal beneficiary of this system.

The 1986 Council meeting took steps to modify the system to give a greater rebate to regions with smaller chapters. Dr. Gayle White moved that regional rebates be made according to a formula that would send three dollars per inductee back to the region of origin. The balance of the five dollars per inductee intended for regional rebates would be apportioned among the regions based on the number of chapters each had. In a long debate filled with parliamentary maneuvering, the Council eventually approved the motion with an amendment from Dr. Terry Box reversing the White formula by rebating two dollars directly and apportioning the remaining three dollars per inductee according to the number of chapters. This proposal became the formula for regional rebates for years to come.[59]

The National Council became involved in some regional and local membership matters through its role as interpreter of the constitution. In 1982, Region VI elected two students to leadership roles, one as their delegate to the National Council and another as the student member of the regional executive committee. The national executive committee ruled this to be unconstitutional, noting that this was supposed to be the same person. The National Council upheld this interpretation.[60]

Local issues included the question of individual identity for the segments of schools that had multiple campuses, Such was the case of Pace University in New York, which had three campuses with Alpha Chi present at each under one umbrella chapter title. The Council agreed to grant individual chapter numbers and designation to each one and New York Delta subdivided into two additional units, New York Lambda and New York Mu.[61]

The Council heard an appeal in 1982 from the chapter at Gardner-Webb College in North Carolina. Their problem, which was shared to a lesser extent with many others, was that older part-time students were monopolizing the top 10 percent of the classes, and moving through them only slowly. Further, while they wanted to be members of Alpha Chi for the recognition value, they did not want to participate in chapter activities. The Council passed this on to the executive committee for resolution. The executive committee considered the matter, and sympathized, but felt that they could do nothing more than point out that the selection process was in the hands of the local institution, and that there was some flexibility in how the selection process could be handled. This interpretation, however, could create difficulties, for the committee received a complaint at the same meeting from a student at Pace who was upset about the variety of the selection criteria applied at the three campuses.[62]

. Local chapters sometimes floundered when they lost a long-time sponsor. Usually, one of the two assistant sponsors allowed by the constitution to be elected annually by the chapter could step forward to take over. Sometimes, however, that did not happen. Alpha Chi recognized that the effectiveness of a chapter was usually a measure of the effectiveness of the sponsor, who provided guidance and continuity from one student generation to the next. To enhance the probability that a trained sponsor would be available, the Council moved to amend the constitution to allow for the appointment of up to three additional sponsors, for a possible total of six. The 1985 national convention approved this amendment.[63]

These matters reflected the interest that local chapters had in making the society better for themselves and for others. Sometimes local issues were in fact purely local and could not be translated into national policy, but the input from the chapters assured that the Council would be kept abreast of changing conditions and needs.

NOTES

[1] *Recorder*, 1981, pp. 57-64.

[2] *Recorder*, 1983, p. 66.

[3] *Recorder*, 1983, pp. 55-63.

[4] *Recorder*, 1985, pp. 56-64.

[5] *Recorder*, 1987, pp. 54-64.

[6] *Recorder*, 1983, p. 68.

[7] *Recorder*, 1983, p. 68.

[8] *Recorder*, 1979, p. 75.

[9] *Recorder*, 1982, p. 65.

[10] *Recorder*, 1983, p. 70.

[11] *Recorder*, 1983, pp. 56-57.

[12] *Recorder*, 1980, p. 71.

[13] *Recorder*, 1983, pp. 56-57.

[14] *Recorder*, 1981, p. 73.

[15] *Recorder*, 1982, p. 64; *Newsletter*, December 1982, pp. 1, 4.

[16] *Recorder*, 1987, p. 66.

[17] *Newsletter*, December 1979, p. 3.

[18] *Recorder*, 1981, p. 73.

[19] *Recorder*, 1982, p. 62.

[20] *Recorder*, 1983, p. 56.

[21] *Recorder*, 1983, p. 74.

[22] *Recorder*, 1985, p. 57.

[23] *Recorder*, 1985, p. 66; 1986, p. 64.

[24] *Newsletter*, March 1987, p. 3.

[25] *Recorder*, 1987, p. 71.

[26] *Recorder*, 1987, p. 78.

[27] *Recorder*, 1985, pp. 66-67.

[28] *Recorder*, 1966, p. 64.

[29] *Recorder*, 1988, p. 58.

[30] *Newsletter*, March 1980, p. 1.

[31] *Recorder*, 1984, pp. 56, 58.

[32] *Recorder*, 1985, p. 73.

[33] *Recorder*, 1986, p. 61.

[34] *Recorder*, 1987, p. 65.

[35] *Recorder*, 1983, p. 73.

[36] *Recorder*, 1984, pp. 66-67.

[37] *Recorder*, 1985, p. 66.

[38] *Manual of Rituals of Alpha Chi*, 1973; *Manual of Rituals of Alpha Chi*, 1986; *Recorder*, 1985, p. 69.

[39] *Recorder*, 1984, pp. 57, 66.

[40] Texas charter #145-214-1, dated May 22, 1985.

[41] *Recorder*, 1985, pp. 57, 66; see also copy of the document itself.

[42] Lorna Wassdorf, office of the Secretary of State of Texas to Robert W. Sledge, July 6, 1992; notes of telephone conversations between Sledge and state officials, June 16, June 19, June 23, June 24, 1992, in a file titled "Government Documents Re Alpha Chi" currently in possession of the author, eventually to be placed in the Alpha Chi archives at Southwestern University.

[43] *Recorder*, 1984, p. 61.

[44] *Recorder*, 1985, p. 57.

[45] *Recorder*, 1984, p. 61.

[46] *Recorder*, 1986, p. 68.

[47] *Recorder*, 1986, p. 62.

[48] *Recorder*, 1987, p. 56, *Newsletter*, December 1987, pp. 1, 4.

[49] *Recorder*, 1984, p. 61.

[50] *Recorder*, 1985, pp. 68-70.

[51] Ibid.

[52] *Recorder*, 1960, p. 45.

[53] *Recorder*, 1987, p. 54; *Newsletter*, March 1987, p. 1; *Newsletter*, December 1987, p. 4.

[54] *Recorder*, 1979, p. 75 and passim.

[55] *Recorder*, 1980, p. 72.

[56] *Recorder*, 1982, pp. 64, 70.

[57] *Recorder*, 1983, p. 74.

[58] *Recorder*, 1986, p. 60.

[59] Ibid.

[60] *Recorder*, 1983, p. 76.

[61] *Recorder*, 1981, p. 66.

[62] *Recorder*, 1982, pp. 64, 71.

[63] *Recorder*, 1984, p. 63, 1985, p. 58.

GENDER

Alpha Chi is, and always has been, predominantly female in its membership.

Members of the National Council of Alpha Chi occasionally receive the assignment of representing the Council in the inauguration of a new chapter of the society. Many times, they form the impression that the new membership class is made up mostly of female students, in the proportion of about two women to one man. Faculty sponsors routinely make the same observation about their own chapters.

That impression is enhanced by a survey of gender distribution among the student members of the National Council. Since 1971, eighty-eight students have been elected to membership on the Council. Of these, fifty-three (60 percent) were female. The class of 1990-92 was completely female. Region VI has never elected a male to the Council. Only Region III has chosen more male students than females to represent it at the national level.

For purposes of this essay, and to test the hypothesis stated above, the national office conducted a spot check of induction classes from representative chapters and representative years.[1] Only coeducational institutions were chosen for the sample. Twenty-eight induction groups were surveyed. Of these, in only two did males predominate. In aggregate, females predominated by a ratio of about two to one (1178 to 578, or 67 percent). The distribution of gender in each of the four years under consideration (1928, 1952, 1974, 1995) was roughly the same, suggesting that the pattern did not change very much over the life of the society.

However, the gender distribution in American colleges and universities has been changing. In 1928 females represented only 39 percent of American baccalaureate degree recipients. In 1952 that figure dipped to 31.5 percent, probably reflecting the last vestiges of the post-war G.I. boom. By the early 1970s, and between 1980 and 1985, the balance shifted to predominantly female. By 1995 about 55 percent of the American baccalaureate degree recipients were female.[2] These numbers emphasize the gender imbalance for the years before 1980.

The flaws of this study are apparent: not everyone who qualifies for Alpha Chi membership accepts; the gender pool of the schools in the sample is unknown; the sample is relatively small. For all its problems, the sample's results and the regularity by which they appear support the impression gained in surveying new membership classes over several decades—Alpha Chi consistently inducts about two females for every male. If this is true, the next question becomes "why is this so?" Someone else can try to answer that.

NOTES

[1] The sample included Southwest Texas State, East Texas State, Hendrix, American International, Anderson, Wartburg, Appalachian State, Pepperdine, Tarleton State, Bridgewater, and Delaware State. The sample years avoided times when wars might skew the data.

[2] *Historical Statistics of the United States* (Washington: U.S. Government Printing Office, 1975), Series H 725-H 754; *Statistical Abstracts of the United States*, published annually by the Bureau of the Census, passim.

CHAPTER 11 (1987-93)
A MATURE SOCIETY

Alpha Chi had come of age. The period of rapid growth continued into the last decade of the twentieth century, but the society had by now come to terms with that expansion and was comfortable with it. If the rapid expansion sometimes meant that chapters could not be properly assimilated and would withdraw from Alpha Chi, that too was accepted.

A more important symbol of growth was the understanding that there no longer needed to be concern about the continuity of leadership. The society revealed its apprehension when Edwin Gaston retired, making him an ex officio member of the executive committee as if they could not carry on without his guidance. Alpha Chi revealed its concern about leadership when Joe Pryor's term as secretary-treasurer approached its end and moved to create a national office for him that would keep his counsel available. Creation of the office of executive director was a move that was coming sooner or later, but its timing showed the society's desire to keep Pryor close at hand.

Now, however, it was becoming clear that there was an abundance of persons who were able to maintain Alpha Chi's status and even bring about useful new initiatives. Some of these capable people were elected to national and regional positions of responsibility, but there were many other competent leaders waiting in the wings.

Leadership

Dean Gayle Webb White came to the presidency of Alpha Chi with energy, ideas, and experience. A National Council member since 1979, she had an unusual credential. She had gone on the Council without receiving the public recognition that goes with serving as a regional officer. She served as an officer in numerous organizations at the state level and, as dean of the School of Business at Southern Arkansas University, was an experienced academic administrator. She was named Arkansas Business Teacher of the Year in 1980.[1] White understood the workings of the executive committee, having held the office of vice president from 1983-87. She plunged immediately into the job of president and began to put her imprint on the society. Her first president's column in the *Newsletter* addressed a concern felt by many, the quality of papers being presented in conventions.

The new executive committee met in New Orleans in August 1987. At that point White announced committee assignments for the coming year, even though the students who would fill some of the slots had not yet been elected. This allowed the faculty members of the committees to be thinking about their task through the year. She added an expansion committee to the existing array, chaired by Dr. Tim Bergendahl of Westfield State College, a man whose energies had made Region VI the fastest growing segment of the society. She proposed that mentors from existing chapters be appointed by the regions to assist new chapters in getting started.[2] At her first National Council meeting as president, Dr. White listed several specific goals for the society during her administration. She aimed for an increase in the endowment from the current $3,000 to $50,000. She wanted to increase the number of alumni chapters and to add fifty new undergraduate chapters in four years. She hoped to visit each of the regions and to redeem several delinquent chapters. White concluded her report on goals by saying she expected other goals to be set and met as time went on.[3]

The vice president for 1987-91 was Dr. Jorge Gonzalez from Berry College in Georgia. Gonzalez, a native of Cuba, was professor of religion at Berry. He was a United Methodist minister with a Ph.D. in biblical studies from Emory University and several publications to his credit.[4] His talent for convention organizing was soon apparent, and he became the most successful master of ceremonies at the convention banquets that the society had seen for some time.

Also new to the executive committee was Sister M. Teresa Brady from the College of White Plains of Pace University in New York. Sister Brady held an M.A. and Ph.D. in English from Fordham University and was director of the Honors Program at her school. She had served a term as Region VI president and two terms as vice president.[5] In or out of office, she used the students of her chapter to publish a regular regional newsletter. At the same convention where she was elected national secretary, her chapter received the President's Cup as Alpha Chi's outstanding chapter. One of her students said of the honor, "We were all excited, but Sister Teresa Brady is the one who really put it together."[6]

The experience of the executive committee was needed when the Council gathered in April 1988. Eleven of the twenty-one members present, including four regional secretary-treasurers, were newly elected from the spring regional meetings. The new secretary-treasurers all had substantial experience in the regions, and the student class of 1988-90 was the most outspoken group to serve on the Council since the first class in 1971-73. The Council was thus flooded with new ideas for new directions, but also had the stability of the veteran leaders to help channel the new energies.[7]

The new student members began their term by raising several questions about how Alpha Chi's money was spent and how it was invested. The direction of this concern was soon apparent, since they caucused after the recess for the evening and prepared a statement that Lee Purcell of Purdue University Calumet presented to the Saturday afternoon session of the Council. From their observations, they concluded that the Council's interest in expansion was driven principally by a desire to build the financial holdings of the society. This, they argued, contributed to "sponsor neglect and chapter inactivity." The document called upon the Council to find "more aggressive and innovative measures to capitalize the general funding of the Society." Further, they called for expansion of the scholarship program in number and value of the awards. This statement was presented to be imbedded in the minutes as a manifesto, with specifics to be provided as the meeting progressed.[8]

Later, student member Sandra Harmon of University of Texas at San Antonio moved to double the number of scholarships awarded in each category to six. After extended debate, an amendment reduced the number to four and was defeated. Another amendment set the number to be granted the next year at five, and this amendment passed, thirteen to eight.[9] In 1989, in accordance with this action, five Benedict Fellows and five Nolle Scholars received recognition and scholarship money.

When Dr. Pryor proposed a 1990 budget that included only three awards in each category, Kimberly Springfield from Stephen F. Austin immediately inquired why there were not five, and Pryor responded that he had taken the previous action to be a one-year policy. The Council agreed, however, that the 1989 action had the effect of being a permanent change unless reversed by subsequent action. That action was soon proposed. The executive committee recommended that the number be

put back to three each. Springfield moved rejection of the recommendation, and was sustained by an eleven to nine vote.[10] In practice, the society routinely thereafter granted five scholarships per category annually
until 1997, when the numbers were doubled.

The students also challenged the site that was proposed for the 1991
convention, Orlando, arguing that the announced hotel prices would be
exorbitant compared to the prices being paid in New Orleans. Several
other possible sites were suggested before the matter was remanded to
the executive committee for decision. Gary Williams of Pepperdine questioned the report of the development committee, echoing the language
of the previous year's manifesto calling for aggressive fundraising. He
felt that the society should be seeking funds from alumni and founda-
tions. When Dr. Wilmoth Carter of Shaw University noted that such
appeals had borne no fruit in the past, Cynthia Garner of Greensboro
College called for "a more positive attitude, focusing on those contributors who could be approached rather than on those that could not."[11]

A bit later in the meeting, the students began to disagree among
themselves. Kimberly Springfield moved that dues be increased by five
dollars and Lee Purcell objected that the focus should be on enhancing
endowment instead of raising dues. Springfield eventually withdrew the
motion. In other areas, Sandra Harmon, picking up on an objection raised
by her sponsor in the general session, suggested that paper ballots be
used for electing National Council members. This matter was referred to
the executive committee. The executive committee devised a voting procedure that was used successfully at the next convention. In fact, despite
some original misgivings, it became a permanent policy.[12] Purcell moved
that the alumni committee investigate the possibility of adding an alumni
member to the National Council. Despite objections, the executive committee considered this proposal, but decided it could not be done since
there was no alumni body to do the electing. Finally, Springfield expressed her concern that Alpha Chi had no anti-discrimination policy.
She asked for the preparation, approval, and distribution of such a policy.
Dr. Michael Sabol of North Adams State called the Council's attention
to the preamble to the constitution, which contained precisely such a
statement.[13] The student class of 1988-90 added a great deal of heat to
the Council proceedings, but with some substantial contributions emerging from it.

Early in 1989 Sister Brady informed Dr. White that she would no longer be able to carry on the duties of secretary due to poor health. Her term as an elected member of the Council expired in 1989, but she would have continued for another two years because of her role as secretary. Dr. Pryor and Dr. Organ carried on in her place, particularly in regard to running the scholarship competition that spring. It was important to elect the next class of faculty Council members early in the 1989 convention so that they could be seated for the Council meeting on Friday afternoon. The voting took place early Friday morning and President White installed the new members immediately.

The election revealed the beginnings of a new trend toward continuity on the Council. That trend was the reelection, after a short period, of former Council members who had rotated off after serving the constitutional limit. Among those chosen was Dr. Robert Sledge of McMurry University, who had laid down the presidency at the previous national convention because of the twelve-year time limit. In later years others who rotated off because of the time limit did the same: Dr. White, Dr. Gonzalez, Dr. Freeman. Dr. Barbara Clark had come back on the Council in 1983 in much the same way, except that she had left the secretary-treasurer's job of Region III in 1982 after eight years on the Council in that role. This trend provided seasoned leadership for the Council. It also left equally competent but less visible talent on the sidelines.

When the Council convened that afternoon, the first order of business was the selection of someone to fill out the remainder of Sister Brady's term as secretary. The choice fell on a surprised and unprepared Rob Sledge, who thus became the first, but not the last, person to hold all three of the national executive committee offices. For the next two years, White, Gonzalez and Sledge were the voting members of the executive committee.[14]

The 1990 regional elections brought a new class of student members to the Council. This group, all females, made useful contributions to the deliberations of the Council, but not quite as spectacularly as had their predecessors. The election of the faculty Council members at the 1991 convention followed the pattern ordained by the Council two years earlier. The nominees were presented to the convention and allowed time briefly to address the assembly. All were present except Dr. Bob Gilliam of Pepperdine, whose case was presented by student delegate Sonia Lau. During and after a candidates' forum, delegates voted by ballot for the balance of the evening, with the poll closing at 11 p.m. The next morning President White announced that no runoff was necessary since four candidates had received the requisite majority of votes. Among them was Dr. Gilliam. Elected to the Council for the first time was former Region II President Dr. Patricia Williams from Sam Houston State University, who would become national vice president two years later. At the end of the convention, Dr. White installed the three elected members who were present, with Gilliam to be confirmed on the Council later.

Both President White and Vice President Gonzalez reached the twelve-year limit in 1993, so a new slate of national officers had to be selected. The election of the new president went smoothly, with Dr. Sledge being returned to the post after a four-year absence. Electing a vice president proved to be more difficult. The task of convention chairman, as everyone knew, was not an easy one. One after another, possible candidates were nominated, and one after another, they declined. Among those suggested, though not in this order, were Dr. Terry Box, Dr. Barbara Clark, Dr. Walden Freeman, Dr. Phillip Holcomb, Dr. Otis McCowan, Dr. Paul Michelson, Dr. Michael Sabol, and Dr. Arthur Shearin. Finally, Dr. Freeman and Dr. McCowan relented and allowed their names to be placed in nomination. The Council elected Dr. McCowan. The secretary's job drew two nominations, Dr. Freeman and Dr. Williams. On vote, Freeman was chosen and the new executive committee took office after being installed the next morning by outgoing President White.[15]

This team served for two years, planning the 1993 convention in Chicago. At Chicago, however, when the Council presented its nominations for the four faculty positions in the class of 1997, a problem arose in that the talent pool was so rich. Among the nominees were the last four national vice presidents, plus another incumbent member, and several able newcomers. When the balloting concluded, two incumbents had been unseated, including the vice president. Although his vice presidential position kept him on the Council, Dr. McCowan believed that the result was a vote of no confidence and offered his resignation as vice president. The Council, loath to accept it, sought to dissuade him. But he insisted, and left the room to allow the Council a chance to discuss it. Very reluctantly the National Council decided to honor his request.[16] He had run as good a convention as any in recent times and the society was the poorer for the loss of his services. He was later described by the hotel staff as "the most organized and thorough planner we have dealt with."[17] The Council elected as McCowan's replacement Dr. Patricia Williams, who brought unprecedented planning and negotiation skills to the position.[18] Her talents would be needed, for the Council was about to lose the services of one of the great names of Alpha Chi, Dr. Joe Pryor.

The National Office

Even before the creation of the office of the executive director, Alpha Chi had felt the need for a full-time national office, headed by a full-time staff person. Dr. Pryor's agreement to assume the position on a half-time basis in 1983 was an interim step toward the accomplishment of the final goal. It was based on Alpha Chi's need, its financial ability, and Dr. Pryor's availability when he retired from the dean's position at Harding.

It was understood by everyone that this was a temporary arrangement, since Dr. Pryor could not be expected to want to continue indefinitely. In 1990 he noted that "the time is fast approaching when Alpha Chi should employ a full-time executive director with appropriate support staff."[19] The society hoped to reach its goal of a $1 million endowment, but probably not before the late 1990s. It was assumed that at least $750,000 had to be in hand in order to support the office without drawing on current income. In an attempt to build the endowment fund more quickly, the Council accepted a motion from Dr. Phil Holcomb's development committee in 1990 to raise the national induction fee by $5 per person, with the entire amount going into the endowment along with a $1 per person allocation made earlier. The $1 per person was originally intended to prime the pump, and was limited to two years. Now it would continue indefinitely, by direction of the National Council. With these appropriations, the endowment fund began to grow at the rate of more than $50,000 a year.[20]

As the fund began to grow rapidly from its 1990 total of about $50,000, it occurred to one Council member that the revenue was now in hand to finance the operations of the society, the scholarship program, and also the amount needed for a full-time national office from current income, while the allocations to endowment continued to mount unabated. In the mind of Dr. Mike Sabol, it was not necessary to wait until the endowment fund alone could support a full-time national office; it could be done out of current revenues without reducing either operations or endowment growth. Generally ignored for the moment, the truth of this observation became increasingly apparent as time went on.[21]

It was not a matter simply of having a full-time employee. The physical necessities of providing office space, office equipment, support services, and secretarial assistance also had to be factored in to the total. Ideally, a location on a friendly college campus might solve some of these problems. Such an offer was already on the table. Dean Bailey McBride extended an invitation to Alpha Chi to locate its national headquarters on the campus of Oklahoma Christian College when the full-time office was established. Implicit in the offer was the provision of office space and at least some support services.[22]

In the interim, however, Dr. Pryor continued to serve as executive director. The 1990 Council authorized him to seek larger office space for his operations and to employ a half-time secretary. Harding had granted him some small space after his retirement in 1989, but since it was not really adequate, he ran much of his operation from his home. Though Editor Organ had a computer by this time,[23] a computer for the executive director's office would modernize the society's operations and create possibilities for greater alumni contact, an issue that was increasingly important to the Council.[24] By the end of the summer, both the computer and the secretary were on board. The secretary was Nancy Hammes, a Harding faculty wife with several hours above her master's degree and twenty years of public school teaching experience. An Alpha Chi alumna herself, she brought intelligence and efficiency to the operation. Her first task was the computerization of Alpha Chi's mailing lists.[25]

President Gayle White applied to Harding's new president, David Burks, a C.P.A. who had been Alpha Chi's auditor until 1986, for office space on the campus, at least for the duration of Pryor's service as executive director. Burks not only acceded to the request, but also gave access to the university's telephone, copying, and postal services. A voice mail service was also installed to take messages when Pryor and Hammes were both off duty.[26]

At the executive committee meeting in 1991, President Sledge announced the formation of a "transition committee," which would investigate the timing and process for shifting from a part-time to a full-time executive director. He charged the committee with discussing other matters, such as underwriting the expense of the office, securing a permanent location for the office, and outlining possible duties for the staff.[27]

At the 1992 National Council meeting, the president appointed Dr. Sabol as chair of the committee, serving with Dr. Robert Blake, Dr. Phillip Holcomb, Dr. Patricia Williams, students Leroy Transfield and Stacy George, plus Dr. Pryor and Dr. Sledge.

While the intent of the Council was to establish an office with a full-time executive director, another possibility emerged for consideration. Dr. Dennis Organ, who was fully conversant with the operation, suggested that he might be willing to undertake the job on a half-time basis, provided that a full-time administrative assistant/secretary could be hired to provide the full business day service that the society needed. Sabol's committee found this plan to be a good one, at least on a trial basis.

Sabol proposed to the Council that, for a six-year trial, the society should establish the post of executive director on a half-time basis and administrative assistant on a full-time basis, at the end of which time an evaluation could be made. Further, he moved that Dr. Organ be employed from June 1 on as associate executive director on a quarter-time basis for a period of no more than two years, by which time Dr. Pryor would have retired. During this transition Dr. Pryor would continue as executive director at the current compensation level. Finally, given the personnel involved, it seemed appropriate to the committee to seek continuation of the agreement with Harding for the trial period. After shortening the trial period to four years, the Council approved the plan.[28]

In further discussions after the meeting, Dr. Pryor set his retirement date as December 31, 1993. At that point, Mrs. Hammes, with the title of administrative assistant, would become full-time, or else an additional staff person would be hired to make a full-time equivalent. Simultaneously, Organ would become executive director, while continuing his duties as editor as a separate category. Harding set aside two rooms in the appropriately named Joseph E. Pryor Science Center as Alpha Chi offices. The society purchased new furniture to fill them. On October 11, 1992, the National Council officers gathered in Searcy to dedicate the facility. Former Council President Dr. Gayle White joined the five current executive committee members, Dr. Sledge, Dr. McCowan, Dean Freeman, Dr. Pryor, and Dr. Organ in a ribbon cutting ceremony.[29]

Finances and Operations

The concern about finances was perhaps not as frantic as the student Council members may have thought, but it was important. The society had always been frugal about expenses. "Our bureaucracy," an Alpha Chi official once wrote, "is smaller and more cost efficient than that of almost any other society in the Association of College Honor Societies."[30] That came as a result of the volunteer hours put in by people at all levels, from the local sponsors through the regional officers to the National Council members and especially the national secretary-treasurer and his staff, who worked for a pittance or for love of the organization. While that was possible for the small society of less than a hundred chapters, the load was quite different as the organization grew toward three hundred. The need for upgrading the services of the national office was very real.

In addition to being frugal, Alpha Chi's leaders took their fiduciary responsibility seriously and tended to err on the side of conservatism in investment policy and appropriation of funds for such things as scholarships.

Three committees guided the National Council in making financial decisions. The first of these was the audit committee, chaired by the national secretary. The 1990 audit committee suggested several changes in the way the national office reported investment income to the Council. A changeover in auditors a bit earlier, with different procedures, may have contributed to the confusion. No funds were unaccounted for; it was simply hard to read the report.[31] Dr. Barbara Clark, a professor of English but also a C.P.A., gave the Council and the national office considerable guidance in producing a more lucid accounting style. Beginning in 1991, the audit committee came to the convention a day early in order to go over the books more thoroughly. The 1991 Council minutes recorded the result:

> The Audit Committee noted that the national office is currently in transition from a bookkeeping style that was appropriate to a comparatively young and small organization to a style befitting the larger and more complex organization that Alpha Chi has become. After making several suggestions to complete the changeover, the committee recorded its appreciation for the work of Alpha Chi's Executive Director, Dr. Joseph E. Pryor; the auditor, Dr. David Tucker; our professional secretary, Mrs. Nancy Hammes; and Dr. Barbara Clark, a member of the committee who visited the national office last fall and facilitated introduction of the new system.[32]

At the 1993 Council meeting, the transition to the new accounting system was virtually complete. The auditor recommended considering a shift from calendar year to a fiscal year coinciding with the academic year, and moving toward a voucher system for disbursing funds. Likewise, he suggested operational guidelines for the routine care of funds in the national office and an updated inventory of physical assets. The Council accepted these recommendations and felt that audit matters were now truly updated.[33]

There had been a development committee at the annual National Council meetings for several years, but the work of those committees had been limited by questions about the society's needs and direction. The committee, led by Dr. Wilmoth Carter, recommended creation of an endowment fund in 1986 and urged solicitation of funds to fill it. The Council agreed and established the fund.[34] The fund attracted a few early contributions and then did not grow much.[35] One of the concerns of the audit committee was that these funds were reported as part of the general investments of the society and the Council was unable to see the progress of the fund.

However, President White appointed Dr. Phil Holcomb to head the development committee. With his energy, and the diversion of the increased induction fees to the fund, it began to grow quickly. Holcomb's chapter made an initial contribution of $1,182 in 1989.[36] By the end of 1991, it stood at $257,176, with a major boost of $120,000 when that sum was transferred from other investment funds. The appropriation of $6 per inductee also quickly swelled the total.[37] On December 31, 1993, the date of Dr. Pryor's retirement, the endowment totaled $466,608.[38] This figure, combined with the regular income that continued to come into the fund, met the guidelines laid down earlier for establishment of a full-time national office.

Proper investment of funds in hand could make a difference in how rapidly Alpha Chi holdings grew. This was of course a difficult task, especially for those with little experience in the area. Further, the responsible parties sought to maximize gains with minimal risks. This created tension and confusion. An initial attempt by President Sledge at establishing an investment policy was little more than a conservative guess at what the proper policy should be. Low returns from these investments led the Council to consider whether a more aggressive policy might not be in order.[39] Honoring this directive, the executive committee developed a more comprehensive and profitable policy at its 1988 meeting.[40] Under the guidance of Dr. Clark, the investment committee over the next few years developed an investment strategy that put up to 50 percent of the society's funds in equities, a riskier but much more successful policy in the bull markets of the 1990s.[41]

Symbols

A representative of the Alpha Chi paraphernalia supplier was present for the 1988 National Council meeting. Dianna Brown addressed some concerns about misplaced orders and pricing of other items. She suggested that the jewelry permit, long used by the society to protect the integrity of its symbols, was anomalous when considered alongside the widespread sale of sportswear and graduation supplies, where it was not required. Dr. Robert Blake moved that the society end the requirement of a jewelry permit before purchase, and the motion passed. This simple act ended a great deal of irksome paperwork for sponsors.

Mrs. Brown asked if a more formal contract between Alpha Chi and the supplier might not be worked out. The two parties were operating under an informal "gentleman's agreement" which might cause problems.[42] The executive committee later that summer received a proposed contract from Brown's and suggested several changes before it was presented to the next Council meeting in 1989.[43] The Council was not prepared to accept a contract at that point, and instead directed the executive committee to consider putting all Alpha Chi materials out for competitive bids. Some Council members urged that whoever the supplier might be, it should rebate some percentage to the society.[44] The executive committee laid the matter to rest temporarily by saying that Alpha Chi did not wish to sign a contract with anyone at that time. It also rejected the notion of rebates and found that the prices and services of Brown's Graduation Supplies and Awards Company were generally satisfactory. At some future date, when the society was prepared to formalize a contract, perhaps competitive bids could be invited.[45]

In 1990 President White appointed one of the new student members of the Council, Michelle Dutson from Southern Utah State College, to investigate the pricing structure of the industry and compare Brown's prices to that. Further, Brown's was no longer so anxious about a contract.[46] Dutson's report in 1991 indicated that she had studied the prices from fourteen suppliers and found that Brown's charges were well within the mainstream.[47] This quieted the concern for the time being. Meantime, Tim Brown had been attending each national convention, selling substantial amounts of memorabilia and often contributing a sizable check to the endowment fund.

Another supplier, Herff-Jones, produced the membership certificates. However, their service seemed to be inconsistent and tardy.[48] Dr. Organ found a simple solution to the matter. Using the computer technology now available, he thought it might be possible to produce high-quality certificates on his own campus. This would eliminate several time-consuming steps in the process and save money as well. The executive committee asked him to try it.[49] He produced several samples that were shared with the executive committee during the year. They chose a style from the selection, and he began to utilize the system. By the time the National Council met in 1993, Pryor was able to report that the new system "worked exceptionally well and had resulted in substantial reduction in costs."[50]

The certificates were redesigned in 1989 at the suggestion of a delegate at the national convention. He proposed that the words "National College Honor Scholarship Society" be employed to give better clarity to the meaning of the certificates.[51] The executive committee happily agreed to this idea and directed that the membership parchments be redesigned accordingly, to go into effect as soon the present supply was expended.[52]

The 1990 Council meeting heard a proposal from student member Heather Hattori that a promotional/orientation videotape be produced for use by the chapters. She acted at the direction of Region II, whom she represented and where the idea originated. Nothing came of the proposal at the time, but the idea remained alive.[53] The following year it bobbed to the surface in the course of other Council deliberations, and when it attracted an affirmative response, Dr. White delegated Dr. Patricia Williams to look into the whole matter.[54]

Williams did more than just investigate. At the 1992 Council meeting, she was accompanied by Dr. Winston Long, a video and film producer with Omni Productions. He informed the Council about the parameters of producing a video and what kinds of options there were. Secretary Freeman reported that "a lively discussion, in which almost everyone participated, followed Dr. Long's departure."[55] The Council leaned toward two productions, one a professional promotional video

174 MATURE SOCIETY

and the other an instructional video that might be produced from within the society. Eventually, Dr. Sabol moved that up to $10,000 be appropriated to produce a "promotional video of B+ quality and at least eight minutes duration." The motion also called for an aggressive search for grants to assist in underwriting the project. After this passed, a further motion authorized student Stacy George to look into the other video with a view to student production.[56]

When the national convention met in Chicago in 1993, Omni crews were on hand to tape the activities. Individual National Council members were taken aside and interviewed for possible inclusion on the tape. Long appeared before the Council to announce that the 1993 distinguished alumnus award recipient, Dan Rather, had agreed to provide narration if possible, but would at least contribute an interview for the production. When taping was completed at the end of the convention, the finished product could be available in as soon as two months. A copy would be sent to Dr. Williams, who would give final approval for production.[57] Williams later reported that she had been unable to find any additional funds, but that the society could likely have a twelve-minute tape for about $15,000. The Council quickly appropriated an additional $5,000.[58] When the executive committee met later that summer, a preliminary copy was ready for viewing. The committee was very pleased and ordered up an additional hundred copies beyond the 330 originally contracted for. Each chapter would receive one, along with an explanatory note from Dr. Pryor.[59]

The second videotape proposal did not fare as well. The seven Council students reported that they had conducted a survey that revealed considerable interest in an instructional tape. There was no time for them to follow through on this, however, and they would leave office before much could be done, so they expressed the hope that the next class would pick up the project.[60] In fact, Stacy George, the principal exponent of the idea, returned to serve at one more meeting, because her replacement had not yet been elected when the 1994 Council met. The next class was divided on their commitment to the idea, and it eventually died.[61]

Conventions

The attendance record set at the 1987 national convention lasted only until the next convention. Alpha Chi returned to New Orleans in 1989 with 635 delegates from 135 chapters in attendance. The featured speaker was to have been Frank F. Fowle III, a dramatic performer who called himself a "modern-day bard" who recited the deeds of heroes. Unfortunately, Mr. Fowle died unexpectedly a few weeks before the convention. Vice President Gonzalez pressed into service one of his colleagues from Berry College, Dr. D. Dean Cantrell. She presented a very timely discussion of the English novelist Jane Austen which was entirely appropriate to the audience.[62]

Following Dr. Cantrell's address Thursday evening, President White and Prof. Olivia Washington presented the 1989 Distinguished Alumni award winner, Dr. Richard Bieker, a professor of economics from Delaware State College. An alumnus of Murray State in Kentucky, he was widely published and served as referee for several journals. He addressed the confession briefly.[63]

The Friday morning schedule packed fourteen concurrent sessions in at 8 a.m. and fourteen more at 9:15 a.m. There followed a business session for the purpose of electing and installing the 1993 class of faculty National Council members. After the business meeting there were two concurrent sessions of the performing arts. Saturday morning there were fewer student papers to choose among, with two sets of only thirteen concurrent sessions each.

In a variation from past conventions, there was no tour scheduled. Instead, since the convention hotel, the Clarion, was within walking distance of the French Quarter and the river, the delegates were simply turned loose on their own Friday afternoon and evening.

The President's Cup winner was announced by Dr. Walden Freeman, chair of the selection committee. The winning chapter was Midwestern State University of Texas. Dr. White made the presentation. After all of the agenda business had ended, President White asked if there was other business. At most Alpha Chi conventions, adjournment would follow within seconds, but not this time. A sponsor stood to denounce the voting procedure, saying that many delegates had voted illegally in the Council elections. He requested that subsequent elections be conducted by ballot. As it happened, the candidate from his chapter had not been chosen. The idea was a good one, however; the change he suggested became standard policy for subsequent conventions. A student delegate attacked what he believed to be the regional and sectarian bias of the organization. The candidate from his chapter also had not been elected.

Dr. White recognized seven more people with complaints and suggestions, several of which resulted in needed changes. Finally "another delegate stood to say that she, for one, had no complaints about the convention. After that comment," the secretary noted, "no one else sought recognition and President White declared the convention adjourned at 12:15 p.m."[64]

Two years later Alpha Chi met at a site that the convention planners hoped would be as attractive as New Orleans. They were wrong. The Orlando convention of 1991 drew only 385 participants. The featured speaker was Dr. Paul Michelson of Huntington College, the secretary-treasurer of Region V. Michelson, a historian specializing in Romanian studies, had been in Romania in December 1989 when the communist regime of Nicolae Ceaucescu ended amidst rioting and assassination. He spoke about his experiences before, during, and after the uprising.[65]

A second of Dr. Pryor's students, Dr. Robert Jones, professor of surgery at Duke, received the Distinguished Alumni Award. Jones was the author of more than a hundred scholarly articles and had served as a visiting professor at eight other universities.[66] Presented by Dr. Pryor, Jones spoke briefly to the convention, expressing his gratitude for the honor.[67]

Because there were fewer presentations, the program was not so crowded as it had been at New Orleans. As in New Orleans, the delegates were given Friday afternoon and evening to enjoy the sights of the nearby Disney World complex, about a ten-minute drive from the Grosvenor, the convention hotel.

At the final business session on Saturday, Dr. Freeman again announced the winner of the President's Cup. "After prolonging the suspense as long as he could," the secretary reported, "Dr. Freeman explained the winner's qualifications and announced that the committee had chosen Kentucky Delta Chapter at Brescia College as the 1991 winner of the President's Cup."[68] In one of her last official acts, President White made the presentation to the delighted Kentuckians. After installing the new Council members and the 1991-95 Council officers, she asked the fateful question again, "Is there any other business to come before us?" No one responded, and she quickly passed the gavel to the new president, Dr. Sledge, who adjourned the convention.

For 1993 the National Council decided it was time to move the national convention north of the Mason-Dixon line. The chosen site was the Bismarck Hotel in downtown Chicago. The National Council held its 1992 meeting there, in preparation for the meeting the following year. All were impressed by the easy access from the airport, the proximity to the sights of the Loop area, and the magnificent theater hall called "Le Pavillon."

The Council set the date as late as they dared, in hopes that the convention would avoid any serious weather problems. As it happened, there was a light snow the day the delegates gathered, and there was some doubt whether the scheduled speaker would arrive. But he managed to fly in from New York and, after much concern on the part of Dr. Patricia Williams, who had secured his services, he took his place. His was one of the most famous names and faces in the country—Dan Rather, anchorman of the CBS Evening News and other television news programs. A 1953 Alpha Chi alumnus of Sam Houston State, he was also the recipient of the Distinguished Alumni Award. After the speech he chatted and signed autographs for the delegates before heading back to catch a plane to Viet Nam where he was scheduled to tape a retrospective with Gen. Norman Schwartzkopf.

Convention attendance stood at 475, representing 119 chapters. Student papers were done in concurrent section of eleven each. Again, no bus tour was scheduled for Friday afternoon, leaving the attendees to explore Chicago on their own. The convention was unique because of the video cameramen taping events and persons throughout the time. The closing business session had another unique moment when Dr. Joseph Pryor stood to receive the applause of the delegates on the occasion of his last convention as executive director. Joined by his wife, Bessie Mae, herself an honorary member of the society and major contributor to registration and executive committee meetings, Dr. Pryor received a clock to which was mounted a plate noting Pryor's offices with Alpha Chi. After a standing ovation, Dr. Pryor recollected some of the events and persons of his thirty-six years with the society.

The president "noted that certain years have marked the ending of epochs in the history of Alpha Chi. . . . [He] then announced the beginning of a new epoch in Alpha Chi's history, one that would receive the active encouragement and support of Dr. Pryor."[69]

NOTES

[1] *Newsletter*, December 1987, p. 1.
[2] *Recorder*, 1987, p. 77.
[3] *Recorder*, 1988, p. 59.
[4] *Newsletter*, November 1993, p. 4.
[5] *Newsletter*, December 1984, p. 4.
[6] *Newsletter*, December 1987, p. 4.
[7] *Recorder*, 1988, p. 57.
[8] *Recorder*, 1988, p. 60.
[9] *Recorder*, 1988, p. 61.
[10] *Recorder*, 1989, pp. 66, 69.
[11] *Recorder*, 1989, p. 67.
[12] *Recorder*, 1991, p. 62.
[13] *Recorder*, 1989, pp. 68-69.
[14] *Recorder*, 1989, p. 65.
[15] *Recorder*, 1991, p. 62.
[16] *Recorder*, 1993, p. 60.
[17] *Recorder*, 1993, p. 68.
[18] *Recorder*, 1993, p. 65.
[19] *Recorder*, 1990, p. 56.
[20] *Recorder*, 1990, pp. 59, 62.
[21] *Recorder*, 1991, p. 61.
[22] *Recorder*, 1989, p. 69.
[23] *Recorder*, 1987, pp. 79, 80.
[24] *Recorder*, 1990, p. 60.
[25] *Newsletter*, December 1990, pp. 1, 4.
[26] *Newsletter*, December 1990, p. 1.
[27] *Recorder*, 1991, p. 70.
[28] *Recorder*, 1992, p. 58.
[29] *Newsletter*, November 1992, pp. 1, 3.
[30] *Newsletter*, November 1992, p. 3.
[31] *Recorder*, 1990, p. 59.
[32] *Recorder*, 1991, pp. 60-61.
[33] *Recorder*, 1993, pp. 61-62, 70.
[34] *Recorder*, 1986, p. 61.
[35] See "Donor Honor Roll" in the *Recorder*, 1992, p. 51 for contributors 1986-1991 and *Recorder*, 1993, p. 51 for donors in 1992.
[36] *Recorder*, 1989, p. 65.
[37] *Recorder*, 1992, p. 63.
[38] *Recorder*, 1994, p. 64.
[39] *Recorder*, 1988, pp. 63-64.

[40] *Recorder*, 1988, p. 68.
[41] See *Recorder*, 1993, pp. 62-63, for example.
[42] *Recorder*, 1988, pp. 57-58.
[43] *Recorder*, 1988, p. 67.
[44] *Recorder*, 1989, p. 67.
[45] *Recorder*, 1989, p. 72.
[46] *Recorder*, 1990, p. 56.
[47] *Recorder*, 1991, p. 61.
[48] *Recorder*, 1992, p. 53.
[49] *Recorder*, 1992, p. 66.
[50] *Recorder*, 1993, p. 57.
[51] *Recorder*, 1989, p. 55.
[52] *Recorder*, 1989, p. 73.
[53] *Recorder*, 1990, pp. 59, 69.
[54] *Recorder*, 1991, p. 60.
[55] *Recorder*, 1992, p. 54.
[56] *Recorder*, 1992, pp. 54, 58.
[57] *Recorder*, 1993, p. 56.
[58] *Recorder*, 1993, p. 63.
[59] *Recorder*, 1993, p. 69.
[60] *Recorder*, 1993, p. 64.
[61] *Recorder*, 1994, pp. 59-60, 61.
[62] *Newsletter*, December 1988, p. 1; *Newsletter*, March 1989, p. 1, 4.
[63] *Newsletter*, March 1989, p. 1; *Recorder*, 1989, p. 51.
[64] *Recorder*, 1989, pp. 54-55.
[65] *Newsletter*, December 1991, pp. 1, 4.
[66] *Newsletter*, December 1990, pp. 1, 4.
[67] *Recorder*, 1991, p. 44.
[68] *Recorder*, 1991, p. 47.
[69] *Recorder*, 1993, p. 46.

JOSEPH EHRMAN PRYOR

When he retired as Alpha Chi's first executive director at the end of 1993, Dr. Joe Pryor could look back on several decades of profoundly successful service to the society. He was the founding sponsor of Arkansas Eta chapter at his beloved Harding College in 1958. In 1959 Region II asked him to accept the post of secretary-treasurer, a responsibility which he fulfilled until 1970 when he succeeded Dr. Nolle as national secretary-treasurer. In 1983 Alpha Chi reorganized its leadership structure and created the office of executive director for the society. The National Council named Pryor to the job and he held it until his retirement in 1993. His service covered half the life of the organization, and for most of that time, he was a member of the national executive committee. Upon his retirement, most of an issue of the *Newsletter* was taken up with tributes to his leadership.[1]

"Dr. Joe" holds other distinctions in the society. He represented the National Council in the inauguration of more than eighty new chapters, which means that he personally oversaw the birth of nearly a fourth of all Alpha Chi chapters. His career as a teacher was such that three of the first six Alpha Chi Distinguished Alumni Award recipients were his chemistry students.

The changes that took place in the society from 1970 to the creation of the professional national office were difficult ones. There is a qualitative difference between managing the daily business of a society with assets of under $100,000 to one whose assets approached a million. There is a qualitative difference between a society which inducted a couple thousand students into a hundred chapters and a society which inducted nearly ten thousand into three hundred chapters. Dr. Pryor saw the society through this transition with grace, instituting most of the needed changes on his own and knowing when and where to seek assistance when he needed it.

Pryor's relationship to Alpha Chi was only one facet of his

busy life. Earning B.A. and B.S. degrees from Harding College, he attended Louisiana State University, where he completed M.A. and Ph.D. work in chemistry. Returning to his alma mater, he became professor of physical science in 1944. In 1960 he was appointed dean and eventually vice president for academic affairs. The science building at Harding is named in his honor. At Harding he served as yearbook advisor for so many prize-winning annuals that he was given the national Distinguished Yearbook Advisor award in 1973. A student athlete himself, he became Harding's athletic representative, serving as the conference president twice and winning enshrinement in the National Association of Intercollegiate Athletics Hall of Fame.[2]

Yet little of this acclaim touches the real essence of the man, which is better defined by his relationship to his church, his family, his students, his colleagues, his friends, and all with whom he comes in contact. In each of these relationships, he is the embodiment of courtesy, honor, and high intelligence. He could accurately be called "Mr. Alpha Chi."[3]

NOTES

[1] *Newsletter*, March 1994, pp. 1-4.

[2] "Pryor, Joseph Ehrman," in *Who's Who in America*, 1978-79 (Chicago: Marquis Who's Who, Inc., [1979]), p. 2630.

[3] *Newsletter*, March 1994, headline, p. 1.

CHAPTER 12 (1994-97)
PASSING THE LAMP

The Million Dollar Mark

Alpha Chi always predicated the creation of a full-time, full-service national office on the availability of funds to underwrite it. Time had shown that amount to be unnecessary, and the national office was fully operational when Dennis Organ became the executive director in January of 1994.

Modern technology was a hallmark of the new operation. In 1994 the National Council authorized installation of an "800 number" that would allow members to call in at no expense to themselves. "The new '800' telephone number seems to be working out well," the new executive director told the executive committee later that year, "and will be publicized in early fall mailings to chapter sponsors."[1] When the staff was out of the office, an automated answering machine took the message. The computer capacity of the office was updated in both hardware and software.[2] Dr. Paul Michelson at Huntington College established an Alpha Chi "home page" on the Internet.[3] Another Alpha Chi web page was done by Southwest Texas State University for its own chapter. An electronic mail address, alphachi@harding.edu, allowed instant contact in electronic print. New Mexico Alpha chapter at New Mexico State University set up a national e-mail forum through alpha-chi@nmsu.edu.[4] Much of this technology had not even been heard of twenty years earlier. Its addition meant that communication and record keeping was substantially upgraded and updated.

The Council took steps to care for financial contingencies affecting the national office staff. In an increasingly litigious age, liability insurance seemed a wise investment. The executive committee asked Dr. Organ to investigate the need in 1995, and he responded the following year with a proposal that would cover the staff to the amount of one million dollars per claim.[5] Additionally, the executive committee, concerned by a recent question about regional funds, directed Dr. Organ to secure bonding for himself and all other financial managers of the society.[6]

Audit committee reports to the National Council recommended that Alpha Chi change auditors. Though the current auditor was entirely satisfactory to the society, the 1994 audit committee suggested informally that his connection with Harding University, the society's host and the executive director's other employer, could be seen as a potential conflict of interest. Accordingly, Dr. Organ shifted Alpha Chi's business later that year to another local firm with no direct connection to either Alpha Chi or the university.[7] Along with a number of other changes, including inauguration of the voucher system and granting more time for the audit committee to work, Alpha Chi now had a financial control system that would serve it well for years to come.[8]

The society began the new regime with the expectation of having a full-time administrative assistant. However, Ms. Nancy Hammes, who was designated for the job, found herself unable to accept more than part-time employment. Accordingly, Dr. Organ hired another Alpha Chi alumna, Ms. Lara Noah, to serve half-time with the title of secretary, staffing the office when Ms. Hammes was off.[9] This arrangement did not last long, before Ms. Hammes accepted a teaching position at a nearby college and resigned the Alpha Chi post. Ms. Noah, who had already made herself indispensable with her computer skills, took over as administrative assistant on a full-time basis, with assistance from a student worker.[10] When it became apparent that this would be a long-term arrangement, Dr. Organ moved, with the approval of the executive committee, to develop a retirement plan for her through TIAA/CREF.[11]

Organ's own job was changed as well. In becoming executive director, he donned an additional hat to supplement his post as editor of publications. The 1994 Council moved to delete the position of editor of publications from the constitution, placing the responsibility for overseeing the publication program of the organization in the hands of the executive director. Dr. Clark Youngblood, in presenting the proposal, noted that the executive director did not have to be the editor, but only to assure that the job was done. The Council made it clear that the new arrangement would not mean that Organ would lose the remuneration he was receiving as editor.[12] In 1967 the society began paying a stipend for the publication of the *Recorder* to Dr. Jess Carnes, who happened also to be vice president. The editor's job was not part of his vice presidential duty; neither now was it part of the executive director's duty, unless it was remunerated separately.

The new era saw a reordering of the publications of Alpha Chi. The *Recorder* had been an annual publication mixing official proceedings and reports with the student papers, poems, and art gleaned from scholarship applications and convention presentations. Beginning with 1995 Dr. Organ produced two issues a year, one dedicated exclusively to proceedings and reports and the other to student presentations. The following year, three issues came out, the third being a journal focusing on alumni matters containing papers from Alpha Chi alumni members and others. A third issue of the *Newsletter*, dedicated to alumni matters, appeared in 1995. Previously, Alpha Chi had published the constitution, the sponsor's handbook, and manual of rituals as three separate documents, amended from time to time as conditions warranted. A new publication titled *The Alpha Chi Handbook, 1996-1998* merged all of these into one volume in the fall of 1996.[13]

By 1997 Alpha Chi had not resolved completely its plans for financial security, but it felt considerably more comfortable than it had a few years earlier. The raising of national induction fees and the diversion of those moneys into endowment caused the endowment fund to rise rapidly. The 1996 National Council, aware that the endowment goal was nearly met, changed the direction of some of the six dollars per initiate previously dedicated to endowment. Dr. Phillip Holcomb, who had worked so diligently to build the endowment, felt confident enough about it to move that two dollars of each induction fee previously committed to endowment now be redirected to the operating fund. When this motion passed, the Council members realized that they had a substantially larger amount of money to work with.[14]

Accordingly, the scholarship committee recommended that the number of Benedict Fellowships and Nolle Scholarships granted in 1997 be increased from the present five each, but without any increase in amount. Jennifer Beekman moved to raise them to seven each, and to increase the grants to $2,500 and $1,500 respectively. Dr. George Pittman moved to amend the Beekman amendment to ten each, at the sums indicated. This motion passed. The scholarship program of the society was thus more than doubled.[15]

Just a little bit later, the alumni committee proposed the creation of a new active alumni scholarship, granting one a year at the level of the Benedict Fellowships. This also was approved, extending the scholarship program still further.[16]

The goal of $1 million in endowment was still a few years away in 1997, but the society's total worth had already crossed that mark as the time for the Philadelphia convention approached. New decisions faced Alpha Chi regarding its stewardship of those assets.

Atlanta Again and Philadelphia

Those who attended the national convention in 1995 remembered the hotel, the town, the speaker, the tours, the program, the traditional excitement of an Alpha Chi convention. The Alpha Chi staff and executive committee remembered Atlanta even more vividly for another reason—the loss of the financial records of the organization. In an otherwise well-hosted gathering, the J.W. Marriott Hotel had a mix-up between their main office and their maintenance staff. Most of Alpha Chi's records, the kind of thing one needs to prepare one's taxes with, were left overnight in the room where the audit committee had been working on them. The room, the society had been told, was secure from outside intrusion.

It was not, however, secure from inside intrusion. When Alpha Chi staff left the room for a while, the hotel maintenance staff entered the room to clean it up, thinking that Alpha Chi was through with it. The cardboard boxes filled with the society's records were tossed into a trash receptacle and carried out to the dumpsters for disposal. When the shocked Alpha Chi staff returned only to find everything gone, the hotel instituted a frantic search and finally discovered what had happened. The search then turned to the dumpsters outside, with hotel staff rummaging through the garbage in a desperate attempt to find the missing records before they were hauled away. Eventually they were successful, and the documents were retrieved.

During their stay in the garbage, however, the records had shared the dumpster with some smelly liquid refuse which had left the papers in less than pristine condition. Attempts at drying them out achieved only partial success, and they had to be boxed up and taken back to the national office where they could be spread around and allowed to dry fully.

Since most of the delegates knew nothing of this, the convention was a grand success. More than 500 delegates from 118 chapters participated. Altogether, there were thirty-four sets of student presentations.

Vice President Patricia Williams and her committee arranged several different tours for Friday afternoon. Though the coordination of these tours was a considerable headache for the planner, the participants enjoyed them immensely. One group went to CNN broadcasting headquarters, another to Coca-Cola headquarters, and some on tours of other parts of the city. Most delegates noticed the feverish activity in the downtown area as Atlanta prepared to host the summer Olympics a year hence.

The guest speaker for the banquet was Leon Harris, anchor for CNN's morning news programs. His topic was "So You Want to Succeed: Who Doesn't?" during which he fascinated the audience with an account of his rise to his current post. Other features of the convention included a student mixer led by Dr. Pug Parris of McMurry University, an activity which coincided with a make-your-own-sundae dessert orgy and the periodic introduction of National Council candidates. Evaluations after the fact showed that this was too much activity at once and subsequent plans avoided that mistake. Dr. Williams also organized the traditional continental breakfast period into "round tables" for delegates who wished to discuss topics relevant to the society.[17]

The National Council in Atlanta had the task of reelecting the national officers for the next four years. Secretary Walden Freeman retired from the VPAA position at his school during the year and did not stand for another term on the Council. The Council named Dr. Sledge and Dr. Williams to another term as president and vice president respectively. To replace Dr. Freeman as secretary, the Council elected Dr. Gayle White for the 1995-99 term. White became the second person to hold all three top elective national offices. Outgoing national secretary Freeman installed the officers near the close of the convention.[18]

Prior to adjournment the 1995 convention heard that the next national meeting would be held in Philadelphia in 1997. The executive committee met in Philadelphia that summer to select a convention hotel and settled on the Adam's Mark Hotel in northwest Philadelphia. The National Council met at the Adam's Mark in the spring of 1996 to further their plans. Philadelphia represented the society's second national meeting in the north and the first time within the bounds of Region VI. It was picked for its historic, cultural, and scientific attractions, as well as for its location.[19]

Projecting into the future, the Council also requested the executive committee to seek sites for the 1999 and 2001 conventions. The Council gave as its preferences either New Orleans or St. Louis in 1999 and either Charleston or Savannah in 2001. The executive committee chose New Orleans for 1999 and met there in the summer of 1996 to select a hotel. They also tentatively agreed that Charleston would be the 2001 host city, depending on arrangements.[20]

Reaching Out to Alumni

For a dozen or more years, interest in developing closer ties with alumni had been building among Alpha Chi's leadership. Much of it came from the desire of the student members of the National Council to maintain some kind of contact with the organization they served. This interest took two forms. One had to do with the development of alumni chapters and the other with more nebulous contacts with alumni of an as-yet-undetermined nature.[21]

Prof. Olivia Washington of Delaware State College took the lead in developing an alumni chapter in her area. When she asked if this was possible, the answer was an emphatic affirmative.[22] Over the next few years, a few alumni chapters began to form. By 1984 Prof. Washington had her northern Delaware alumni chapter up and running.[23] Others expressed interest. Region IV considered the possibility in 1984, and Sister M. Teresa Brady was discussing the idea for the northern part of Region VI beginning in 1986.[24] A new chapter in Indianapolis began in 1991 under the leadership of Dr. Herbert W. Cassel. And in 1993 Dr. Pryor inaugurated a new alumni chapter at Alice Lloyd College, called the "Caney Creek Community Center Alumni Chapter."[25]

The first alumni chapter of Alpha Chi was established in San Antonio before World War II. It had remained active until the early 1960s, sending delegates and reports to the regional conventions and supporting the society in other ways. Since that time, nothing had been heard from them in the national office or in Region I, and it was assumed that the chapter had expired.[26]

At the Region I convention at Texas Lutheran College in 1996, there suddenly appeared a delegation from the San Antonio alumni chapter. Not only were they not defunct, but they had been active through the years, supporting scholarship and holding regular meetings. A scrapbook of their activities attested to the validity of a thriving and vigorous group of substantial size. They were immediately added to the mailing list.[27]

In addition to alumni chapters, the society also sought other ways of building rapport with alumni. This proved to be difficult because nobody knew quite how to go about it. The establishment of a distinguished alumni award was one small step toward greater alumni recognition. President Sledge, in his first report to the National Council in 1984, listed four goals he thought the society should strive toward. The second of these was "service to alumni and alumni service to the society."[28] To that end he appointed an alumni committee from the Council membership in 1986, chaired by Dr. Jorge Gonzalez. The committee began to generate ideas immediately and reported them to the Council, but little action was taken for several years as the Council tried to discern a direction for the emphasis.[29]

When Gonzalez became vice president in 1987, new President Gayle White continued the committee under the leadership of Dr. Clyde Barrett from Peru State. Barrett led a discussion group of alumni (some of whom were chapter sponsors) at the 1989 convention. This gathering encouraged the Council to continue to investigate the process.[30]

The lack of current mailing addresses by which to reach alumni was always the principal rock upon which these initiatives foundered. Beginning in 1991, however, the Council began to think in terms of building a computerized list of alumni as a sample for test projects. Since that task would be labor intensive, especially in the beginning, it had been deemed impossible. But the advent of new computer technology and the prospect of a full-time national office made it seem more possible. In 1991 and 1992, Council discussions of the alumni services centered around the forthcoming full-time national office.[31]

When Dr. Dennis Organ became assistant executive director and heir apparent to Dr. Pryor's post, he began to give alumni affairs some thought. His initial reaction was negative, but he heard at the Association of College Honor Societies meetings that Phi Kappa Phi had a vigorous alumni program. Organ visited their headquarters and came away convinced that this was an important new direction for Alpha Chi. He came to believe that an alumni program was a natural way to build Alpha Chi's reputation and prestige by keeping the society's value for members alive after their college days were ended.[32] His thinking and his initiative gave impetus to an idea that was languishing for want of direction. In the summer of 1993, at the executive committee's meeting at the Swissotel in Atlanta, he expressed his ideas with great enthusiasm:

From Alpha Chi's standpoint, such alumni membership could enhance our emphasis on undergraduate programs by offering contacts and resources on which Alpha Chi and its members might draw. Moreover, continued alumni contact with Alpha Chi would remind graduates of the society and its goals.[33]

The executive committee responded by appropriating funds for the computer upgrade that would be needed and charged the alumni committee at the 1994 meeting to produce a constitutional amendment that would allow for a new type of membership in the society, namely, "active alumni members." Dr. Clark Youngblood now chaired the alumni committee and his group worked hard at the matter in 1994. From their labors came a plan for implementation, including the requisite constitutional changes and a recommendation that one of the benefits of the new status should be access to the society's publications.[34]

The national convention approved the proposed constitutional changes in Atlanta in 1995 and Organ revealed his plans for implementation. In addition to receipt of the standard Alpha Chi publications, the active alumni member would receive two additional periodicals. One was a third annual issue of the *Newsletter*, published each summer and dedicated to alumni and spring graduates. This was handled through the existing editorial arrangement. The second proposal included other changes. The executive director recommended that the *Recorder* be reduced in size and published three times a year. One issue would contain undergraduate art and papers. Another would be a "proceedings issue" which would serve as the official record of the society. The third would be an alumni issue, devoted to issues that might interest that constituency and drawing from a wide range of contributors. He urged that the society seek another person to serve as editor of the alumni *Recorder*. The Council approved these proposals.[35]

In July 1995 Dr. Organ reported to the executive committee that he had issued a call for applicants for the position of alumni editor and recommended the approval of the application of Dr. Todd H. Stebbins from William Penn College. The executive committee confirmed this appointment. Organ also announced that he was assembling an editorial board of six members to assist Dr. Stebbins.[36] Subsequently, Organ announced the board's membership: Dr. Roxanne L. Sullivan, Bellevue

University; Dr. Mark Malinauskas, Murray State University; Prof. William Zahka, Widener University; Dr. Paul Michelson, Huntington College; Dr. Stephen Rowe, West Liberty State College; and Dr. Joyce MacKinnon, University of New England. The first issue appeared in the summer of 1996 and was deemed a superior product.[37] A summer alumni edition of the *Newsletter* first appeared in 1995.

In one more reach toward Alpha Chi alumni, Dr. Youngblood's committee proposed to the 1996 National Council that an alumni fellowship be set up for one award per year, on a level comparable to the Benedict awards. The proposal received the approval of the Council.[38]

Thus, Alpha Chi embarked on a new emphasis, reiterating all the while that its primary mission was to recognize and undergird undergraduate scholarship.

Winners and Stars

The Friday morning program at the Atlanta convention included a speech by the 1995 Distinguished Alumni Award winner, Dr. Mary Wheat Gray, a graduate of Nebraska Alpha Chapter at Hastings College, one of the first two schools outside the southwest to join Alpha Chi in 1949. Dr. Gray, a mathematician, a lawyer, and board chair of Amnesty International, used her statistical skills to dispel some mistaken ideas about government and society in our time.[39]

In 1996 the National Council's awards committee announced that the 1997 recipient of the Distinguished Alumni award would be Dr. Joe Hightower of Rice University, yet another of Dr. Joe Pryor's scientific protégés from Harding University. With M.S. and Ph.D. degrees from Johns Hopkins, Hightower was a prolific contributor to the literature of his field of chemical engineering and a humanitarian with several civic awards in Houston.[40]

The President's Cup for 1995, emblematic of the outstanding chapter over the past three years, went to Tarleton State University in Stephenville, Texas. The president handed the cup to the chapter as the climax of the closing business session at the Atlanta convention. The 1996 regional meetings nominated several contenders for Tarleton's successor at the Philadelphia convention of 1997. These were Angelo State University, Southwest Texas State University, Sam Houston State University, Carson-Newman College, Freed-Hardeman University, Northwest Missouri State University, Culver-Stockton College, and Alice Lloyd College.

In an attempt to provide encouragement to chapters whose accomplishments were significant, but not quite up to President's Cup nomination, the 1994 awards committee led by Dr. Gayle White proposed the creation of a category called "star chapters." The committee established a set of criteria for qualification, with the understanding that chapters who met the standards would receive a certificate and recognition at the next national or regional convention after their selection. The first of these chapters was announced in 1996. They included the chapters at Alice Lloyd College, Anderson University, Angelo State University, Appalachian State University, Belmont University, Berry College, Brescia College, Carson-Newman College, Dominican College, East Central University, George Fox College, Harding University, Huntington College, Lander University, Lee College, Northwest Missouri State University, Pace University at Plesantville, Point Park College, Roanoke College, Robert Morris College, Sam Houston State University, Shaw University, Southeastern Oklahoma State University, Southern Arkansas University, Southwest Texas State University, Stephen F. Austin State University, University of Central Arkansas, University of Southern Colorado, and William Carey College.[41] After the first granting of this recognition at the regional meetings of 1996, "the regional secretary-treasurers reported that the Star Chapter awards had been successful."[42]

Passing the Lamp to the Next Generation

As Alpha Chi observed the seventy-fifth anniversary of its founding in 1997, it could look back over a history that was filled with a few disappointments and many more accomplishments. Most of the positive contributions of the society could be attributed to the work and dedication of the faculty sponsors. It was a truism in the society that the success of any given chapter was an almost exact measure of the skill and commitment of the sponsor. Student generations, which came and went every two years, gave Alpha Chi its spirit, but they could not provide the continuity needed to build and maintain the chapter's survival, much less its usefulness as a servant of the scholars of the institution. The sponsors were the ones who passed Alpha Chi's lamp of learning from hand to hand.

Beyond the local chapters, the history of Alpha Chi has been the story of sponsors who have given even more. As one looks back over the life of the society for seventy-five years, one can pick out figures whose dedication and vision brought the society to its present size and usefulness—Benedict, Nolle, Gooden, Schwab, Shook, Wiley, Gaston, Carnes, Pryor, and others. Not one of them, as it turned out, was indispensable. As each one drifted off the stage, a new generation of faculty and student leaders emerged to take up the lamp of Alpha Chi and carry it forward with new ideas and new energies. Today's generation, too, will move on in its time, and when it does, it will pass the lamp of leadership to those who perhaps are the student members of today.

NOTES

[1] *Recorder*, 1994, pp. 53, 65.

[2] *Recorder*, 1994, p. 52; *Recorder*, Proceedings Issue, 1996, p. 3.

[3] *Recorder*, Proceedings Issue, 1996, p. 3; *Newsletter*, Fall 1996, p. 4. Address was www.huntcol.edu:80/~pmichels/ax.html.

[4] *Newsletter*, November 1994, p. 4.

[5] *Recorder*, Proceedings Issue, 1995, p. 32; *Recorder*, Proceedings Issue, 1996, p. 11.

[6] *Recorder*, Proceedings Issue, 1996, p. 11.

[7] *Recorder*, 1994, p. 65.

[8] *Recorder*, 1994, pp. 56, 65; *Recorder*, Proceedings Issue, 1995, pp. 24-25; *Recorder*, Proceedings Issue, 1996, pp. 5-6.

[9] *Recorder*, 1994, pp. 51, 52.

[10] *Recorder*, 1994, p. 65.

[11] *Recorder*, Proceedings Issue, 1996, p. 11.

[12] *Recorder*, 1994, p. 59; *Recorder*, Proceedings Issue, 1995, p. 6.

[13] *Recorder*, Proceedings Issue, 1996, pp. 3, 11.

[14] *Recorder*, Proceedings Issue, 1996, p. 6.

[15] *Recorder*, Proceedings Issue, 1996, p. 7.

[16] *Recorder*, Proceedings Issue, 1996, pp. 7-8.

[17] *Recorder*, Proceedings Issue, 1995, pp. 2-8; convention program; *Newsletter*, March 1995, p. 1; *Newsletter*, November 1995, pp. 1-2, 4.

[18] *Recorder*, Proceedings Issue, 1995, pp. 6, 26-27; *Newsletter*, November 1995, p. 4.

[19] *Newsletter*, Fall 1996, pp. 1, 4.

[20] *Recorder*, Proceedings Issue, 1996, p. 11.

[21] *Recorder*, 1983, pp. 75-76.

22 *Recorder*, 1983, pp. 75-76.

23 Ibid.

24 *Recorder*, 1984, p. 80; *Recorder*, 1985, p. 63; *Recorder*, 1988, pp. 62-63; *Recorder*, 1991, p. 83.

25 *Recorder*, 1994, p. 52.

26 *Recorder*, 1986, p. 63.

27 *Recorder*, Proceedings Issue, 1996, p. 21.

28 *Recorder*, 1984, p. 58.

29 *Recorder*, 1986, p. 63; *Recorder*, 1987, p. 70.

30 *Recorder*, 1989, pp. 68-69, *Recorder*, 1992, p. 55.

31 *Recorder*, 1991, p. 71; *Recorder*, 1992, p. 55.

32 *Recorder*, 1993, p. 58; Handwritten note, February 6, 1997.

33 *Recorder*, 1993, pp. 69-70.

34 *Recorder*, 1994, pp. 59-61.

35 *Recorder*, Proceedings Issue, 1995, pp. 23-25.

36 *Recorder*, Proceedings Issue, 1995, p. 31.

37 *Recorder*, Alumni Issue, 1996, passim.

38 *Recorder*, Proceedings Issue, 1996, pp. 7-8.

39 *Recorder*, Proceedings Issue, 1996, p. 2, *Newsletter*, November 1994, pp. 1, 4)

40 *Newsletter*, Summer 1996, p. 1.

41 *Recorder*, 1994, p. 57; *Newsletter*, February 1996, p. 1.

42 *Recorder*, Proceedings Issue, 1996, p. 6.

Focus On . . .

ALUMNI

Alpha Chi has never quite known what to do with its alumni. As a general honor society, the society had no central common theme other than scholarship and character. For many students, membership was a matter only of paying their initiation fee and accepting their certificate. For others, however, there was a desire to associate themselves with the society after graduation.

Alumni in the San Antonio area began talking about this possibility by 1934, and established an unauthorized association in 1935.[1] In 1941 the society issued a charter to the San Antonio group as Texas Alpha Alumni chapter.[2] At the 1942 Alpha Chi meeting at Our Lady of the Lake, the Alpha Alumni chapter helped host the society and presented a report and a set of proposed by-laws. Dr. Nolle, in printing the minutes of the meeting, took special note of the report, saying, "Because it pictures so completely the activities of the chapter and may serve to inspire other alumni groups to similar endeavor, the Annual Report of the Executive Board of Alpha Alumnus [sic] Chapter is printed in full in the Appendix."[3] The chapter held meetings quarterly with an average attendance of fifty-six per meeting in 1941.[4]

World War II may have dampened enthusiasm for alumni chapters somewhat, but the 1949 meeting of the society at Incarnate Word granted a charter for a chapter in the "Lower Rio Grande Valley" of Texas. When the local chapter at McMurry College also asked for an alumni charter for its graduates, the society decided to send the whole matter to a committee. The San Antonio chapter was still active and hosted a tour of the city of San Antonio for the delegates.[5] In 1950 the society amended its constitution to extend the provisions for alumni chapters.[6] Among other things, the amendment granted the right to create alumni chapters to the regional councils, of which it was expected there would soon be two. All these provisions were found in the new Article XV of the constitution.[7]

From time to time over the next decade, the San Antonio chapter sent reports to the society. As late as 1966 the *Recorder* carried a report from the chapter, noting that it still held regular meetings and that it was awarding scholarship grants.[8] Then, for some reason, contact between the alumni chapter and the society was lost for thirty years. Contact was reestablished when delegates from the San Antonio chapter appeared at the 1996 meeting of Region I at Texas Lutheran College, thirty miles from San Antonio, and announced that they had been active and thriving for the whole time.

Other alumni chapters have also been formed over the years: in Delaware, in Indianapolis, and in Caney Creek, Kentucky. Alpha Chi's recent emphasis on alumni will embrace these chapters and others yet to be formed.

NOTES

[1] Harry Y. Benedict to Grace Carter Keeling, May 1, 1935, Benedict Papers, University of Texas at Austin, Box 2B64. In the letter, Benedict responded to an initiative from Mrs. Keeling for creation of an alumni chapter in San Antonio. The president approved the idea and offered Nolle's help in effecting it. "I should advise a rather simple organization with hardly any dues or cost in addition to the necessary 'meal ticket.' Not barring talks on various subjects, the general theme of the meetings ought to be the obligations to the social order of colleges and universities and their ex-students. The purpose of founding colleges was to send out into the general public graduates who would serve as a yeast to leaven the whole loaf."

[2] Proceedings, 1941, p. 3, 7. These pages suggest that the chapter was already recognized; personal card, Maurice H. Sochia, president of the chapter in 1996 claims March 29, 1941 as the charter date. The Proceedings of the following year (p. 14) indicate that the charter was awarded along about that time, but also that the group had been active for some years previous.

[3] *Proceedings*, 1942, p. 5.

[4] *Proceedings*, 1942, p. 14.

[5] *Proceedings*, 1949, p. 4.

[6] *Proceedings*, 1950, pp. 5-6.

[7] Alpha Chi Constitution, amended to April 1, 1950.

[8] *Recorder*, Spring 1966, p. 37.

AFTERWORD

Most history is the story of change. The story of continuity and stability and tradition mostly goes ignored. That which stays the same is seldom remarked, just as news reporting focuses on the disasters that do happen, not on those which are averted.

Alpha Chi's story, as told here, speaks of change—but the truly important thing may be its continuity in such matters as symbols, leadership styles (if not leadership structures), the dynamics of the faculty-student-curriculum relationships, the concept of education and the value of excelling at it, the criteria for membership, the gender balance. All of these are similar throughout the story.

Thus the accounts of twenty-five chapters in Texas seventy-five years ago are similar to the accounts of three hundred-plus chapters nationwide today, though the numbers, the geographic provenance, the times, may be different.

Some of the things that have changed in seventy-five years include the following:

(1) The baccalaureate focus in 1922 was on the liberal arts. There were very few specialized "vocational" programs in undergraduate colleges, apart from the one very important exception of teacher training. A college degree was usually seen as a credential for access to the upper levels of social and economic opportunity. Students wanted to know how their education would help them cope with the intellectual circles they expected to participate in.

By contrast, today's Alpha Chi includes persons in very specialized curricula. Many, perhaps most, of today's students ask of their collegiate experience the very pragmatic question, "How well will this help me earn a living?" The trend to specialization is also reflected in the dropping of "themes" for student presentations, which any Alpha Chi student, regardless of discipline, was once expected to have the ability to address in written prose. Today's presentations are centered on the idiosyncrasies of the individual disciplines and cater to the student's specialized strengths. In 1956 the society was already wrestling with this question under the theme of the year, "Is the Scholar a Specialist?"

(2) The age level of persons joining Alpha Chi is higher. Today, colleges have many more "non-traditional" students. This raises the average age of Alpha Chi members, especially since a high percentage of older students excel at their studies and thus qualify for Alpha Chi membership in greater percentages. Moreover, seventy-five years ago, many students completed high school at the age of sixteen. (In Texas, persons graduated from high school after eleven years of classes until about 1950.) And it is not only a matter of chronological age. The level of sophistication created by access to "adult" subjects and to world-wide information resources means that twenty-year-olds in 1997 have had a wider exposure to the world's multiple layers than had their sheltered, insular counterparts of seventy-five years before.

(3) The varieties of race, religion, culture, and, maybe, social class that form the background of Alpha Chi members are much broader today. It is a much more diverse, probably more secular, collection of people.

(4) The age gap has been democratized. Faculty-student relations are now much less formal, and respect for the ivory tower much more limited, than in earlier years. Students have been admitted to the centers of power, forming almost a third of the National Council, the principal governing body of the society. Since 1941 students have formed the centerpiece of the conventions. Before 1941 meetings consisted of faculty papers and presentations. Since World War II conventions have been built around student presentations and performances.

History is also most often the story of elites, of those who save their records, of those who lead, of the national rather than the local. Alpha Chi's history as told here is regrettably the same because time and resources and access did not allow the author to delve into the lives of individual chapters and individual persons. He knows that his student experience of Alpha Chi was much more the story of his local chapter than of the one national meeting he happened to attend because it was on his campus. Besides, the aggregate of private experience is hard to distill; the public event is easier to discuss and understand than the totality of private events. What an invitation to join Alpha Chi meant to the student is more significant than who was elected regional vice president, but the former subject is practically impossible to extract while the latter information is readily at hand.

Open questions still underline the gap that exists in Alpha Chi between the vision and the reality. What is Alpha Chi doing, what can Alpha Chi do to lift up the forgotten half of its goals, the issue of character? What can Alpha Chi do to make scholarship effective for good? What are the limits of geographic growth for the society? Where are the appropriate arenas of intellectual growth? What does it mean to be a member, given that there may not be much difference except grades between the inductees and their peers? Where is Alpha Chi going, and where should it go?

APPENDIX 1: NATIONAL OFFICERS

Presidents
Elected by the Convention
1922-23 John C. Granbery (Southwestern) title is "Chairman" for one year
1923-24 John C. Granbery (Southwestern) title is now "President"
1924-25 E.H. Sparkman (Baylor University)
1925-26 Earl Huffor (Sam Houston)
1926-27 J.C. McElhannon (Baylor College)
1927-28 Alfred H. Nolle (Southwest Texas)
1928-29 W.P. Davidson (Southwestern)
1929-30 Bessie Shook (North Texas State)
1930-31 O.T. Gooden (Hendrix College)
1931-32 Julius Olsen (Simmons College)
1932-33 James Marcus Bledsoe (East Texas State Teachers College)
1933-34 John Lord (Texas Christian University)
Elected by the National Council
1934-37 Harry Y. Benedict (Texas) (died, May, 1937)
1937-40 no president (VP Lord functioned in the role)
1940-45 Homer P. Rainey (Texas)
1945-49 no president (VP Lord functioned in the role)
1949-66 Paul J. Schwab (Trinity University)
1966-67 John L. McMahon (Our Lady of the Lake College)
1967-79 Edwin W. Gaston Jr. (Stephen F. Austin State)
1979-83 James Divelbiss (Westmar College)
1983-87 Robert W. Sledge (McMurry College)
1987-91 Gayle Webb White (Southern Arkansas University)
1991-99 Robert W. Sledge (McMurry University)

Vice Presidents
Elected by the Convention
1923-24 S.I. Hornbeak (Trinity University)
1924-25 Alfred H. Nolle (Southwest Texas State Teachers College)
1925-26 Julius Olsen (Simmons College)
1926-27 John Lord (Texas Christian University)
1927-28 Edna Graham (West Texas State Teachers College)
1928-29 Bessie Shook (North Texas State Teachers College)
1929-30 O.T. Gooden (Hendrix College)
1930-31 Julius Olsen (Simmons College)
1931-32 Edna Graham (West Texas State Teachers College)
1932-33 John Lord (Texas Christian University)
1933-34 Julia Luker (McMurry College)
Elected by the National Council
1934-48 John Lord (Texas Christian University)
1948-54 T.E. Ferguson (Stephen F. Austin State College)
1954-66 John L. McMahon (Our Lady of the Lake College)
1966-67 office vacant, McMahon having become president)
1967-75 Jess G. Carnes (Trinity University)
1975-79 James Divelbiss (Westmar College)
1979-81 Bailey McBride (Oklahoma Christian College)
1981-83 Robert W. Sledge (McMurry College)

1983-87 Gayle Webb White (Southern Arkansas University)
1987-91 Jorge Gonzalez (Berry College)
1991-93 Otis McCowan (Belmont College)
1993-99 Patricia Williams (Sam Houston State University)

Secretary-Treasurers
1923-28 H. Y. Benedict (University of Texas) (elected president of UT in midsummer 1928 and resigned as secretary-treasurer; Alpha Chi president Nolle served in interim)
1929-69 Alfred H. Nolle (Southwest Texas State Teachers College)
1970-83 Joseph E. Pryor (Harding College)

Executive Directors
1983-93 Joseph E. Pryor (Harding University)
1994-   Dennis M. Organ (Harding University)

Editors of Publications
1932   "Minutes" - Alfred H. Nolle (Southwest Texas State)
1933-56 *Proceedings* - Nolle
1957-66 *Recorder* - Autrey Nell Wiley (Texas Women's University)
1967-75 *Recorder* - Jess Carnes (Trinity University)
1976-   *Recorder* - Dennis M. Organ (Harding University)

Minutes Secretaries for Conventions
1922   (a) Christine Hutchinson (Texas Woman's College)
1922   (b) Harry Y. Benedict (University of Texas)
1923   Benedict
1924   Benedict
1925   Benedict
1926   Benedict
1927   Ethel B. Garrett (Sam Houston State Teachers College)
1928   Garrett
1929   Garrett
1930   I.M. Blackburn (Louisiana College)
1931   Bessie Shook (North Texas State Teachers College)
1932   Shook
1933   Shook
1934   Shook
1935   Shook
1936   Shook
1937   Shook
1938   Shook
1939   Shook
1940   Shook
1941   Shook
1942   Shook
1943   No meeting because of the war

1944	No meeting	
1945	No meeting	
1946	Shook	
1947	Shook	
1948	No meeting because of bad weather	
1948	Shook	
1949	Shook	
1950	Shook	
1951	Alma Lueders (Southwest Texas State) vice the absent Shook	
1952	Shook	
1953	Shook	
1954	Shook	
1955	Shook	
1956	Region I	Julia Luker (McMurry College)
	Region II	C.F. Sheley (Stephen F. Austin State)
1957	Shook	
1958	Region I	Jennie Tate (McMurry College)
	Region II	Sheley
1959	Shook	
1960	Region I	Tate
	Region II	Joseph E. Pryor (Harding College)
1961	A.B. Wacker (Our Lady of the Lake College)	
	Region I	Tate
	Region II	Pryor
1962	Region I	Otto O. Watts (Hardin-Simmons University)
	Region II	Pryor
1963	Jess Carnes (Trinity University)	
	Region I	Loretta Schmidt (school unknown)
	Region II	Pryor
1964	Region I	Ruth Ann Scott (school unknown)
	Region II	Pryor
1965	no name signed to national convention minutes	
	Region I	Anita Richter (Texas Lutheran College)
	Region II	Pryor
1966	Region I	no name signed to minutes
	Region II	Pryor
1967	Joseph E. Pryor (Harding College)	
	Region I	Martha Harmonson (Wayland Baptist College)
	Region II	Pryor
1968	Region I	Watts
	Region II	Pryor
1969	Pryor	
	Region I	Jess Carnes (Trinity University)
	Region II	Pryor
1970	Region I	Wendell Cain (West Texas State University)
	Region II	Pryor

From 1971-1983, the national secretary-treasurer kept the minutes of the national conventions and the elected regional secretary-treasurers took the minutes for the respective regional meetings. In 1983, a reorganization of the society's leadership structure created the offices of executive director and secretary of the national council. The latter kept the national minutes from that time forward.

Secretaries of the National Council

Appointed by the presiding officer
1934-48 Council did not meet enough to keep minutes
1949-64 Bessie Shook (North Texas State Teachers College)
1965 Woodrow W. Pate (Centenary College)
1966-69 Joseph E. Pryor (Harding College)
Elected by National Council
1970-83 Joseph E. Pryor (Harding University)
1983-87 Barbara R. Clark (Oglethorpe University)
1987-89 Sr. M. Teresa Brady (Pace - White Plains)
1989-91 Robert W. Sledge (McMurry University)
1991-95 Walden S. Freeman (Schreiner College)
1995-99 Gayle Webb White (Southern Arkansas University)

APPENDIX 2: MEETING SITES

1922 Southwestern University (February 22)
1922 University of Texas (April 21, Education Bldg, Room 223)
1923 University of Texas (Education Bldg, Room 207)
1924 Baylor University
1925 Sam Houston State Teachers College
1926 Southwestern University
1927 Texas Christian University
1928 Howard Payne College
1929 North Texas State Teachers College
1930 East Texas State Teachers College
1931 Baylor College
1932 Simmons College (co-hosts Abilene Christian, McMurry)
1933 Southwest Texas State Teachers College
1934 Texas State College for Women
1935 University of Texas
1936 Incarnate Word College
1937 West Texas State Teachers College
1938 Arkansas State Teachers College
1939 Texas College of Arts and Industries
1940 Southwestern University
1941 Stephen F. Austin State Teachers College
1942 Our Lady of the Lake College
1943 meeting cancelled because of wartime travel restrictions
1944 meeting cancelled
1945 meeting cancelled
1946 Southwest Texas State Teachers College
1947 Sam Houston State Teachers College
1948 cancelled due to weather; set for North Texas State Teachers College
1949 Incarnate Word College
1950 North Texas State Teachers College
1951 Louisiana College
1952 Baylor University
1953 Southwestern University

1954	Sul Ross State Teachers College
1955	Incarnate Word College
1956	Region I	Abilene Christian College
	Region II	Texas Christian University
1957	Our Lady of the Lake
1958	Region I	Texas Western College
	Region II	East Texas State Teachers College
1959	Texas Woman's University
1960	Region I	West Texas State Teachers College
	Region II	Harding College
1961	Centenary College
1962	Region I	Trinity University
	Region II	Texas Wesleyan College
1963	Midwestern University
1964	Region I	Wayland Baptist College
	Region II	Hendrix College
1965	Hardin-Simmons University
1966	Region I	Texas Lutheran College
	Region II	Ouachita Baptist University
1967	Stephen F. Austin State College
1968	Region I	West Texas State University
	Region II	College of the Ozarks
1969	East Central Oklahoma State College
1970	Region I	Southwestern University
	Region II	Texas Wesleyan College
1971	Holiday City (Holiday Inn) Memphis, TN (attendance 192)
1972	Region I	Abilene Christian College
	Region II	Southern State College (Southern Arkansas Univ.)
	Region III	Atlanta, GA
	Region IV	Wartburg College
	Region V	Anderson College
1973	Hilton Inn, St. Louis, MO (attendance 206)
1974	Region I	Mary-Hardin-Baylor College
	Region II	Harding College
	Region III	Atlanta, GA
	Region IV	Dana College
	Region V	meeting cancelled
	Region VI	American International College
1975	Atlanta American Motor Hotel, Atlanta, GA (attendance 231)
1976	Region I	McMurry College
	Region II	Houston Baptist University
	Region III	Atlanta, GA
	Region IV	William Woods College
	Region V	Anderson College
	Region VI	North Adams State College
1977	St. Anthony Hotel, San Antonio, TX (attendance 251)
1978	Region I	Texas Lutheran College
	Region II	Oklahoma City, OK
	Region III	Atlanta, GA
	Region IV	Westmar College
	Region V	Huntington College
	Region VI	College of White Plains, Pace University
1979	Grand Hotel, New Orleans, LA (attendance 424)

1980   Region I   Tarleton State University
        Region II   University of Texas at Arlington
        Region III   Atlanta, GA
        Region IV   Kansas Wesleyan University
        Region V   Huntington College
        Region VI   Marymount Manhattan College
        Region VII   Pepperdine University
1981   Maxwell House, Nashville, TN (attendance 382)
1982   Region I   Southwestern University
        Region II   Centenary College (Louisiana)
        Region III   Charleston, SC
        Region IV   Southwest Baptist University
        Region V   College of Mt. St. Joseph
        Region VI   Boston, MA
        Region VII   Pepperdine University
1983   Hilton Palacio del Rio, San Antonio, TX (attendance 406)
1984   Region I   Angelo State University
        Region II   Southern University
        Region III   Atlanta, GA
        Region IV   Peru State College
        Region V   Illinois State University
        Region VI   Philadelphia, PA
        Region VII   Pepperdine University
1985   Hyatt Regency, Louisville, KY (attendance 362)
1986   Region I   Midwestern State University
        Region II   Harding University
        Region III   Charleston, SC
        Region IV   Buena Vista College
        Region V   Indiana Central University
        Region VI   Marymount Manhattan College
        Region VII   Pepperdine University
1987   Fort Magruder Inn, Williamsburg, VA (attendance 515)
1988   Region I   Texas Lutheran College
        Region II   Sam Houston State University
        Region III   Atlanta, GA
        Region IV   Columbia College
        Region V   Huntington College
        Region VI   Albany, NY
        Region VII   Pepperdine University
1989   Clarion Hotel, New Orleans, LA (attendance 689)
1990   Region I   Abilene Christian University
        Region II   Oklahoma Christian University of Science and Arts
        Region III   Savannah, GA
        Region IV   Friends University
        Region V   Kendall College
        Region VI   Baltimore, MD
        Region VII   Pepperdine University
1991   Grosvenor Resort Hotel, Lake Buena Vista (Orlando), FL (attendance 390)
1992   Region I   University of Texas at San Antonio
        Region II   Shreveport, LA
        Region III   Atlanta, GA
        Region IV   Bellevue College
        Region V   Alice Lloyd College

Region VI   Philadelphia, PA
Region VII Southern Utah University
1993   Bismarck Hotel, Chicago, IL (attendance 475)
1994   Region I   Tarleton State University
        Region II   Nacogdoches, TX
        Region III   Knoxville, TN
        Region IV   University of Southern Colorado
        Region V   Brescia College
        Region VI   Cambridge, MA
        Region VII   Grand Canyon University
1995   J.W. Marriott Hotel, Lenox Square, Atlanta, GA (attendance 490)
1996   Region I   Texas Lutheran College
        Region II   Harding University
        Region III   Charlotte, NC
        Region IV   Northwest Missouri State University
        Region V   Anderson University
        Region VI   Baltimore, MD
        Region VII   George Fox College
1997   Adam's Mark Hotel, Philadelphia, PA

APPENDIX 3: NATIONAL SCHOLARSHIPS

B - Harry Yandell Benedict Memorial Scholarship/Fellowship
N - Undergraduate Scholarship (variously known as Alpha Chi Scholarship,
    National Council Scholarship, and, from 1970, Alfred H. Nolle Scholarship)

1938	B	Arthur L. Cunkle	Arkansas State Teachers College
1939	B	Jett Clinton Arthur	chapter not known
1940	B	Harold M. Wisely	Stephen F. Austin State Teachers College
1941	B	John Reesing	Baylor University
	B	Nell Green	West Texas State Teachers College
1942-49	awards not given, though they were discussed		
1950	B	Reinhold Lucke, Jr.	Southwest Texas State Teachers College
1951-53	no record of awards found		
1954	B	W.T. Witt	chapter not known
1955	no record of award found		
1956	B	Richard Libera	chapter not known
1957	B	Allen E. Schmidt	Hardin-Simmons University
	N	Lillian M. Cunningham	Hastings College
	N	Calvin McKaig	Baylor University
1958	N	Beverly Kelly	Lander College
1959	N	Kathryn Cantrell	Lander College
1960	no record of award found		
1961	B	Bobby Jack Frye	Wayland Baptist College
	N	Donna Layton	Dana College
1962	B	Jereldine Cross	Wayland Baptist College
	N	Joseph Halperin	American International University
1963	B	Gloria Joyce Adams	North Texas State University
	N	Elizabeth Nielson	Dana College
1964	B	Anthony Clay Cecil	Southwestern University
	N	no record of award found	

1965	B	James Andrew Means	Hendrix College
	N	Michael Edwin Moody	Hastings College
1966	B	Don George Scroggin	Centenary College
	N	Sandra Lee Cummings	Murray State University
1967	B	Maurice Bondurant	Murray State University
	N	Stephen Bohling	Dana College
1968	B	Dale E. Work	Harding College
	N	David Werner	Sioux Falls College
1969	B	Keith Matzen	Hastings College
	N	Kerrilyn Corder	Hastings College
1970	B	Arthur L. Shearin	Harding College
	N	Cynthia A. Chance	Tennessee Wesleyan College
1971	B	William C. Acord	Northeastern State College
	B	Donna K. Wolfe	Harding College
	N	Billy W. Bristow	Arkansas College
	N	Linda Erickson	St. Scholastica College
1972	B	Sheridan C. Barker	Carson-Newman College
	B	Norman D. Hamlin	Azusa Pacific College
	B	John T. Maple	Oklahoma Christian College
	N	Donald L. Jackson	Oklahoma Christian College
	N	Marjorie J. Meimburg	Azusa Pacific College
	N	Kaj Neve	Dana College
1973	B	Kathryn A. Erfurth	Trinity University
	B	Carol LaMay	North Adams State College
	B	Gayle L. Biehunko	Incarnate Word College
	N	Kathryn Coleman	Tarleton State College
	N	Mark Menefee	Trinity University
	N	Marilyn Martin	Hendrix College
1974	B	Mark J. Benedict	Trinity University
	B	William R. Brown	Louisiana College
	B	John O. Simmons	Harding College
	N	Gena Dagel	Trinity University
	N	Stephen L. Goble	Carson-Newman College
	N	Connie L. Parker	Tennessee Wesleyan College
1975	B	Robert N. Brown	Louisiana College
	B	Kathleen A. Harris	Wartburg College
	B	Ramona Mohamed	Lincoln University
	N	Kathy Saccoman	College of St. Scholastica
	N	Janet Smith	Harding College
	N	Marilyn Veselka	Sam Houston State University
1976	B	Gregory Milliron	Pepperdine College
	B	Kenneth Neller	Harding College
	B	Susan Theut	Lake Superior State College
	N	Charles Ellis	Carson-Newman College
	N	Daniel Francis	Westminster College
	N	Susan Wolter	College of Mt. St. Joseph
1977	B	Robert Degges	Carson-Newman College
	B	David Francis	Westminster College
	B	Que Russell Grigson	Ouachita Baptist University
	N	Sharon Barclay	Carson-Newman College
	N	Cathy Simmons	Bridgewater College
	N	Lucia Tredici	Trinity University
1978	B	Lovey K. Johnson	York College of Pennsylvania

	B	Sherri McInnis	Louisiana College
	B	Harold D. Tallant, Jr.	Carson-Newman College
	N	Marty G. Bell	Belmont College
	N	Elizabeth L. Leonard	Roanoke College
	N	Dana Pack	Dallas Baptist College
1979	B	Pamela Barnett	McMurry College
	B	Steven J. Breiner	Appalachian State University
	B	Everett D. LaFon	Christian Brothers College
	B	Robert R. Miller	Bridgewater College
	N	Cheryl Messore	Medaille College
	N	Sheila Mitchell	Jamestown College
	N	Kevin Pope	Harding College
	N	Pamela Snapp	Anderson College
1980	B	Robert Corrigan	Trinity University
	B	Gillian Gremmels	Wartburg College
	B	Allen B. Jetmore	Westminster College
	B	Mary K. Vyskocil	Dominican College
	N	Bill Hefley	Harding University
	N	Claudia Lewis	Abilene Christian University
	N	Alan Spearman	Berry College
1981	B	Charles Brown	Austin College
	B	Terri Enigk	Concord College
	B	Daniel Ulrich	Bridgewater College
	N	Debbie Dillard	Texas Wesleyan College
	N	Timothy Howard	Berry College
	N	Frank Telegadas	Bridgewater College
1982	B	Valerie Aydlett	Old Dominion University
	B	Elizabeth Eudy	Ouachita Baptist University
	B	Tim Howard	Berry College
	N	Douglas Punke	Arkansas College
	N	Wendy Sheldon	Trinity University
	N	Cynthia Swart	Anderson College
1983	B	Rebecca Burton	Carson-Newman College
	B	Harry Hawthorne	Louisiana College
	B	George James III	Angelo State University
	B	Ray Kenny	Northeastern Illinois University
	N	Susan M. Killam	Christopher Newport College
	N	Terri E. Sidaris	Berry College
	N	LeAnn Sorrell	Christian Brothers College
1984	B	Jeffrey Howe	Menlo College
	B	Alan D. Strange	Centenary College of Louisiana
	B	Rosilee Walker	Baylor University
	N	Susan L. Hamon	Trinity University
	N	Norman E. Madden	Harding University
	N	Melanie Wright	Texas Lutheran College
1985	B	Stephen Bittrich	Texas Lutheran College
	B	Richard L. Gibson	Baylor University
	B	Lenette Taylor	University of Central Arkansas
	N	Brian Divelbiss	Westmar College
	N	Jeffrey Peterson	Abilene Christian University
	N	Paul Raybon	Berry College
1986	B	Melinda Beavers	University of Texas at Tyler
	B	John Mansoor	Louisiana College

	B	Tyagan Miller	University of Southern Indiana
	N	Peter Clark	Baylor University
	N	Anita Lowe	Brescia College
	N	Ting Sun	Austin College
1987	B	Julie D. Campbell	Midwestern State University
	B	Peter Y. Clark	Baylor University
	B	Thomas Young	McMurry College
	N	Alberto Roca	Trinity University
	N	Paula Trainer	Flagler College
	N	Jeffrey Wood	Huntington College
1988	B	Jon B. Scales	Midwestern State University
	B	Karen Turner	Indiana University Southeast
	B	Stephanie Tyler	East Texas State University
	N	Amy Becker	Trinity University
	N	Tamara Hoffner	Catawba College
	N	Wendy Nelson	Flagler College
1989	B	Susan Dindot	Southwestern University
	B	Eric Eberts	Abilene Christian University
	B	Peter B. Marsh	Pepperdine University
	B	Christina Smith	Huntington College
	B	Claudia Zuch	SUNY at Brockport
	N	Michael J. Ashton	Trinity University
	N	Carolyn A. Christopher	Mars Hill College
	N	Dee Ann Gailey	Angelo State University
	N	Angela C. Martindale	Kansas Wesleyan University
	N	Angela B. Pate	Stephen F. Austin State University
1990	B	Stuart L. Greer	Wayland Baptist University
	B	Daniel Lubetsky	Trinity University
	B	Geri Lyon-Grande	College of White Plains, Pace University
	B	Richard Swallows	Louisiana College
	B	Russell Swanson	Flagler College
	N	James L. Bond	Oklahoma Christian Univ. of Science and Arts
	N	Luigina Cavaggioni	Marymount Manhattan College
	N	Michael Glenn	Northeastern Illinois University
	N	Kelly McElrath	Baylor University
	N	James Samsel	University of Texas at San Antonio
1991	B	Beverly Bertke	Brescia College
	B	Grace Guiffrida	Pace University at Pleasantville
	B	Michelle Hutt	Mars Hills College
	B	Gary Latham	Christian Brothers College
	B	Yuri Zats	Menlo College
	N	Joel Baxter	Oklahoma Christian Univ. of Science and Arts
	N	Joe D. Gregson	Mesa State College
	N	Lucy Snyder	Angelo State University
	N	Lucy Taft	Baylor University
	N	William Webb	Anderson University
1992	B	Michael P. Gray.	University of Texas at Tyler
	B	Joe D. Gregson	Mesa State College
	B	Kelly A. McElrath	Baylor University
	B	Mamta D. Somaiya	Houston Baptist University
	B	Stefani Thieszen	Hastings College
	N	Erin C. Hatch	Centenary College of Louisiana
	N	Marilyn Kravatz	Dominican College

	N	Silas N. Langley	Fresno Pacific College
	N	Sean W. Meade	Wartburg College
	N	Holly B. Woleslagle	Geneva College
1993	B	Kimberly D. Beane	Elon College
	B	Tyson R. Browning	Abilene Christian University
	B	Julie M. Jackson	Christian Brothers University
	B	Scott Lange	Northeastern Illinois University
	B	Manish K. Mamnani	New Mexico State University
	N	Luana M. Adams	Abilene Christian University
	N	Christi Jo Ehrig	Southwest Texas State University
	N	Patricia Hickson	Angelo State University
	N	Shelby W. Hough	Pembroke State University
	N	Virginia E. Thompson	Centenary College of Louisiana
1994	B	Dianna Cooper	University of Indianapolis
	B	Debrah Harris	Missouri Western State College
	B	Donna Kelly	North Adams State College
	B	Ashley Stiegler	Southwestern University
	B	Doris Strouse	Geneva College
	N	Laura Berrong	Mars Hill College
	N	Samuel D. Cox	Carson-Newman College
	N	Sara T. Hutchison	Bridgewater College
	N	Kimberly M. Mathiot	Northeastern Illinois University
	N	Slade Sullivan	Abilene Christian University
1995	B	Amy H. Amy	Harding University
	B	Robin Clonce	East Central University
	B	David B. Clubb	Elon College
	B	Tanja W. Jovanovic	Oklahoma Christian U. of Science and Arts
	B	Joel A. Nichols	Abilene Christian University
	N	Brian C. Graves	Mars Hill College
	N	Jennifer P. Hoffman	Flagler College
	N	L. Zoe Payne	Southwest Texas State University
	N	Anna M. Shirey	Berry College
	N	Francisco C.R. Silva	Wingate University
1996	B	David W. Bennett	Lindsey Wilson College
	B	Julie D. DeWoody	Harding University
	B	Brian C. Graves	Mars Hill College
	B	Lee M. Johnson	St. Ambrose University
	B	R. Gregory Tebbetts	Lyon College
	N	Craig N. Brewer	Austin College
	N	Bridgett A. Crocker	Shenandoah University
	N	Melissa Jo Hancock	Milligan College
	N	Dana C. Imhof	Adrian College
	N	Donna C. McCafferty	Southwest Texas State University

APPENDIX 4: FACULTY NATIONAL COUNCIL MEMBERS, 1934-96

(dates after 1996 indicate end of current term for incumbents; asterisks indicate Council members who died in office)

Atkinson, Wm. Eugene, Tarleton State College	1976-84
Atteberry, James L., Harding College	1967-69
Bally, L.H., Northeastern State College	1947-63*
Barrett, Clyde J., Peru State College	1986-92
Beck, Norman. Texas Lutheran College	1984-88
Benedict, Harry Y., University of Texas	1934-37; president, 1934-37*
Bergendahl, Timothy J., North Adams State College, Westfield State College	1975-88
Blake, Robert G., Elon College	1982-94, 1995-99
Box, Terry, Stephen F. Austin State	1983-87, 1989-93
Brady, Sr. M. Teresa, College of White Plains at Pace University	1981-89; secretary, 1987-89
Braun, Penelope, Columbia College	1989-93
Cain, Wendell, West Texas State	1967-76
Carnes, Jess G., Trinity University	1967-79; vice president 1967-75
Carter, Wilmoth A., Shaw University	1977-89
Clark, Barbara R., Oglethorpe University	1974-82, 1983-95; secretary, '83-87
Clifford, F. Burr, Southwestern University	1964-69
Condaris, Christine, North Adams State	1993-97
Cook, Kenneth E., Anderson College	1978-82
Crenshaw, Troy C., Texas Christian University	1950-55, 1956-57
Davis, Edward L., American International	1972-75*
de Schweinitz, George, West Texas State	1965
Divelbiss, James, Westmar College	1970-83; vice president 1975-79; president, 1979-83
Dudzinski, Sr. Mary Lucia, College of Mt. St. Joseph	1982-86
Edris, David M., Peru State College	1992-2000
Ericson, Joe E., Stephen F. Austin State	1969-71
Ferguson, T.E., Stephen F. Austin State	1949-58; vice president, 1949-54
Ford, E. Lee, Centenary College	1956-66
Frashier, Loyd D., Pepperdine University	1971-84
Freeman, Walden S., William Woods College	1976-86
Schreiner College	1987-95; secretary, 1991-95
Gadaire, Charles R., American International	1957-73
Gaston, Edwin W., Stephen F. Austin State	1962-79; president, 1967-79
Gilliam, Bob J., Pepperdine University	1984-88, 1991-95
Gonzalez, Jorge A., Berry College	1979-91, 1993-97; vice president, 1987-91
Gooden, O.T., Hendrix College	1935-40, 1949-55
Graham, Patricia A., U. of Texas San Antonio	1995-99
Griffin, Howard, Sam Houston State	1977-79
Hall, Thelma, Shorter College	1996-2000
Harris, David L., Henderson State	1955-56
Holcomb, Phillip A., Angelo State University	1988-2000
Howard, Claud, Southwestern University	1934-37, 1940-50

Huffor, Earl, Sam Houston State 1941-51
Jones, Eugene W., Wayland Baptist College 1964-65
Lardner, Peter, Flagler College 1994-96
Legge, John W., Blackburn College 1974-78
Lewis, Lemoine G., Abilene Christian College 1969-71
Logan, Susan H., Appalachian State 1971-81
Lord, John, Texas Christian University .... 1934-48; vice president, 1934-48*
Luker, Julia, McMurry College 1951-56
McBride, Bailey B., Oklahoma Christian .... 1970-84; vice president, 1979-81
McCowan, Otis B., Belmont College .... 1989-93; vice president, 1991-93
Mack, Mattie Swayne, West Texas State 1953-58
McMahon, John, Our Lady of the Lake College ..... 1952-71; vice president, 1954-66;
                                                     president, 1966-67

Sr. Mary Clement, Incarnate Word College 1934-35
Michelson, Paul E., Huntington College 1986-98
Mills, R.A.,Texas Technological College 1942-47, 1949-53
Nolle, Alfred H., Southwest Texas State 1934-1969;
                                                  secretary-treasurer, 1934-69

Odom, Charles L., Centenary College 1936-46
Olsen, Julius, Hardin-Simmons University 1937-42
Pate, Woodrow W., Centenary College 1964-75
Peterson, Clell T., Murray State 1970-74
Philbeck, Ben E., Carson-Newman College 1970-77
Pittman, George C., Mississippi College 1995-99
Platt, Robert M., McMurry College 1966-67
Pryor, Joseph E., Harding University .... 1959-83; secretary-treasurer, '70-83
Rainey, Homer P., University of Texas .... 1940-45; president, 1940-45
Robbins, Orville, East Central Oklahoma State 1981-85
Sabol, Michael A., North Adams State 1988-2000
Schwab, Paul J., Trinity University .... 1949-66; president, 1949-66*
Scully, Daniel W., Adrian College 1971-77
Sessions, Kyle, Illinois State University 1985-89
Shearin, Arthur L., Harding University 1988-96
Sheley, C.F., Stephen F. Austin State 1955-59
Shook, Bessie, North Texas State 1938-66*
Sixbey, George L., Arkansas State Teachers 1958-61
Sledge, Robert W., McMurry University 1973-87, 1989-99;
                                                  vice president, 1981-83;
                                                  president, 1983-87, 1991-99;
                                                  secretary, 1989-91

Smith, Billy P., Hardin-Simmons University 1969-71
Watts, Otto O., Hardin-Simmons University 1958-68
Weaver, Gilbert, John Brown University 1984-88
White, Gayle Webb, Southern Arkansas 1979-91, 1993-99;
                                                  vice president, 1983-87;
                                                  president, 1987-91;
                                                  secretary, 1995-99

Whitley, S.H., East Texas State 1934-36
Wiley, Autrey Nell, Texas State Col. for Women 1946-71
Williams, Patricia A., Sam Houston State .... 1991-99; vice president, 1993-99
Witt, Paul C., Abilene Christian College 1949-64
Yarbrough, Trisha, East Central University 1996-2000
Youngblood, Clark R., Grand Canyon Univ. 1988-2000

APPENDIX 5: REGIONAL OFFICERS

Regional Presidents and Vice Presidents

1934	Region I	P	Edna Graham, West Texas State Teachers College
		VP	Charles L. Odom, Centenary College
1935		P	P.R. Clugston, Arkansas State Teachers College
		VP	Clyde T. Reed, Texas College of Arts and Industries
1936		P	Julia Luker, McMurry College
		VP	R.A. Mills, Texas Technological College
1937		P	R.A. Mills, Texas Technological College
		VP	J.H. Wisely, Stephen F. Austin State Teachers College
1938		P	Charles L. Odom, Centenary College
		VP	Claud Howard, Southwestern University
1939		P	Claud Howard, Southwestern University
		VP	Elsie Jenison, Texas State College for Women
1940		P	Paul C. Witt, Abilene Christian College
		VP	J.H. Wisely, Stephen F. Austin State Teachers College
1941		P	Autrey Nell Wiley, Texas State College for Women
		VP	J.R. Manning, Texas College of Arts and Industries
1942		P	J.H. Wisely, Stephen F. Austin State Teachers College
		VP	L.A. Bally, Northeastern State College
1943			no meeting because of war; officers continued
1944			no meeting; officers continued
1945			no meeting; Wisely died May 26, 1945; Bally functioned as president through the 1946 meeting.
1946		P	Paul Schwab, Trinity University
		VP	Charles G. Smith, Baylor University
1947		P	J.R. Manning, Texas College of Arts and Industries
		VP	Mattie S. Mack, West Texas State Teachers College
1948			no meeting because of weather; officers continued
1949		P	Mattie S. Mack, West Texas State Teachers College
		VP	Otto O. Watts, Hardin-Simmons University
1950		P	Otto O. Watts, Hardin-Simmons University
		VP	Elsie Bodemann, East Texas State Teachers College
1951		P	J. E. Caldwell, Louisiana College
		VP	Myrtle Brown, North Texas State Teachers College
1952		P	Myrtle Brown, North Texas State Teachers College
		VP	E. Lee Ford, Centenary College
1953		P	Troy C. Crenshaw, Texas Christian University
		VP	Sr. Margaret Rose, Our Lady of the Lake College
1954		P	E. Bruce Thompson, Baylor University
		VP	Annie Lee Knox, Texas Wesleyan College
1955	Region I	P	Gertrude Horgan, Incarnate Word College
		VP	J.R. Manning, Texas College of Arts and Industries
	Region II	P	E. Lee Ford, Centenary College
		VP	Elsie Bodemann, East Texas State Teachers College
1956	Region I	P	Lloyd A. Nelson, Texas Western College
		VP	Stather Elliott Thomas, Sul Ross State Teachers College
	Region II	P	Elsie Bodemann, East Texas State Teachers College
		VP	Dolphus Whitten, Jr., Henderson State College
1957	Region I	P	Stather Elliott Thomas, Sul Ross State Teachers College

		VP	Alma Lueders, Southwest Texas State Teachers College
	Region II	P	Dolphus Whitten, Jr., Henderson State College
		VP	Hattie Propst, Northeastern State College
1958	Region I	P	Stather Elliott Thomas, Sul Ross State Teachers College
		VP	Jennie Tate, McMurry College
	Region II	P	Dolphus Whitten, Jr., Henderson State College
		VP	Hattie Propst, Northeastern State College
1959	Region I	P	Ples Harper, West Texas State Teachers College
		VP	Sr. Margaret Rose, Our Lady of the Lake College
	Region II	P	H. Howard Hughes, Texas Wesleyan College
		VP	Richard E. Yates, Hendrix College
1960-62	Region I	P	Jess G. Carnes, Trinity University
		VP	Eugene W. Jones, Wayland Baptist College
	Region II	P	Richard E. Yates, Hendrix College
		VP	Woodrow W. Pate, Centenary College
1963-64	Region I	P	Eugene W. Jones, Wayland Baptist College
		VP	George de Schweinitz, West Texas State Teachers Col.
	Region II	P	Woodrow W. Pate, Centenary College
		VP	Edwin Gaston, Jr., Stephen F. Austin State Teachers Col.
1965-66	Region I	P	George de Schweinitz, West Texas State Teachers College, 1965
		P	Robert M. Platt, McMurry College, 1966
		VP	Robert M. Platt, McMurry College, 1965
	Region II	P	Edwin Gaston, Jr., Stephen F. Austin State Teachers Col.
		VP	E.B. Speck, East Central State College
1967-68	Region I	P	Wendell Cain, West Texas State Teachers College
		VP	Russell Kemp, Texas Lutheran College, 1967
		VP	Lemoine G. Lewis, Abilene Christian College, 1968
	Region II	P	James L. Atteberry, Harding College
		VP	Joe E. Ericson, Stephen F. Austin State Teachers College
1969-71	Region I	P	LeMoine G. Lewis, Abilene Christian College
		VP	Norman W. Spellman, Southwestern University
	Region II	P	Joe E. Ericson, Stephen F. Austin State University
		VP	Lee Morgan, Centenary College
1970-72	Region III	P	Susan H. Logan, Appalachian State University
		VP	Leonard Rowlett, Lincoln Memorial University
	Region IV	P	John O. Chellevold, Wartburg College
		VP	Kenneth P. Smith, Sterling College
	Region V	P	Daniel W. Scully, Adrian College
		VP	Ralph A. Cornell, Huntington College
1971-73	Region I	P	Norman W. Spellman, Southwestern University
		VP	Robert C. Fain, Tarleton State College
	Region II	P	Lee Morgan, Centenary College
		VP	William Trigg, Arkansas Polytechnic College
1972-74	Region III	P	Shelton E. Stewart, Lander College
		VP	Walter B. Shurden, Carson-Newman College
	Region IV	P	Richard S. Jorgensen, Dana College
		VP	Walden S. Freeman, William Woods College
	Region V	P	Kenneth E. Cook, Anderson College
		VP	John W. Legge, Blackburn College
	Region VI	P	Frank K. Flaumenhaft, University of New Haven
		VP	Fred J. Parent, Nasson College
1973-76	Region I	P	Robert C. Fain, Tarleton State College

		VP	Robert W. Sledge, McMurry College
	Region II	P	William Trigg, Arkansas Polytechnic College
		VP	Don R. Byrnes, Houston Baptist College
1974-76	Region III	P	Walter B. Shurden, Carson-Newman College
		VP	Jorge A. Gonzalez, Berry College
	Region IV	P	Walden S. Freeman, William Woods College
		VP	Donald Good, William Penn College
	Region V	P	Clell T. Peterson, Murray State University
		VP	Benjamin Ulrich, Jr., Parks College of St. Louis University
	Region VI	P	Fred J. Parent, Nasson College
		VP	Timothy J. Bergendahl, North Adams State College
1976-78	Region I	P	Robert W. Sledge, McMurry College
		VP	Iva M. Fussell, Mary Hardin-Baylor College
	Region II	P	Don R. Byrnes, Houston Baptist College
		VP	Charles McDowell, University of Texas at Tyler
	Region III	P	Jorge A. Gonzalez, Berry College
		VP	Leland L. Nicholls, Appalachian State University
	Region IV	P	George Hinkle, Westminster College
		VP	Wayne G. Marty, Westmar College
	Region V	P	Benjamin Ulrich, Jr., Parks College of St. Louis University
		VP	Sr. Marita Greenwell, Brescia College
	Region VI	P	Muriel Dollar, Caldwell College
		VP	Sr. M. Theresa Brady, College of White Plains
1978-80	Region I	P	Iva M. Fussell, Mary Hardin-Baylor College
		VP	Ronald Hiner, Panhandle State University
	Region II	P	Charles McDowell, University of Texas at Tyler
		VP	Myrna Hammons, Northeastern Oklahoma State Univ.
	Region III	P	Winona Bierbaum, Mars Hill College
		VP	Robert G. Blake, Elon College
	Region IV	P	Wayne G. Marty, Westmar College
		VP	Roger M. Clites, Kansas Wesleyan University
	Region V	P	Sr. Marita Greenwell, Brescia College
		VP	Paul E. Michelson, Huntington College
	Region VI	P	Sr. M. Theresa Brady, College of White Plains
		VP	Sr. Miriam Catherine Nevins, Dominican Col. of Blauvelt
1980-82	Region I	P	Norman Beck, Texas Lutheran College
		VP	Phillip A. Holcomb, Angelo State University
	Region II	P	Myrna Hammons, Northeastern Oklahoma State Univ.
		VP	Kan Luther, Texas Wesleyan College
	Region III	P	Robert G. Blake, Elon College
		VP	Otis McCowan, Belmont College
	Region IV	P	Janet Juhnke, Kansas Wesleyan University
		VP	Betty Heifner, Southwest Baptist College
	Region V	P	Paul E. Michelson, Huntington College
		VP	Margaret Noble, Defiance College
	Region VI	P	Sr. Miriam Catherine Nevins, Dominican Col. of Blauvelt
		VP	Sr. M. Theresa Brady, College of White Plains
	Region VII	P	Dale Robertson, Brigham Young University of Hawaii
		VP	Bob J. Gilliam, Pepperdine University
1982-84	Region I	P	Phillip A. Holcomb, Angelo State University
		VP	William Clark Stevens, Abilene Christian University
	Region II	P	Kan Luther, Texas Wesleyan College
		VP	Don England, Harding University
	Region III	P	Otis McCowan, Belmont College

		VP	Camilla Hoy, Greensboro College
	Region IV	P	Donald H. Welsh, Valley City State University
		VP	Richard Lampe, Buena Vista College
	Region V	P	Kenneth E. Cook, Anderson College
		VP	Kyle E. Sessions, Illinois State University
	Region VI	P	Olivia W. Washington, Delaware State College
		VP	Michael A. Sabol, North Adams State College
	Region VII	P	Bob J. Gilliam, Pepperdine University
		VP	Max E. Stanton, Brigham Young University of Hawaii
1984-86	Region I	P	Jeff Campbell, Midwestern State University
		VP	Peter Petersen, West Texas State University
	Region II	P	Don England, Harding University
		VP	Joe Guenter, University of Arkansas at Monticello
	Region III	P	Camilla Hoy, Greensboro College
		VP	Peter Lardner, Flagler College
	Region IV	P	Clyde Barrett, Peru State College
		VP	John Palan, Marymount College of Kansas
	Region V	P	Kyle E. Sessions, Illinois State University
		VP	Herbert Cassel, Indiana Central University
	Region VI	P	Michael A. Sabol, North Adams State College
		VP	Olivia W. Washington, Delaware State College
	Region VII	P	Max E. Stanton, Brigham Young University of Hawaii
		VP	Loyd D. Frashier, Pepperdine University
1986-88	Region I	P	Peter Petersen, West Texas State University
		VP	James Nichols, Abilene Christian University
	Region II	P	Joe Guenter, University of Arkansas at Monticello
		VP	Patricia Williams, Sam Houston State University
	Region III	P	Peter Lardner, Flagler College
		VP	Frances Garner, Mobile College
	Region IV	P	Richard Lampe, Buena Vista College
		VP	Penelope C. Braun, Columbia College
	Region V	P	Herbert Cassel, Indiana Central University
		VP	Gwendolyn Applebaugh, Indiana University Southeast
	Region VI	P	Olivia W. Washington, Delaware State College
		VP	Michael A. Sabol, North Adams State College
	Region VII	P	Scott Stein, Warner Pacific College
		VP	Clark Youngblood, Grand Canyon College
1988-90	Region I	P	James R. Nichols, Abilene Christian University
		VP	Carl E. Hall, University of Texas at El Paso
	Region II	P	Patricia Williams, Sam Houston State University
		VP	Terry Box, Stephen F. Austin University
	Region III	P	Frances Garner, Mobile College
		VP	Peter C. Reichle, Appalachian State University
	Region IV	P	Penelope C. Braun, Columbia College
		VP	Kathryn M. Boyle, Friends University
	Region V	P	Kenneth E. Cook, Anderson University
		VP	William Chandler, Concordia College Wisconsin
	Region VI	P	William Zahka, Widener University
		VP	Christine Condaris, North Adams State College
	Region VII	P	Max E. Stanton, Brigham Young University of Hawaii
		VP	Loyd D. Frashier, Pepperdine University
1990-92	Region I	P	Carl E. Hall, University of Texas at El Paso
		VP	Patricia Graham, University of Texas at San Antonio
	Region II	P	Terry Box, Stephen F. Austin University

		VP	Orville Robbins, East Central (Okla.) University
Region III	P		Peter C. Reichle, Appalachian State University
		VP	George Pittman, Mississippi College
Region IV	P		Kathryn M. Boyle, Friends University
		VP	Roxanne L. Sullivan, Bellevue College
Region V	P		Thomas Mihail, Purdue University
		VP	Kenneth M. Mitchell, Alice Lloyd College
Region VI	P		Christine Condaris, North Adams State College
		VP	Sally Hanna-Jones, Capitol College
Region VII	P		James W. Harrison, Southern Utah State College
		VP	Max E. Stanton, Brigham Young University of Hawaii

1992-94
Region I	P		Patricia Graham, University of Texas at San Antonio
		VP	Jim Kirby, Tarleton State University
Region II	P		John Maple, Oklahoma Christian U. of Science and Arts
		VP	Marette Jackson, University of Central Arkansas
Region III	P		George Pittman, Mississippi College
		VP	Ellen Millsaps, Carson-Newman College
Region IV	P		Roxanna L. Sullivan, Bellevue College
		VP	John Ryan, University of Southern Colorado
Region V	P		Kossuth M. Mitchell, Alice Lloyd College
		VP	Robert E. Cinnamond, Brescia College
Region VI	P		Sally Hanna, Capitol College
		VP	William Zahka, Widener University
Region VII	P		Max E. Stanton, Brigham Young University of Hawaii
		VP	James W. Harrison, Southern Utah University

1994-96
Region I	P		Jim Kirby, Tarleton State University
		VP	David Horton, St. Edward's University
Region II	P		Kenneth Chinn, Southeastern Oklahoma State University
		VP	Trisha Yarbrough, East Central (Okla.) University
Region III	P		Ellen Millsaps, Carson-Newman College
		VP	Robert Morgan, Gardner-Webb University
Region IV	P		John Ryan, University of Southern Colorado
		VP	Richard Frucht, Northwest Missouri State University
Region V	P		Robert E. Cinnamond, Brescia College
		VP	Blake Janutolo, Anderson University
Region VI	P		William Zahka, Widener University
		VP	Sally Hanna, Capitol College
Region VII	P		Susan Shaw, George Fox College
		VP	Kathleen Lamkin, University of La Verne

1996-98
Region I	P		David Horton, St. Edward's University
		VP	Pug Parris, McMurry University
Region II	P		Terrell Tebbetts, Lyon College
		VP	Suzanne Pundt, University of Texas at Tyler
Region III	P		Robert Morgan, Gardner-Webb University
		VP	Floyd Tesmer, Strayer College
Region IV	P		Richard Frucht, Northwest Missouri State University
		VP	Christine Cotton, Columbia College
Region V	P		Blake Janutolo, Anderson University
		VP	Helen Sands, University of Southern Indiana
Region VI	P		Sara E. Hanna, Capitol College
		VP	Kenneth LaSota, Robert Morris College
Region VII	P		Kathleen Lamkin, University of La Verne
		VP	Janet Melnyk, George Fox University

Regional Secretary-Treasurers

| Region I | 1934-59 | Alfred H. Nolle, Southwest Texas State Teachers College |
| | 1959-68 | Otto O. Watts, Hardin-Simmons University |

Region II	1955-59	C.F. Sheley, Stephen F. Austin State Teachers College
	1959-70	Joseph E. Pryor, Harding College
	1970-84	Bailey B. McBride, Oklahoma Christian

Region I	1969-76	Wendell Cain, West Texas State College
	1976-84	Eugene Atkinson, Tarleton State University
	1984-88	Norman Beck, Texas Lutheran College
	1988-2000	Phillip A. Holcomb, Angelo State University

Region II	1969-84	Bailey E. McBride, Oklahoma Christian College
	1984-88	Gilbert B. Weaver, John Brown University
	1988-96	Arthur L. Shearin, Harding University
	1996-2000	Trisha Yarbrough, East Central University

Region III	1970-74	Ben F. Philbeck, Carson-Newman College
	1974-82	Barbara R. Clark, Oglethorpe University
	1982-94	Robert G. Blake, Elon College
	1994-96	Peter Lardner, Flagler College
	1996-2000	Thelma Hall, Shorter College

Region IV	1970-76	James Divelbiss, Westmar College
	1976-86	Walden S. Freeman, William Woods College
	1986-92	Clyde J. Barrett, Peru State College
	1992-2000	David M. Edris, Peru State College

Region V	1970	James A. Parr, Murray State University
	1970-74	Clell T. Peterson, Murray State University
	1974-78	John W. Legge, Blackburn College
	1978-82	Kenneth E. Cook, Anderson College
	1982-86	Mary Lucia Dudzinski, College of Mt. St. Joseph
	1986-98	Paul E. Michelson, Huntington College

Region VI	1972-75	Edward L. Davis, American International College
	1975-88	Timothy J. Bergendahl, Westfield State College
	1988-2000	Michael A. Sabol, North Adams State College

Region VII	1980-84	Loyd D. Frashier, Pepperdine University
	1984-88	Bob J. Gilliam, Pepperdine University
	1988-2000	Clark R. Youngblood, Grand Canyon University

Student Representatives to the National Council

Elected At-Large by the National Convention

Joy Crouch	East Central State College	1971
Jackie DeVore	Lander College	1971
John Maple	Oklahoma Christian College	1971
John Ragle	McMurry College	1971
Lawrence Rasmussen	Dana College	1971
Sandra DeVries	Houston Baptist College	1973
Tara Ann Kelly	George Mason University	1973
Swaid Swaid	Harding College	1973
Connie Tague	Westmar College	1973
Ronald Thompson	Kentucky Wesleyan College	1973
Sherry Crum	Tarleton State College	1975
Curtis Linge	Harding College	1975
Gregory Milliron	Pepperdine College	1975
Shelaine Nelson	William Woods College	1975
Donna Newhart	Brescia College	1975
Larry Pike	Mars Hill College	1975

Elected by Regions

Angela Kreidel	Abilene Christian College	1978	I
Rebecca Risinger	Sam Houston State College	1978	II
Marc Niemeller	Greensboro College	1978	III
Brian Proctor	Westmar College	1978	IV
Phil Burkett	Huntington College	1978	V
Ivana Tallerico	College of White Plains, Pace Univ.	1978	VI
*Nina Sethi	Pepperdine College	1979	
Patrick Crowder	Angelo State College	1980	I
Thomas Harkrider	Texas Wesleyan College	1980	II
Greg Hawthorne	Berry College	1980	III
Allison VanMeter	Kansas Wesleyan College	1980	IV
Debra Wolford	Brescia College	1980	V
Chilufya Konie	College of White Plains, Pace Univ.	1980	VI
James Kinsel	Menlo College	1980	VII
David Hutchison	McMurry College	1982	I
Anna Verzinski	Stephen F. Austin State College	1982	II
Mark Oldham	Greensboro College	1982	III
Margaret Gerhart	Marymount College of Kansas	1982	IV
Theresa Willett Howard	Brescia College	1982	V
Kate Cunningham	College of White Plains, Pace Univ.	1982	VI
Marilyn Misch	Pepperdine College	1982	VII
Jeffrey Peterson	Abilene Christian College	1984	I
Opoku Boahene	East Central Oklahoma State Univ.	1984	II
Robert Winstead	Berry College	1984	III

* Elected by the National Council Chapters (Region VII not yet formed)

William Rodgers	Westminster College (Missouri)	1984	IV
Myra Wright	Indiana University Southeast	1984	V
Nancy Seyfried	Delaware State University	1984	VI
Shelley Slinn	Columbia Christian College	1984	VII
Julie Campbell	Midwestern State University	1986	I
Larry Murphy	John Brown University	1986	II
Craig A. Bell	Johnson C. Smith University	1986	III
Stephanie Netsch	Columbia College	1986	IV
Kathy Ann Sloan	Indiana University Southeast	1986	V
Deborah Schiffer	Wesley College	1986	VI
Thea Wilshire	Pepperdine University	1986	VII
Sandra Harmon	University of Texas at San Antonio	1988	I
Kimberly Springfield	Stephen F. Austin State Univ.	1988	II
Cynthia Garner	Greensboro College	1988	III
Stephen B. Evans	Columbia College	1988	IV
Lee Purcell	Purdue University Calumet	1988	V
Linda Zettlemoyer	Delaware State University	1988	VI
Gary Williams	Pepperdine University	1988	VII
Molly Isbell	Texas Lutheran University	1990	I
Heather Hattori	Stephen F. Austin State Univ.	1990	II
Chrissy Vaughn	Gardner-Webb University	1990	III
Anna Gotangco	Columbia College	1990	IV
Jamie Douglas	University of Indianapolis	1990	V
Peung Vongs	College of White Plains, Pace Univ.	1990	VI
Michelle Dutson	Southern Utah University	1990	VII
Nancy Meza	University of Texas at San Antonio	1992	I
Shannon Scott	Stephen F. Austin State Univ.	1992	II
Marty L. White	Gardner-Webb University	1992	III
Krista Shanstrom	University of Southern Colorado	1992	IV
Paula S. Morman	Alice Lloyd College	1992	V
Stacy G. George	Capitol College	1992	VI
Leroy G. Transfield	Brigham Young University of Hawaii	1992	VII
Devesh Raj	Angelo State University	1994	I
Sarah Minor	Oklahoma Christian University.	1994	II
Eric Newsome	Freed-Hardeman University	1994	III
Jennifer Shroyer	University of Southern Colorado	1994	IV
Chad Lewis	University of Indianapolis	1994	V
Francesca DeFranco	College of White Plains, Pace Univ.	1994	VI
Eric Hart	Grand Canyon University	1994	VII
Patrice Poage	Tarleton State University	1996	I
Kelli Doolen	Southeastern Oklahoma State Univ.	1996	II
Michael Galkovsky	Freed-Hardeman University	1996	III
Jennifer Beekman	Northwest Missouri State Univ.	1996	IV
Chelsea Poppe	Urbana University	1996	V
Brenda Cappy	Point Park College	1996	VI
Sara Waldal	George Fox University	1996	VII

APPENDIX 6: AWARDS

Distinguished Alumni Award

1987   John Michael White, Professor of Chemistry, University of Texas
         Nominee and Alumnus of Harding University

1989   Richard Francis Bieker, Professor of Economics, Delaware State College
         Nominee of Delaware State College, Alumnus of Murray State
         University

1991   Robert H. Jones, Cardiac Surgeon; Professor of Surgery, Duke University
         Nominee and Alumnus of Harding University

1993   Dan Rather, Anchor and Managing Editor, CBS Evening News
         Nominee and Alumnus of Sam Houston State University

1995   Mary Wheat Gray, Professor of Mathematics, American University; Board
         Chair, Amnesty International
         Nominee and Alumna of Hastings College

1997   Joe W. Hightower, Professor of Chemical Engineering, Rice University
         Nominee and Alumnus of Harding University

President's Cup (Outstanding Chapter Award)

1987   College of White Plains, Pace University, New York Delta

1989   Midwestern State University, Texas Alpha Gamma

1991   Brescia College, Kentucky Delta

1993   Sam Houston State University, Texas Omicron

1995   Tarleton State University, Texas Alpha Kappa

APPENDIX 7: ROSTER OF CHAPTERS

Charter dates in some cases may err by one or two years because of incomplete records or delay between application and inauguration of a chapter.

1	Southwestern University Texas Alpha	1923	33	Northeastern State University Oklahoma Alpha	1938
2	University of Mary Hardin-Baylor Texas Beta	1922	34	American International College Massachusetts Alpha	1949
3	Baylor University Texas Gamma	1923	35	Hastings College Nebraska Alpha	1949
4	Texas Presbyterian College * Texas Delta	1923	36	Midwestern State University Texas Alpha Gamma	1952
5	Trinity University Texas Epsilon	1923	37	University of Central Oklahoma Oklahoma Beta	1952
6	West Texas A&M University Texas Zeta	1923	38	Henderson State University Arkansas Epsilon	1953
7	University of North Texas Texas Eta	1923	39	University of Arkansas at Monticello Arkansas Zeta	1955
8	Texas Woman's University Texas Theta	1923	40	Texas Lutheran University Texas Alpha Delta	1956
9	Southwest Texas State University Texas Iota	1923	41	Harding University Arkansas Eta	1957
10	Austin College Texas Kappa	1923	42	Lander University South Carolina Alpha	1957
11	Texas A & M University - Commerce Texas Lambda	1924	43	Westminster College of Salt Lake City Utah Alpha	1958
12	Texas Wesleyan University Texas Mu	1924	44	Southern Arkansas University Arkansas Theta	1958
13	Our Lady of the Lake University Texas Nu	1924	45	Pan American University at Edinburg * Texas Alpha Epsilon	1958
14	Texas Christian University * Texas Xi	1924	46	East Texas Baptist University Texas Alpha Zeta	1958
15	Sam Houston State University Texas Omicron	1924	47	Valdosta State University Georgia Alpha	1958
16	Howard Payne University * Texas Pi	1926	48	Wayland Baptist University Texas Alpha Eta	1958
17	Hardin-Simmons University Texas Rho	1926	49	Anderson University Indiana Alpha	1958
18	Stephen F. Austin State University Texas Sigma	1926	50	Mississippi College Mississippi Alpha	1959
19	St. Edward's University Texas Tau	1926	51	Wartburg College Iowa Alpha	1960
20	McMurry University Texas Upsilon	1926	52	Lyon College Arkansas Iota	1960
21	University of the Incarnate Word Texas Phi	1926	53	Dana College Nebraska Beta	1960
22	Sul Ross State University Texas Chi	1926	54	Tusculum College Tennessee Alpha	1960
23	Centenary College of Louisiana Louisiana Alpha	1926	55	Appalachian State University North Carolina Alpha	1962
24	Hendrix College Arkansas Alpha	1927	56	East Central University Oklahoma Gamma	1962
25	Abilene Christian University Texas Psi	1927	57	Union University Tennessee Beta	1962
26	Texas A&M University - Kingsville Texas Omega	1928	58	Nasson College * Maine Alpha	1964
27	Texas Tech University * Texas Alpha Alpha	1928	59	Franciscan University of Steubenville Ohio Alpha	1964
28	Ouachita Baptist University Arkansas Beta	1928	60	Adrian College Michigan Alpha	1964
29	Louisiana College Louisiana Beta	1930	61	Sterling College Kansas Alpha	1965
30	University of Central Arkansas Arkansas Gamma	1932	62	Murray State University Kentucky Alpha	1965
31	University of the Ozarks Arkansas Delta	1932	63	William Penn College Iowa Beta	1965
32	University of Texas at El Paso Texas Alpha Beta	1937	64	University of Sioux Falls South Dakota Alpha	1967

Asterisks denote chapters that are now defunct.

65	Westmar University Iowa Gamma	1967
66	Huntington College Indiana Beta	1967
67	Langston University Oklahoma Delta	1967
68	Oklahoma Christian University of Science and Arts Oklahoma Epsilon	1967
69	William Woods University Missouri Alpha	1967
70	University of Southern Colorado Colorado Alpha	1967
71	Nazareth College * Kentucky Beta	1967
72	East Carolina University * North Carolina Beta	1967
73	Davis & Elkins College West Virginia Alpha	1968
74	University of Texas at Arlington Texas Alpha Theta	1968
75	Tennessee Wesleyan College Tennessee Gamma	1968
76	Barton College North Carolina Gamma	1968
77	Talladega College Alabama Alpha	1968
78	Pepperdine University California Alpha	1968
79	University of Maine at Farmington * Maine Beta	1968
80	Angelo State University Texas Alpha Iota	1968
81	Carson-Newman College Tennessee Delta	1968
82	Lincoln Memorial University Tennessee Epsilon	1968
83	St. Mary of the Plains College * Kansas Beta	1968
84	Elon College North Carolina Delta	1968
85	University of Tampa Florida Alpha	1969
86	Ricker College * Maine Gamma	1969
87	Kentucky Wesleyan College Kentucky Gamma	1969
88	Olivet College Michigan Beta	1969
89	University of New Haven * Connecticut Alpha	1969
90	Tarleton State University Texas Alpha Kappa	1969
91	Eureka College Illinois Alpha	1969
92	Berry College Georgia Beta	1969
93	St. Ambrose University Iowa Delta	1969
94	California Baptist College California Beta	1969
95	Concord College West Virginia Beta	1969
96	College of St. Scholastica * Minnesota Alpha	1969
97	Azusa Pacific University California Gamma	1969
98	Fort Wright College * Washington Alpha	1969
99	Widener University Pennsylvania Alpha	1970
100	Arkansas Tech University Arkansas Kappa	1970
101	Brigham Young University of Hawaii Hawaii Alpha	1970
102	Buena Vista University Iowa Epsilon	1970
103	Voorhees College South Carolina Beta	1971
104	Dillard University Louisiana Gamma	1971
105	North Adams State College Massachusetts Beta	1971
106	University of the Americas * Mexico Alpha	1971
107	Caldwell College New Jersey Alpha	1971
108	Defiance College Ohio Beta	1971
109	West Virginia Institute of Technology West Virginia Gamma	1971
110	Blackburn College Illinois Beta	1971
111	Bluefield State College West Virginia Delta	1971
112	Grand Canyon University Arizona Alpha	1971
113	Ladycliff College * New York Alpha	1971
114	Lee College Tennessee Zeta	1971
115	Lincoln University Pennsylvania Beta	1971
116	William Carey College Mississippi Beta	1971
117	Warner Pacific College Oregon Alpha	1971
118	Parks College of Saint Louis University Illinois Gamma	1971
119	Houston Baptist University Texas Alpha Lambda	1971
120	Mars Hill College North Carolina Epsilon	1971
121	Belmont University Tennessee Eta	1972
122	Oglethorpe University Georgia Gamma	1972
123	Gardner-Webb University North Carolina Zeta	1972
124	George Mason University Virginia Alpha	1972
125	Culver-Stockton College Missouri Beta	1972
126	Averett College Virginia Beta	1973
127	Southwest Baptist University Missouri Gamma	1973
128	Shaw University North Carolina Eta	1973
129	Oklahoma Panhandle State University Oklahoma Zeta	1973
130	Lake Superior State University Michigan Gamma	1973
131	North Carolina A&T State University North Carolina Theta	1973
132	Bridgewater College Virginia Gamma	1973
133	Lubbock Christian University Texas Alpha Mu	1974
134	Dallas Baptist University Texas Alpha Nu	1974
135	St. Thomas Aquinas College New York Beta	1974

136	Roanoke College Virginia Delta	1974
137	Brescia College Kentucky Delta	1974
138	University of Hartford Connecticut Beta	1974
139	Old Dominion University Virginia Epsilon	1975
140	Marymount College of Kansas * Kansas Gamma	1975
141	Bowie State University Maryland Alpha	1975
142	Medaille College New York Gamma	1975
143	Tift College * Georgia Delta	1975
144	Jamestown College North Dakota Alpha	1975
145	College of Mount St. Joseph Ohio Gamma	1975
146	Elizabeth City State University North Carolina Iota	1975
147	Menlo College California Delta	1975
148	College of White Plains, Pace University *	1975
	New York Delta	
149	Jackson State University Mississippi Gamma	1975
150	Our Lady of Holy Cross * Louisiana Delta	1975
151	University of North Carolina at Pembroke North Carolina Kappa	1975
152	Westminster College Missouri Delta	1975
153	Christian Brothers University Tennessee Theta	1975
154	Piedmont College Georgia Epsilon	1975
155	University of South Alabama Alabama Beta	1975
156	Mercy College New York Epsilon	1976
157	Southern University Louisiana Epsilon	1976
158	John Brown University Arkansas Lambda	1976
159	Johnson C. Smith University North Carolina Lambda	1976
160	Spring Garden College * Pennsylvania Gamma	1976
161	University of Texas at Tyler Texas Alpha Xi	1976
162	York College of Pennsylvania Pennsylvania Delta	1976
163	Christopher Newport University Virginia Zeta	1976
164	Columbia College Missouri Epsilon	1976
165	Methodist College North Carolina Mu	1976
166	Thomas College Maine Delta	1977
167	Freed-Hardeman University Tennessee Iota	1977
168	High Point University North Carolina Nu	1977
169	Dominican College New York Zeta	1977
170	Greensboro College North Carolina Xi	1977
171	Morehead State University * Kentucky Epsilon	1977
172	Kansas Wesleyan University Kansas Delta	1977
173	Illinois State University Illinois Delta	1977
174	University of Mobile Alabama Gamma	1977
175	Grace College Indiana Gamma	1977
176	Mississippi Valley State University Mississippi Delta	1977
177	Flagler College Florida Beta	1977
178	Oregon Institute of Technology Oregon Beta	1977
179	University of Arkansas at Pine Bluff Arkansas Mu	1978
180	Delaware State University Delaware Alpha	1978
181	Bellevue University Nebraska Gamma	1978
182	Catawba College North Carolina Omicron	1978
183	Bethune-Cookman College Florida Gamma	1978
184	Southern University at New Orleans Louisiana Zeta	1978
185	Concordia College New York Eta	1978
186	University of Texas at Brownsville Texas Alpha Omicron	1978
187	Valley City State University * North Dakota Beta	1978
188	Marist College New York Theta	1978
189	Mount Vernon Nazarene College Ohio Delta	1978
190	Virginia Intermont College Virginia Eta	1978
191	Taylor University Indiana Delta	1979
192	Tri-State University Indiana Epsilon	1979
193	Marymount Manhattan College New York Iota	1979
194	Mount Vernon College D.C. Alpha	1979
195	Indiana University Southeast Indiana Zeta	1979
196	Colby-Sawyer College New Hampshire Alpha	1979
197	Arizona State University * Arizona Beta	1979
198	Limestone College South Carolina Gamma	1980
199	Mount Senario College * Wisconsin Alpha	1980
200	Robert Morris College Pennsylvania Epsilon	1980
201	Tougaloo College Mississippi Epsilon	1980
202	Wingate University North Carolina Pi	1980
203	Peru State College Nebraska Delta	1980
204	University of New England Maine Epsilon	1980
205	Mount Saint Mary College New York Kappa	1980
206	Ferrum College Virginia Theta	1980
207	New Mexico State University New Mexico Alpha	1981

208	Aurora University Illinois Epsilon	1981		244	Touro College New York Nu	1983
209	Westfield State College Massachusetts Gamma	1981		245	University of Baltimore Maryland Gamma	1983
210	Southern Wesleyan University South Carolina Delta	1981		246	Loretto Heights College * Colorado Beta	1983
211	Northern Kentucky University Kentucky Zeta	1981		247	Eastern College Pennsylvania Iota	1983
212	Columbia Christian College * Oregon Gamma	1981		248	University of Indianapolis Indiana Eta	1984
213	Benedict College South Carolina Epsilon	1981		249	Northland College Wisconsin Beta	1984
214	David Lipscomb University Tennessee Kappa	1981		250	Charleston Southern University South Carolina Zeta	1984
215	Roger Williams University Rhode Island Alpha	1981		251	Columbia Union College Maryland Delta	1984
216	Daniel Webster College New Hampshire Beta	1981		252	University of Dubuque Iowa Zeta	1984
217	Georgia Southwestern State University Georgia Zeta	1981		253	St. Mary's College of California * California Epsilon	1984
218	Oklahoma City University Oklahoma Eta	1981		254	Judson College Illinois Eta	1984
219	Pace University New York Lambda	1981		255	Barry University Florida Epsilon	1984
220	Pace University Westchester New York Mu	1981		256	Wesley College Delaware Gamma	1984
221	University of Texas at San Antonio Texas Alpha Pi	1981		257	Purdue University Calumet Indiana Theta	1984
222	Edinboro University of Pennsylvania Pennsylvania Zeta	1981		258	Spelman College Georgia Eta	1985
223	Bloomfield College New Jersey Beta	1981		259	Notre Dame College New Hampshire Delta	1985
224	Barrington College * Rhode Island Beta	1982		260	Schreiner College Texas Alpha Sigma	1985
225	Northeastern Illinois University Illinois Zeta	1982		261	Pontifical Catholic Univ. of Puerto Rico Puerto Rico Alpha	1985
226	Point Park College Pennsylvania Eta	1982		262	Cathedral College * New York Xi	1985
227	Augsburg College Minnesota Beta	1982		263	Faulkner University Alabama Delta	1985
228	Harris-Stowe State College Missouri Zeta	1982		264	Southern Utah University Utah Beta	1985
229	Centenary College New Jersey Gamma	1982		265	Friends University Kansas Epsilon	1985
230	St. Augustine's College North Carolina Rho	1982		266	University of Southern Indiana Indiana Iota	1985
231	College of the Southwest New Mexico Beta	1982		267	University of West Alabama Alabama Epsilon	1986
232	Hawthorne College * New Hampshire Gamma	1982		268	SUNY College at Brockport New York Omicron	1986
233	Capitol College Maryland Beta	1982		269	Cumberland University Tennessee Lambda	1986
234	Green Mountain College Vermont Alpha	1982		270	Philadelphia Col. of Pharmacy & Science Pennsylvania Kappa	1986
235	Goldey Beacom College Delaware Beta	1982		271	Nyack College New York Pi	1986
236	Howard University * D.C. Beta	1982		272	Graceland College Iowa Eta	1986
237	Norwich University Vermont Beta	1982		273	Williams Baptist College Arkansas Nu	1986
238	Concordia University at Austin Texas Alpha Rho	1983		274	University of Houston - Clear Lake Texas Alpha Tau	1986
239	Hawaii Pacific University Hawaii Beta	1983		275	Southeast Missouri State University * Missouri Eta	1986
240	Castleton State College Vermont Gamma	1983		276	St. Andrews Presbyterian College North Carolina Sigma	1986
241	Thiel College Pennsylvania Theta	1983		277	Indiana University - Kokomo Indiana Kappa	1986
242	Southeastern Oklahoma State University Oklahoma Theta	1983		278	Saginaw Valley State University Michigan Delta	1986
243	Warner Southern College Florida Delta	1983		279	Indiana Institute of Technology Indiana Lambda	1986

280	Teikyo Post University	1986
	Connecticut Gamma	
281	Dowling College	1986
	New York Rho	
282	Florida Memorial College	1986
	Florida Zeta	
283	Strayer College	1987
	D.C. Gamma	
284	Southern Connecticut State University	1987
	Connecticut Delta	
285	Fresno Pacific University	1987
	California Zeta	
286	Park College	1987
	Missouri Theta	
287	Concordia University Wisconsin	1987
	Wisconsin Gamma	
288	Kendall College	1987
	Illinois Theta	
289	Nova Southeastern University	1987
	Florida Eta	
290	Alice Lloyd College	1987
	Kentucky Eta	
291	West Coast University	1988
	California Eta	
292	Mesa State College	1988
	Colorado Gamma	
293	Grand View College	1988
	Iowa Theta	
294	Villa Julie College	1988
	Maryland Epsilon	
295	Missouri Southern State College	1989
	Missouri Iota	
296	Montreat College	1989
	North Carolina Tau	
297	University of Maine at Fort Kent	1989
	Maine Zeta	
298	Hannibal-LaGrange College	1989
	Missouri Kappa	
299	Missouri Western State College	1990
	Missouri Lambda	
300	Northwest Missouri State University	1990
	Missouri Mu	
301	Capital University	1990
	Ohio Epsilon	
302	Tomlinson College *	1990
	Tennessee Mu	
303	Geneva College	1990
	Pennsylvania Lambda	
304	Shorter College	1990
	Georgia Theta	
305	Mount Olive College	1990
	North Carolina Upsilon	
306	Clearwater Christian College	1990
	Florida Theta	
307	Pine Manor College	1990
	Massachusetts Delta	
308	Montana State University - Billings	1991
	Montana Alpha	
309	University of South Florida at Sarasota	1991
	Florida Iota	
310	Shenandoah University	1991
	Virginia Iota	
311	Texas A&M University - Corpus Christi	1991
	Texas Alpha Upsilon	
312	Urbana University	1991
	Ohio Zeta	
313	Cornerstone College	1992
	Michigan Epsilon	
314	Edward Waters College	1992
	Florida Kappa	
315	York College	1992
	Nebraska Epsilon	

316	Endicott College	1992
	Massachusetts Epsilon	
317	George Fox University	1992
	Oregon Delta	
318	Mount Ida College	1992
	Massachusetts Zeta	
319	New Hampshire College	1993
	New Hampshire Epsilon	
320	University of La Verne	1993
	California Theta	
321	Southeastern College of the	
	Assemblies of God	1994
	Florida Lambda	
322	Milligan College	1994
	Tennessee Nu	
323	Wilkes University	1994
	Pennsylvania Mu	
324	West Liberty State College	1994
	West Virginia Epsilon	
325	Oakwood College	1994
	Alabama Zeta	
326	Lindsey Wilson College	1994
	Kentucky Theta	
327	Saint Vincent College	1994
	Pennsylvania Nu	
328	Southwest State University	1994
	Minnesota Gamma	
329	William Tyndale College	1995
	Michigan Zeta	
330	Sue Bennett College	1995
	Kentucky Iota	
331	MidAmerica Nazarene College	1995
	Kansas Zeta	
332	California State University, Bakersfield	1995
	California Iota	
333	Carthage College	1996
	Wisconsin Delta	
334	Franklin Pierce College	1995
	New Hampshire Zeta	
335	Central Methodist College	1996
	Missouri Nu	
336	University of Kentucky	1996
	Kentucky Kappa	
337	Emmanuel College	1996
	Georgia Iota	
338	Newbury College	1996
	Massachusetts Eta	
339	Cascade College	1996
	Oregon Epsilon	
340	The American College	1996
	Georgia Kappa	
341	Thomas College	1996
	Georgia Lambda	

	Texas Alpha Alumnus Chapter	1941
	Indianapolis Alumni Chapter	1990
	Southern Region VI Alumni Chapter	1991
	Caney Creek Community Center	
	Alumni Chapter	1993

INDEX

Index does not include items in appendices.

A

A.H. Fetting Company 16
Abernethy, Francis E. 105, 134
Abilene Christian University 20, 29, 32, 61,
    64, 67, 77, 78, 81, 85, 123, 124, 139, 152
Addams, Jane 22
Adrian College 88, 112, 124, 125
Alice Lloyd College 187, 191
Allen, Lloyd Green 68
Alpha Beta Phi 67
Alpha Chi Handbook, 1996-1998 184
Alpha Pi Omega 67
alumni chapter 71, 72
alumni fellowship 190
American Association of University
    Professors 60
American International College 71, 72,
    86, 88, 97, 105, 117, 123
Anderson University 86, 87, 116, 191
Angelo State University 109, 138, 190, 191
Appalachian State University 88, 112, 124,
    191
archives iii, 146
Arizona State University 129
Arkansas Tech University 116
Arkansas State Teachers College 32, 33, 48,
    57, 58, 67, 87
Association of College Honor Societies
    47, 86, 87, 188
Atkinson, William Eugene 89
Atlanta national conventions 121-22, 128,
    132-33, 134, 185-86, 189, 190
Atlantic Christian College 110
Atteberry, James L. 104, 105, 111
Austin College 13, 14, 59, 67, 137
Azusa Pacific College 110

B

Bally, L.H. 63, 64, 70, 75, 88, 92
Barden, John G. 111
Barnard College 12
Barrett, Clyde 188
Baxter, Batsell 32

Baylor College 10, 13, 14, 18, 19, 26-
    28, 67 (*see University of Mary Hardin-
    Baylor*)
Baylor University 13, 14, 16, 18, 64, 67,
    74, 77
Beekman, Jennifer 184
Bell, Craig A. 137
Bellevue University 189
Belmont University 191
Benedict, Harry Y. v, 6-8, 10-14, 16-21, 24-
    27, 29, 32, 34, 35, 37, 40, 42, 44-48, 51-
    59, 69, 92, 100, 192
Benedict Scholarship (Fellowship) 58, 65,
    75, 97, 125, 184
Bergendahl, Timothy C. 117, 123, 162
Berry College 110, 152, 162, 175, 191
Bethune-Cookman College 129
Bieker, Richard 175
Binnion, R.B. 67
Birdwell, A.W. 67
Bishop, Charles McTyeire i, 2, 8, 22, 27,
    60
Bishop, Eugene Hendrix 2
Blake, Robert G. 169, 172
Bledsoe, J.M. 33
Boahene, Opoku 137
Bodemann, Elsie 78, 83
Bohmfalk, Paul 58
Boorstin, Daniel J. 134
Box, Terry J. 155, 166
Brady, Sr. M. Teresa 117, 153, 162-65, 187
Bralley, F.M. 67
Brandstetter, J. Morey 47
Brescia College 129, 152, 176, 191
Bridgewater College 129
Brigham Young University—Hawaii 129,
    138, 149
Brown's Awards Company 147-48, 172-73
Brown, Myrtle 74, 75
Bruce, W.H. 67, 68
Bucknell University 59
Burkett, Phil 123
Burks, David B. 168
Burr, Aaron 80

William Woods College 110, 127
Williams, Patricia 166, 169, 173-74, 177, 186
Williams, Gary 164
Williamsburg national convention 139, 142-43, 153
Wilson, Woodrow 67, 68, 153
Winstead, Robert 152
Wisely, J.H. 53, 61, 63
Witt, Paul 61, 64, 70-73, 81, 84, 86-88
Wong, Chumei 137
Woodrow Wilson Foundation 85
Woods, Bliss 3

Y

Yale University 12, 80
Yates, Richard E. 89, 94
Youngblood, Clark 183, 189-90

Z

Zahka, William 190
Zats, Yuri 138